AMPHIBIANS AND REPTILES

of the

CHICAGO AREA

MILK SNAKE (*Lampropeltis triangulum triangulum*)
A young individual; adult milk snakes are not such a bright red

FOX SNAKE (*Elaphe vulpina vulpina*)
A young individual; colors in the adult are not so bright

Amphibians and Reptiles
of the
Chicago Area

By Clifford H. Pope
CURATOR OF AMPHIBIANS AND REPTILES

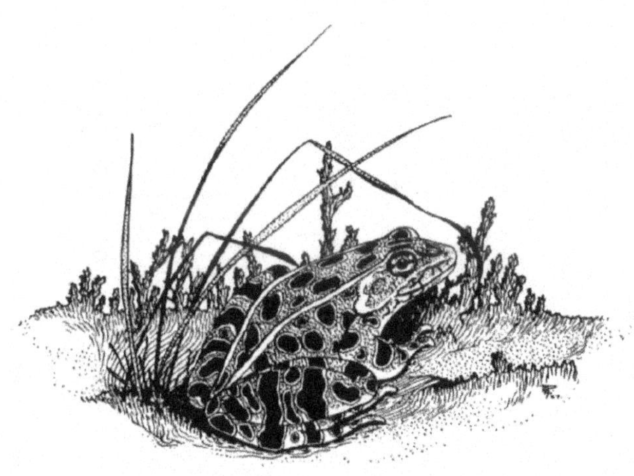

CHICAGO NATURAL HISTORY MUSEUM

1947

A PATHFINDER BOOK REPRINT EDITION

Originally published in 1947 by Chicago Natural History Press

Printed in the United States of America

ISBN: 979-8869033253

CONTENTS

	PAGE
LIST OF ILLUSTRATIONS	7
INTRODUCTION	11
IDENTIFICATION	13

AMPHIBIANS

SALAMANDERS	17
Identification	19
Mudpuppy (*Necturus maculosus maculosus*)	21
Newt (*Triturus viridescens louisianensis*)	24
Jefferson's Salamander (*Ambystoma jeffersonianum*)	29
Spotted Salamander (*Ambystoma maculatum*)	34
Marbled Salamander (*Ambystoma opacum*)	41
Tiger Salamander (*Ambystoma tigrinum tigrinum*)	46
Red-backed Salamander (*Plethodon cinereus*)	52
Four-toed Salamander (*Hemidactylium scutatum*)	55
Two-lined Salamander (*Eurycea bislineata bislineata*)	57
Siren (*Siren intermedia nettingi*)	61
FROGS	65
Identification	67
American Toad (*Bufo americanus americanus*)	69
Fowler's Toad (*Bufo woodhousii fowleri*)	81
Cricket Frog (*Acris gryllus*)	86
Swamp Tree Frog (*Pseudacris nigrita triseriata*)	90
Spring Peeper (*Hyla crucifer crucifer*)	95
Tree Frog (*Hyla versicolor versicolor*)	100
Wood Frog (*Rana sylvatica*)	105
Bullfrog (*Rana catesbeiana*)	111
Green Frog (*Rana clamitans*)	121

CONTENTS 6

PAGE

Pickerel Frog (*Rana palustris*) 127
Leopard Frog (*Rana pipiens pipiens*) 133

REPTILES

LIZARDS 145
Glass-Snake (*Ophisaurus ventralis*) 146
Six-lined Race-Runner (*Cnemidophorus sexlineatus*) 149
Blue-tailed Skink (*Eumeces fasciatus*) 153

SNAKES 160
Identification 162
Hog-nosed Snake (*Heterodon contortrix contortrix*) 165
Green Snake (*Opheodrys vernalis blanchardi*) 169
Blue Racer (*Coluber constrictor flaviventris*) 171
Pilot Black Snake (*Elaphe obsoleta obsoleta*) 174
Fox Snake (*Elaphe vulpina vulpina*) 177
Bull Snake (*Pituophis sayi sayi*) 179
Milk Snake (*Lampropeltis triangulum triangulum*) 184
Graham's Water Snake (*Natrix grahamii*) 188
Kirtland's Water Snake (*Natrix kirtlandii*) 189
Queen Snake (*Natrix septemvittata*) 192
Common Water Snake (*Natrix sipedon sipedon*) 194
DeKay's Snake (*Storeria dekayi wrightorum*) 200
Red-bellied Snake (*Storeria occipitomaculata occipitomacu-
lata*) 201
Butler's Garter Snake (*Thamnophis butleri*) 204
Plains Garter Snake (*Thamnophis radix*) 208
Ribbon Snake (*Thamnophis sauritus proximus*) 211
Common Garter Snake (*Thamnophis sirtalis sirtalis*) . . . 213
Massasauga (*Sistrurus catenatus catenatus*) 220

TURTLES 226
Identification 228
Musk Turtle (*Sternotherus odoratus*) 230
Snapping Turtle (*Chelydra serpentina serpentina*) 234
Spotted Turtle (*Clemmys guttata*) 238
Blanding's Turtle (*Emys blandingii*) 241
Common Box Turtle (*Terrapene carolina carolina*) 244
Ornate Box Turtle (*Terrapene ornata*) 249
Map Turtle (*Graptemys geographica*) 252
Painted Turtle (*Chrysemys picta marginata*) 255
Troost's Turtle (*Pseudemys scripta troostii*) 260
Soft-shelled Turtle (*Amyda spinifera spinifera*) 263

INDEX 267

LIST OF ILLUSTRATIONS

PLATES   FACING PAGE

1. Milk Snake 1
   Fox Snake 1

2. Nest of Mudpuppy 13

3. Eggs of Mudpuppy 50
   Typical Home of the Mudpuppy 50

4. Jefferson's Salamander 58
   Four-toed Salamander 58
   Red-backed Salamander 58

5. Color Change of the Tree Frog 162

6. Hog-nosed Snake 170
   Eggs of Green Snake 170

7. Adult Blue Racer 174
   Juvenile Blue Racer 174

8. Queen Snake 190
   Pilot Black Snake 190
   Bull Snake 190
   Kirtland's Water Snake 190

9. Common Water Snake 206
   DeKay's Snake 206
   Plains Garter Snake 206

10. Ribbon Snake 222
    Massasauga 222

FACING
PAGE

11. Snapping Turtle 238
    Common Box Turtle 238
    Troost's Turtle 238
    Blanding's Turtle 238

12. Map Turtle . . . . : . 254
    Soft-shelled Turtle 254
    Spotted Turtle 254
    Musk Turtle 254
    Painted Turtle 254

TEXT FIGURES

PAGE

 1. Map of the Chicago Area 10
 2. The Naso-labial Groove of Salamanders 19
 3. Tongue of Two-lined Salamander 20
 4. Mudpuppy 22
 5. Courtship of Salamanders 27
 6. Egg-laying of Salamanders 31
 7. Spermatophores of Spotted Salamander 36
 8. Spotted Salamander 37
 9. Egg Clusters of Spotted Salamander 39
10. Spermatophore of Marbled Salamander 42
11. Brooding of Eggs by Salamanders 43
12. Tiger Salamander 47
13. Larva of Tiger Salamander 49
14. Siren 62
15. Eggs and Larvae of American Toad 73
16. Slough of American Toad 77
17. Fowler's and American Toads 83
18. Fowler's Toad Feigning Death 85
19. Cricket Frog 87
20. Swamp Tree Frog 91
21. Female Swamp Tree Frog Approaching Male 92
22. Spring Peeper 96
23. Eggs of Spring Peeper 97
24. Wood Frog 106
25. Bullfrog 112
26. Mouth of Bullfrog 113
27. Laying Position of Bullfrogs 114
28. Egg Cluster of Bullfrog 115
29. Green Frog 121

PAGE

30. Laying Stages of Green Frog 123
31. Pickerel Frog 128
32. Leopard Frog 134
33. Development of Leopard Frog 137
34. Glass-Snake Brooding Eggs 147
35. Six-lined Race-Runner Courting and Copulating 150
36. Blue-tailed Skink Retrieving Egg 155
37. Method of Counting Snake Scales 163
38. Bull Snake Removing Loose Dirt from Pocket Gopher's
     Burrow 181
39. Bull Snake Killing Pocket Gopher 182
40. Range of Bull Snake 183
41. Range of Common Water Snake 199
42. Ranges of Garter Snakes 207
43. Courtship of Plains Garter Snake 209
44. Shell of Musk Turtle 231
45. Shell of Snapping Turtle 235
46. Shell of Blanding's Turtle 241
47. Shell of Common Box Turtle 245
48. Plastron of Ornate Box Turtle 250
49. Shell of Map Turtle 253
50. Shell of Troost's Turtle 261

FIG. 1. Map of the Chicago area.

This book is written for those already interested in natural history and for individuals who derive keen pleasure from constantly becoming better acquainted with their environment. The aim is to arouse interest in reptiles and amphibians by showing that each kind has its own habits, worthy of special and detailed attention. Technical terms and scientific jargon have been avoided, but numerous details are included because much of the fascination of animal behavior lies in its complexity.

Our knowledge is so incomplete that it is not possible to give a full account of a single local species, and the amateur thus has a good opportunity to experience the thrill of making original observations. There is no hobby superior to that of the naturalist who combines trips into the open country with study of good books and the care of a vivarium during the winter months.

The "Chicago area" includes fifteen counties in Illinois and Indiana, one in Michigan, and three in Wisconsin (see Fig. 1). No point within this area is more than seventy miles from the center of Chicago. It is surprising that as many as fifty-two kinds of reptiles and amphibians live in this area, along with 4 per cent of the entire country's human population. Only six states are inhabited by so many people.

For a region with little variation in altitude, our local area is unusually interesting. This is largely because it lies at the transition zone between hardwood forest and prairie. Many of the local animals found to the west are unknown farther east, and vice versa (Figs. 40 and 42). In some cases, intergradation between subspecies occurs here. Some knowledge of the physiography of our area is a great help to anyone planning to look for reptiles and amphibians in their native haunts. No better account is needed than F. M. Fryxell's *The Physiography of the Region of Chicago* (University of Chicago Press, in 1927), or J. H. Bretz's *Geology of the Chicago Region* (Illinois Geological Survey, Part I, Bulletin 65, 1939).

Years ago, Karl P. Schmidt, now Chief Curator of Zoology in the Chicago Natural History Museum, began a series of popular accounts of local reptiles and amphibians. The three of these now published treat all the groups except the snakes. The present work includes much new knowledge, adds an account of the snakes, and is more comprehensive and detailed than the leaflets. The Chicago Academy of Sciences has issued various lists of the reptiles and amphibians of the Chicago area, with the names of places where they have been found. These should be consulted for details of distribution.

I am deeply indebted to Leon L. Pray for the drawings of the frogs and reptiles and the paintings of the amphibians and turtles, and to Miss Peggy Collings for the salamander drawings. Albert A. Enzenbacher painted the snakes shown in color and D. Dwight Davis took the photographs of snakes that, together with the color plates by Mr. Enzenbacher, have been reproduced here through the kind permission of G. P. Putnam's Sons. They are from the *Field Book of Snakes*. Mr. Pray is on the taxidermy staff of the Chicago Natural History Museum, Miss Collings and Mr. Davis are on its zoological staff. I am very grateful to my wife, Sarah H. Pope, for reading both manuscript and proof.

DISCOVERY OF THE NEST OF A MUDPUPPY (*Necturus maculosus maculosus*)
The eggs may be seen attached to the stone at the water-line

The recognition of substances and objects, be they animal, vegetable, or mineral, is a major consideration in all sorts of endeavor. The chemist has tests for chemicals, and the housewife quickly picks out good foods. The student of natural history must be able to identify kinds or "species" of animals and plants.

I have reduced the recognition of our fifty-two local amphibians and reptiles to its simplest terms by including many illustrations and avoiding anatomical technicalities. Diagnostic details or "characters" are arranged in "keys" so that the worker, by making a series of choices, is quickly led to the right name.

Any two- or four-legged animal of the Chicago area that is neither furred nor feathered must be a reptile or an amphibian. The "glass-snake" (in reality a limbless lizard) and the snakes do not have legs but are recognized by their smooth, scaly skin to which dust and dirt do not adhere.

Body never pancake-shaped, in every case covered with scale-
less skin that is either smooth and moist or dry and
warty..Amphibians
   Tail present throughout life; limbs about equal in length.
                        Salamanders, p. 17
   Tail present only in larval (tadpole) stage; hind limbs much
     larger and longer than fore limbs................Frogs, p. 65
Body enclosed in a short, rigid, or a flexible pancake-shaped
     shell, or covered with dry scaly skin................Reptiles
Body long and flexible.
   Movable eyelids present........................Lizards, p. 145
   Movable eyelids lacking.........................Snakes, p. 160
Body not elongate, enclosed in a hard, rigid, or a flexible,
     pancake-shaped shell........................Turtles, p. 226

AMPHIBIANS

Salamanders confuse the layman more than any other amphibians or reptiles. This is because they are light-shunning, moisture-loving creatures resembling lizards in form. It is not surprising that the salamander is commonly known as the wood or spring "lizard." Perhaps we should revert to the rough and ready method of instruction used by the famous sixteenth century artist, Benvenuto Cellini. One day, when a salamander appeared on his hearth, he pointed to it as he gave his young son a violent slap, by way of impressing the animal on the youth's plastic mind. This incident gives a clue to the origin of the belief that salamanders live in fire. It was easy to assume that one found crawling on the hearth had actually wandered from the hot coals rather than from the reserve pile of wood drying near-by.

The more we observe a salamander the more easily we become convinced that its resemblance to a lizard is superficial. The sun-loving lizard has a dry, scaly skin, the secretive salamander a scaleless one that, in most species, is moist and cannot withstand exposure to sun. The lizard's egg, essentially like a bird's in structure, is laid on land; as a rule, salamander eggs are deposited in water and scarcely differ from those of a frog. Most salamanders, therefore, begin life in water as larvae with external gills, something no lizard ever does. The layman would be far better off to think of a salamander as a tailed frog.

Although the eggs of salamanders, like those of other backboned animals higher than the amphibians, are fertilized before being laid, the male does not deposit sperm directly into his mate's body. The transfer of these male reproductive cells is accomplished only after the sexes have performed a courtship dance, the details of which vary from species to species. The male concludes his part of the performance by depositing "spermatophores," tiny, stump-shaped bits of mucus capped by masses of sperm (Figs. 7 and 10), which the female promptly picks up with the lips of her vent or cloaca. The study of "courtship patterns" of the various species of local salamanders is a fascinating pastime as well as a worthwhile scientific undertaking. Our knowledge of the siren's life history is incomplete, but there is anatomical evidence that it is one of the few existing species—and the only local one—practicing external fertilization similar to that of fishes.

Among all the groups of reptiles and amphibians no other is so predominantly North American, the salamander fauna of the southeastern states being the richest in the world. These amphibians are not abundant in our region but small populations of several interesting species do occur here. Since all salamanders are harmless, they can be handled without restraint.

The salamanders comprise the Order Caudata of the Class Amphibia.

A complete account of the species inhabiting the United States can be found in Sherman C. Bishop's *Handbook of Salamanders* (1943). A general but highly technical treatment of the Caudata is contained in *The Biology of the Amphibia*, written by G. Kingsley Noble and published in 1931.

The identification of adult salamanders should give no trouble to anyone who has learned to look for a naso-labial groove (Fig. 2). Larval salamanders are readily recognized as such by their external gills and the early development of all the limbs. Frog larvae or tadpoles

FIG. 2. Naso-labial groove, apparent in red-backed salamander (right) as a line running downward from nostril to mouth. This character is lacking in the tiger salamander (left).

(except during the first few days after hatching when they are still minute in size) have concealed gills; their limbs develop late and the front pair remain hidden in the gill cavity until metamorphosis. The naso-labial groove is not present in larval salamanders, so identification before transformation is difficult. In some cases, consideration of size and habitat will help.

Hind limbs present.

    Bushy external gills present; can live only in water.

                                      Mudpuppy, p. 21

    External gills absent; does, or at least can live out of water.

        Naso-labial groove lacking (Fig. 2).

            Sides with red spots but without vertical grooves. Newt, p. 24

            Sides with numerous vertical grooves but without red spots.

                Black above with bluish flecks especially profuse on sides . . . . Jefferson's Salamander, p. 29

                Black above with two rows of yellow or orange spots along back . . . . Spotted Salamander, p. 34

                Black above with light bands across back.

                        Marbled Salamander, p. 41

                Black above with many irregular yellow spots that fuse along edge of belly . . . . . . Tiger Salamander, p. 46

        Naso-labial groove present (Fig. 2).

            Hind foot with four toes . . . . . . Four-toed Salamander, p. 55

            Hind foot with five toes.

                Tongue attached to floor of mouth.

                        Red-backed Salamander, p. 52

                Tongue set on stalk (Fig. 3) . . Two-lined Salamander, p. 57

Hind limbs lacking . . . . Siren, p. 61

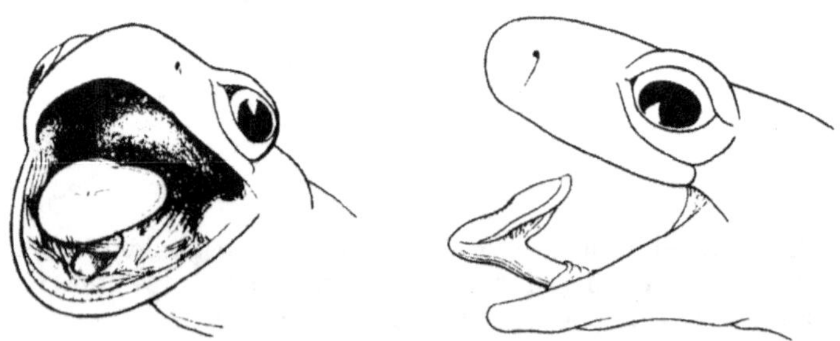

FIG. 3. Tongue of two-lined salamander. Left: Front view with the mouth open. Right: The tongue and its stalk as seen from one side.

MUDPUPPY

Necturus maculosus maculosus

Plates 2 and 3 and Figure 4

Recognition.—Any local salamander four or more inches long with four instead of five toes on the hind limb is a mudpuppy. A pair of light stripes down the back and bushy external gills distinguish small mudpuppies from four-toed salamanders. The latter never exceed a length of four inches, do not have the light dorsal stripes, and lose their slender external gills before the body and tail are an inch long.

The Sexes.—There are no conspicuous sexual differences. Two nipple-like projections directed rearward are present in the vent of the male only.

Reproduction.—Although many nests have been found, no one has ever seen mudpuppies courting, mating, or depositing eggs under natural conditions. Captives have been observed to perform a simple courtship dance, and spermatophores have been deposited in aquaria.

The nests (Plate 2) are shallow hollows beneath the submerged part or whole of any object such as a stone or log, and the eggs (Plate 3) are always several inches to a few feet below the surface. In streams and rivers, nests are near rifts but not in the swiftest water and the opening is invariably on the downstream side. Nesting females avoid very small streams.

When depositing her eggs, the salamander turns her belly upward and sticks one egg at a time to the surface above her. The eggs adhere separately but form a close cluster not more than a foot across (Plate 3). The egg is a light yellow sphere barely ¼ inch in diameter enclosed in an elastic membrane and a few gelatinous layers. A nest contains from 18 to 140 or more eggs; counts of much more than a hundred may be based on complements of two animals. Females guard their nests.

Mating takes place in the autumn and possibly at other times as well; laying in late May and the first half of June. The incubation period, from six to nine weeks, varies with the temperature, warm water hastening the process.

The large Lake Michigan population seems to make annual migrations up the inflowing streams and rivers.

FIG. 4. Adult mudpuppy, seen from above.

Detailed records of such movements are wanting and much to be desired; according to Cagle, adults of southern Illinois enter sloughs and backwaters of the Mississippi and Muddy rivers during May to spawn in relatively shallow water.

Growth and Age.—The hatchling measures $\frac{7}{8}$ of an inch. Individuals reach sexual maturity between their seventh and eighth years at a length of 7 or 8 inches. Seventeen inches is the maximum size but most adults are approximately a foot long.

Two of these salamanders survived eight years and ten months in the London Zoological Gardens, six others from five to eight years. Senning recently found that age can be determined by studying growth rings in certain bones of the skull. He tells the age with accuracy to the fifteenth or sixteenth year and believes that mudpuppies live at least twenty-three years.

Habits.—There is a marked tendency to be nocturnal in clear water, whereas in muddy or weed-choked water this tendency is not so evident. Observers have been surprised to see mudpuppies moving about under the ice in winter for they may remain active the year around.

Food.—The mudpuppy is not a very discriminating feeder for it will devour many kinds of small animals. Examination of hundreds of stomachs shows that crayfish, aquatic insects and their larvae, fish, and annelid worms are mainstays of the diet.

Economic Importance.—The latest investigator concludes that this salamander is not a menace to food fish so its wholesale destruction is not warranted. Thousands are caught every year to serve as material for dissection in zoology classes of schools and colleges. Thus the species plays a useful role in education.

Habitat.—Thoroughly aquatic habits require the mudpuppy to live in permanent bodies of water. It thrives in such diverse situations as stagnant drainage ditches, muddy, weed-choked streams, hill or mountain creeks, and cold, clear lakes. Locally it may be found in the Des Plaines, Du Page, and Fox rivers, and in Chicago parks in lagoons connected with Lake Michigan (Plate 3).

Captivity.—As a rule, salamanders start life as aquatic animals with external gills but soon lose the gills and become at least partly terrestrial. The captive mudpuppy is interesting as an example of a salamander that, in one sense, never grows up but remains a larva all its life. Other animals of value should not be confined with it because of its voracious feeding habits.

Occurrence.—There are local records for Cook, Du Page, Kane, and McHenry counties in Illinois, and Lake and Porter counties in Indiana. The species is widely distributed in the region of the Great Lakes and in the Mississippi drainage from the Arkansas River northward. The population of Lake Winnebago, Wisconsin, has been recently set off as a subspecies, *stictus.*

Reference.—The Salamanders of New York. By Sherman C. Bishop. New York State Museum Bulletin, No. 324, 1941. An **excellent general account.**

NEWT
Triturus viridescens louisianensis
Figure 5

Recognition.—This is the only local salamander that lacks a series of vertical grooves on the side of the body. The back and sides are olive, the belly light yellow; the body and tail are everywhere dotted with black, the dotting being especially conspicuous on the belly; a row of small red spots is more or less in evidence along the upper sides.

The Sexes.—The male has on the side of the head a row of pits, the hedonic glands, which are lacking in the female. During the breeding season the male develops dark, horny excrescences on the inner side of the hind legs and the tips of the adjacent toes. At this time, too, the cloaca protrudes noticeably and numerous tubules may be seen in it. The cloaca of the breeding female is a little protuberant and has converging ridges with dark, horny edges.

Bishop gives additional sexual differences for northeastern *Triturus viridescens viridescens*, but material from the Chicago region is so scant that these differences are not discernible in it.

Reproduction.—Virtually nothing is known about the reproduction of the local newt except that two males with well-developed nuptial excrescences on the hind limbs were collected at Miller, Lake County, Indiana, on May 3, 1930, and three females distended with eggs were taken at the same place on April 17, 1932. These specimens are now in the Chicago Natural History Museum. Cagle has recently reported the courtship of newts in a small pool in Union County, southern Illinois, on February 28; eggs were found in this pool a few days later.

The following abbreviated account of reproduction in the northeastern *Triturus viridescens viridescens* will serve as a guide to the study of the local subspecies, which undoubtedly has habits much like those of its north-eastern relative.

The male takes the initiative in an elaborate courtship during which the female is first stalked repeatedly and finally seized from above in the region of the fore legs by the hind limbs of the male (Fig. 5c). Amid much jerking and shifting about, the male rubs the side of the head against the snout of the female and waves his tail, presumably setting up a current toward the head of his mate (Fig. 5d). The rubbing by the hedonic glands of the cheek not only quiets the female but induces her to follow when he dismounts and moves ahead to deposit spermatophores.

The fascinating and varied courtships of different newts have considerable phylogenetic significance (see the discussion of this subject by R. E. Smith: Copeia, 1941, pp. 255–262).

Eggs are deposited in quiet or sluggish water and are stuck, one at a time, to stems, leaves, or other submerged objects. An average egg is $\frac{1}{16}$ of an inch in diameter, light to dark brown at one pole, light yellowish green at the other. It has three envelopes. The outermost is not spherical, measuring barely $\frac{3}{16}$ of an inch in one diameter, $\frac{1}{16}$ less in the other.

A study of the sperm cycle by Ifft and others has shown that the male develops sperm through the summer and discharges them in the autumn during breeding activities which are described as "false" because they do not include deposition of eggs. The testes are normally inactive through the winter but again discharge sperm in the spring. Temperature is the principal factor influencing the sperm cycle, since, at all seasons, a drop below 53° F. prevents sperm development or discharge, and temperatures above this point induce, even in winter, sperm formation; a rise to about 73° F. in winter causes sperm discharge.

Mating and laying take place in April and May. The period of incubation lasts from twenty to thirty-five days under natural conditions, from ten to sixteen at room temperature.

Growth and Age.—The northeastern newt, *Triturus viridescens viridescens*, hatches at a length of approximately ⁵⁄₁₆ of an inch, passes through a larval stage lasting some eighty-four days, and transforms into a bright orange, terrestrial "red eft," a stage in which it cannot live in water and has a skin highly repellent to it. After two, three, or even four seasons spent on land, profound changes adapt the skin to aquatic respiration, and the newt returns to water where it breeds for the first time and spends the rest of its life.

The land stage is unknown in the Chicago area and also apparently on the Louisiana Gulf Coast and in the Mississippi Valley. This fact, in conjunction with certain color characters, links our local newts to those of the Mississippi and western Gulf Coast regions known as *Triturus viridescens louisianensis*. The problem is complicated by the occurrence on Long Island, New York, and in other eastern localities, of colonies that also fail to produce red efts. These colonies, however, resemble their northeastern neighbors in other respects.

Two females from Miller, Indiana, distended with eggs, measure from tip to tip $3\frac{5}{16}$ and $3\frac{7}{16}$ inches, their respective lengths from snout to vent being $1\frac{11}{16}$ and $1\frac{3}{4}$ inches. Corresponding measurements for two males, also from Miller, having nuptial excrescences on the hind limbs, are $3\frac{1}{8}$, $3\frac{3}{16}$, and, for both, $1\frac{9}{16}$ inches. Some idea of adult size may be gained from the measurements of this small series, which is mentioned above under the discussion of reproduction. Although these females are the longer, the series is too small to form a basis for comparison of length in the sexes. It is the male in *Triturus viridescens viridescens* that has the greater average length.

A red eft reported by Hausman lived in a terrarium for seven years, a record of longevity for the species.

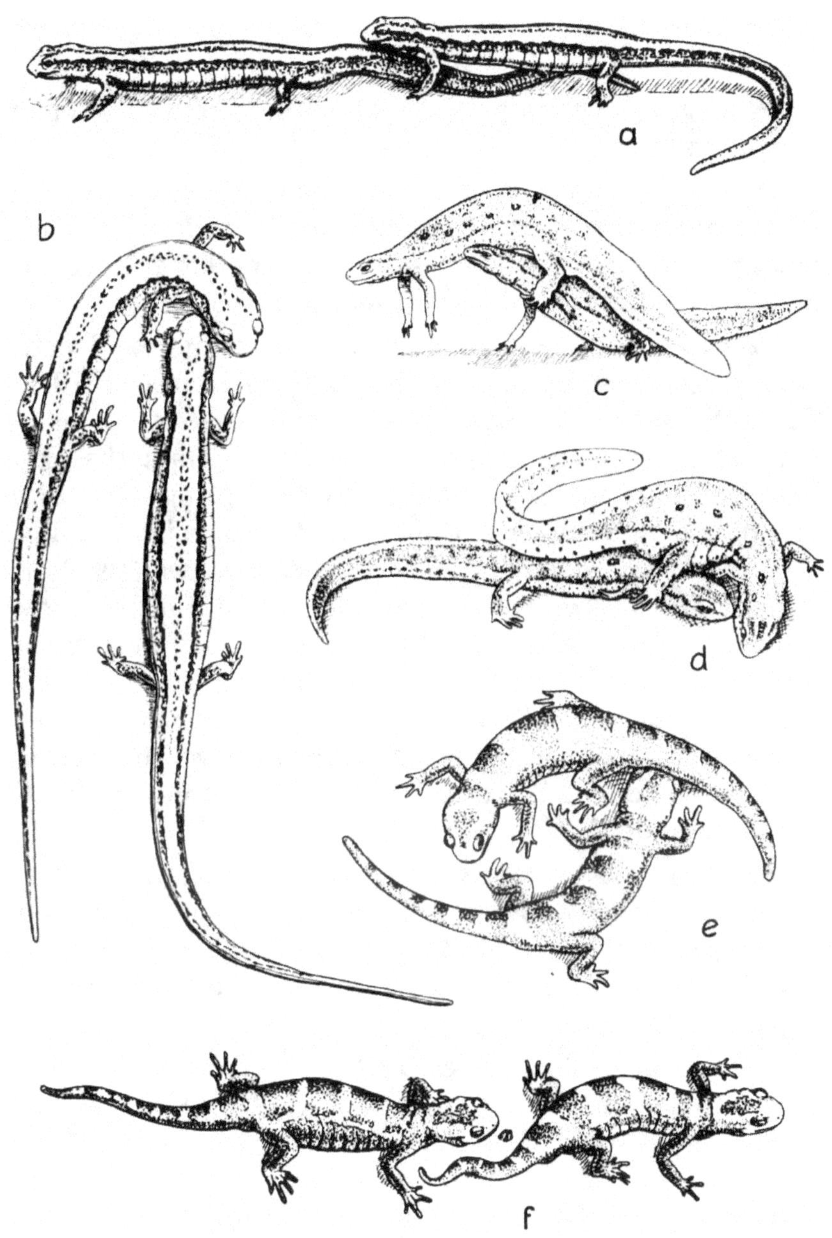

FIG. 5. Courtship of salamanders. *a* and *b:* Two-lined salamander. *c* and *d:* Newt. *e* and *f:* Marbled salamander (spermatophore between pair in *f*). *a, b, e,* and *f* after Noble and Brady; *c* and *d* after Bishop.

Habits.—A thoroughly aquatic frequenter of sluggish or still water.

Food.—Presumably the local newt, like its relative of the northeastern states, eats a great variety of small, aquatic animals. Detailed studies of the latter's feeding habits have been made by Hamilton and others.

Habitat.—The newt is known to be numerous locally only in certain small ponds of the Indiana Dunes at Miller. Cat-tails grow in these ponds, and the salamanders may be taken from masses of decaying debris that has been raked from the bottom. In the spring of 1942 I caught a single individual north of Chicago in a sunny, grass-bordered, woodland pond only one or two feet deep, the bottom covered with aquatic plants. Countless crayfish and a few sunfish also lived in this pond of extreme southern Lake County south of Deerfield Road and between Portwine Road and the Des Plaines River. Another search failed to bring a second newt to light, so perhaps the crayfish are to be blamed for the scarcity of the salamanders.

Captivity.—Newts breed readily in well-planted, sunny aquaria. They soon learn to take bits of liver or fish from the fingers and to haunt the part of the aquarium where food is offered. No other salamander is so hardy and so easy to observe in captivity.

Occurrence.—The species, *Triturus viridescens*, is widely distributed over the eastern part of the United States and adjacent Canada. One subspecies has the northeastern states as its area of distribution, another, *Triturus viridescens dorsalis*, occurs on the coastal plain of the Carolinas, and a third, *Triturus viridescens louisianensis*, lives in the Mississippi region. Grobman has recently determined that the two northern forms intergrade in Michigan, *louisianensis* occurring in the western part of the upper peninsula and the southwestern part of the lower. In the Chicago area, newts have been found in Cook and Lake counties, Illinois; Walworth County,

Wisconsin; and Lake County, Indiana. Only in the last county are they known to be common.

Reference.—The Salamanders of New York. By Sherman C. Bishop. New York State Museum Bulletin, No. 324, 1941. An excellent general account.

JEFFERSON'S SALAMANDER
Ambystoma jeffersonianum
Plate 4 and Figure 6

Recognition.—The bluish black or dark brown ground color of this species is usually broken by numerous bluish white flecks that tend to be concentrated on the sides. When these flecks are absent, difficulty may arise through confusion with the uniformly colored phase of the red-backed salamander. This difficulty is readily cleared by search for a naso-labial groove (evident under a lens as a fine line from the nasal opening to the mouth), which is present only in the red-backed salamander.

The Sexes.—During the breeding season, the swollen vent of the male protrudes noticeably, whereas the female's vent is never more than slightly swollen and protuberant. The following differences, though only comparative, help in sexing series of breeding specimens. The tail of the male is longer and flatter, the head broader and flatter, the limbs longer and thicker, and the body shorter. If the limbs of one side are pressed along the body toward each other, the toes usually overlap in the male but fail to do so in the female.

Reproduction.—Breeding starts in early spring when the adults, aroused by continuous warm rains or melting snows, emerge from hibernation and migrate to the breeding ponds or pools. If suitable conditions persist, the migration may develop into a virtual stampede, but ordinarily the return of cold weather interferes to make migration a protracted process. Although normally nocturnal, this movement is often continued into daylight hours by individuals caught without shelter; such stragglers are in danger of being frozen to death or killed by the sun before they can reach cover.

Almost any woodland pool or pond may be chosen as a breeding site, since these amphibians exhibit little or no ability to distinguish between temporary and permanent bodies of water. Not infrequently a pool that dries before the larvae metamorphose is chosen year after year even though permanent water lies near-by.

In courtship involving a single pair, the male, after grasping his mate by the armpits with his fore limbs, vigorously rubs with his chin first the top and sides of her head and then her snout. His body and tail undulate and his grip may be shifted to a point in front of her fore limbs. Finally, he swims ahead, and the female, if sufficiently aroused, follows and applies her snout to his cloaca. He then extends the limbs and again undulates body and tail while a spermatophore is extruded and attached to any object on the bottom such as a leaf or stone. The female advances and picks up with her cloaca either the entire spermatophore or only its head.

Bishop saw many more females than males in one New York breeding aggregate and believes that the courtship pattern is modified by such a lack of balance between the sexes. In a Pennsylvania aggregate, the males greatly outnumbered the females. It is clear that further observations are needed.

When ready to lay, the female selects during the night a twig or stem a few inches below the surface and places her body along it. She then either stretches the fore limbs out or holds them by her sides and extends the hind limbs backward, pressing the thighs against either side of the vent. If the support is horizontal or nearly so, she does not cling to it but maintains a precarious balance in her awkward position. As the eggs are extruded, her back is arched and her elevated tail is sometimes moved from side to side (Fig. 6). The eggs, laid singly at the rate of about

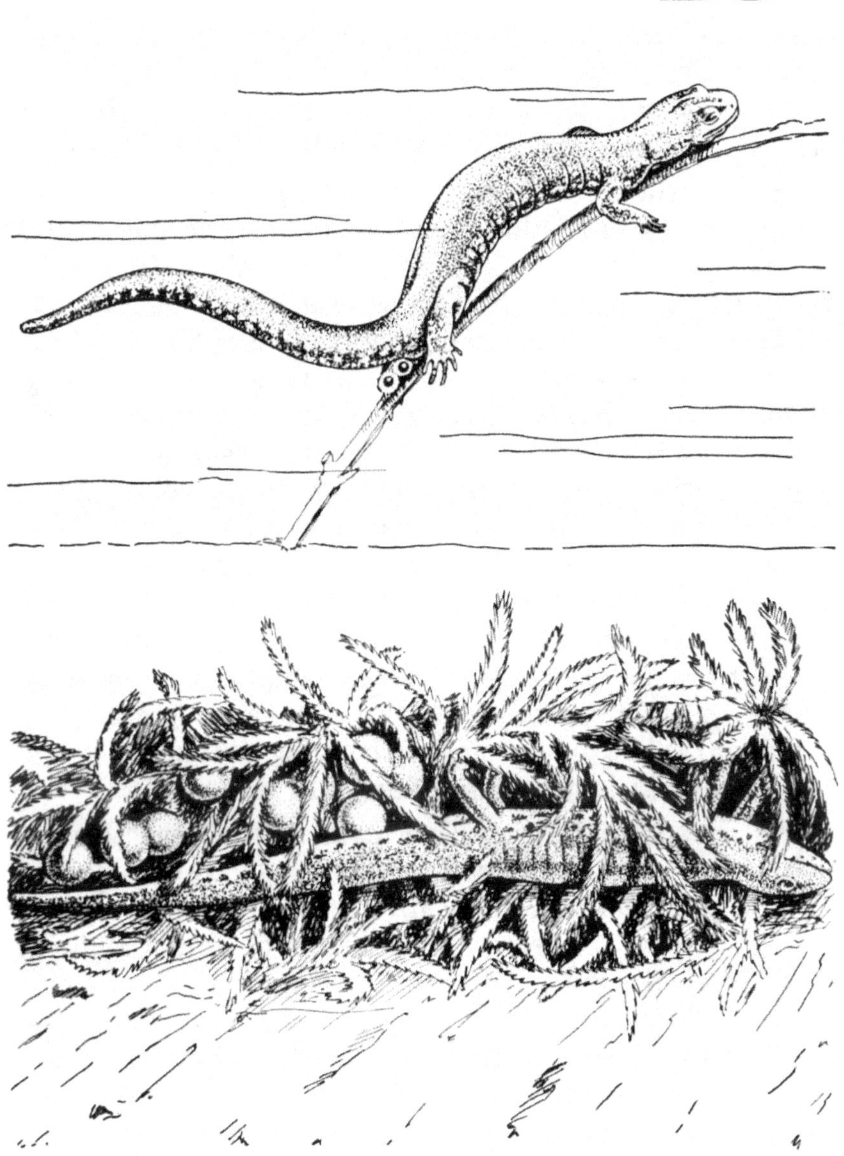

FIG. 6. Egg-laying of salamanders. Above: Jefferson's salamander. Below: Four-toed salamander as found on May 11. After
Bishop.

four per minute, stick to the support and to each other.
After approximately sixteen have appeared, the female
rests many minutes or even a few hours before shifting
her position and starting a new batch.

At first the clear mucus surrounding the eggs has little
volume, and a single batch extends along one side of the
support or forms a spiral around it. With the rapid
absorption of water, the mucus swells so much that a
cylindrical mass an inch in diameter and 2 or 3 inches long
promptly takes shape, the supporting twig or stem forming
its long axis; before the eggs hatch, the dimensions of the
mass increase still more. Occasionally a female does not
move much while laying, and her entire complement
quickly swells into a single elongate mass 10 or 12 inches
in length. The number of eggs in a complement varies
from 100 to almost 300. The egg itself is barely $\frac{1}{8}$ of an
inch in diameter, light at one pole but dark at the other.
It is surrounded by three or four envelopes and a layer of
mucus, the diameter of the outer envelope being nearly $\frac{3}{16}$
of an inch. The green color of the mucus of most old egg
masses is caused by a unicellular plant (see p. 37).

As already stated, this species is aroused each spring
by the first long thaw or warm rainy spell. The few available records indicate that, in the latitude of Chicago,
mating takes place between the middle of March and the
tenth of April, the exact time varying with the season.
Laying follows soon after mating. The incubation period
is thirty to forty-five days in central New York but eggs
kept at room temperature hatch in two weeks. No observations have been made in the Chicago area. In other
parts of the range where this species occurs with the
spotted salamander, it lays about five days before the
first spotted salamanders arrive to breed.

Growth and Age.—The average hatchling is half an
inch long and has a rod-like projection, the balancer, on
either side equally distant from the eye and the gills. The
balancers persist from ten to sixteen days and are useful

in supporting the body. The gills of the mature larva are conspicuous, the head is broad, and the high tail crests or fins extend (on the upper side) some distance along the back. The larval period may last 125 days, or drying of the breeding pools or ponds may shorten it to eight weeks. There is a correlated variation in the size of the mature larvae; some metamorphose when only $1\frac{7}{8}$ inches long, others not until they are fully an inch longer. · Sexual maturity is attained about twenty-one months after transformation, at a total length of $4\frac{1}{2}$ to $5\frac{1}{2}$ inches. The average fully grown adult measures $6\frac{3}{8}$ inches from tip to tip, the largest $7\frac{1}{4}$. The tail and body are about equal in length or else the body is a trifle longer. No one knows what age is attained.

Habits.—Although nocturnal, this salamander ventures abroad on dark days. It burrows in loose soil and leaf mold or makes its abode in a cavity under a log, flat stone, or some other prone object. The larval habits are like those of the marbled salamander.

Food.—The adults eat insects and their larvae, earthworms, millipeds, and spiders; the larvae eat various small, aquatic creatures or even smaller larvae of their own or related species.

Habitat.—In general this salamander frequents woodlands, but near the Great Lakes it also inhabits marshy areas of lake beaches and dunes, hiding under drift débris.

Occurrence.—In the dune region at the southern tip of Lake Michigan, Jefferson's salamander abounds, and it is found, much less frequently, in the wooded region northwest of Chicago. There are records for Cook and Lake counties, Illinois; Lake, Porter, and La Porte counties, Indiana; and Berrien County, Michigan. It may occur in other parts of our area that were originally forested.

The general distribution includes southeastern Canada and the northeastern United States westward to Minnesota and southward to Virginia. Preferring a cold climate, the species is abundant only in the northern part of its range or in the higher altitudes farther south. The northern seaboard states are an exception, for in parts of them it is rare or even absent.

Reference.—The Salamanders of New York. By Sherman C. Bishop. New York State Museum Bulletin, No. 324, 1941. An excellent general account.

SPOTTED SALAMANDER

Ambystoma maculatum

Figures 7–9

Recognition.—Two irregular rows of conspicuous, dull yellow to bright orange spots extending along the back distinguish this species from other local salamanders. The ground color of the back is deep bluish black and the slate-colored sides are never bordered below by a row of spots that tend to fuse. Compare the description of the tiger salamander (p. 46).

The Sexes.—During the breeding season the males may be recognized by their swollen, protuberant vents and darker bellies. At all seasons, the following differences will help to separate the sexes: In the male, the body and tail are longer and more slender; if the limbs of one side are pressed along the body toward each other, the toes of this sex touch or are separated by a short space, whereas in the female they are always separated by a considerable space. The head of the female is broader, more convex above, and less pointed. There are also a few minor differences.

Reproduction.—Breeding starts in early spring when the adults, aroused by continuous, warm rains or melting snows, emerge from hibernation and migrate by night to some woodland pond or pool. If suitable conditions persist, the migration may develop into a virtual stampede, but ordinarily the return of cold weather interferes to make migration a protracted process. The males usually arrive a day or two ahead of the females and a few days later than any Jefferson's salamanders of the same area.

Although this salamander is one of the most familiar amphibians of our country, there is difference of opinion about its courtship pattern. Wright and Allen long ago saw males rubbing the tops of their heads along the whole lower surfaces of the females and depositing spermatophores immediately thereafter. Recently, Mohr has stated that the courtship differs in no important detail from that of Jefferson's salamander, a species in which the male mounts the female.

When large numbers happen to reach a breeding site at one time, a spectacular nuptial dance ensues, but observers have been unable to make out exactly what takes place. In two of three cases reported the males outnumbered the females, whereas in the third the sexes were present in equal numbers.

A male has been observed to deposit twenty-two spermatophores in forty-five minutes, and it has been estimated that forty constitute the full complement of a single individual. Groups of 100 or more have been found in an area two or three feet across, but this is twice the usual number and groups of only a few are not rare. A linear series often means that a male has straddled a stick and deposited along it at regular intervals. Spermatophores are ordinarily found in shallow water. Figure 7 shows a group of them in situ as well as a single one greatly enlarged.

The process of laying has been observed more than once. During the night a female approaches a slanting stick or stem and selects a point on it six inches to a foot or two below the surface of the water. She takes hold at this point with her hind feet, places the body in a semi-erect position, and proceeds slowly to apply one egg after another without appreciably shifting her position. Usually the fore limbs are spread widely apart, but they sometimes grasp the support; the tail is extended. From thirty to

more than sixty minutes are required for the deposition
of a single cluster, and a female presumably produces two
or three clusters in a season. This species has been known
to lay on land, like the marbled salamander.

At first a cluster is an inch or less in diameter but the
protective mucus swells so rapidly by absorption of water
that the diameter increases four or five fold in about an

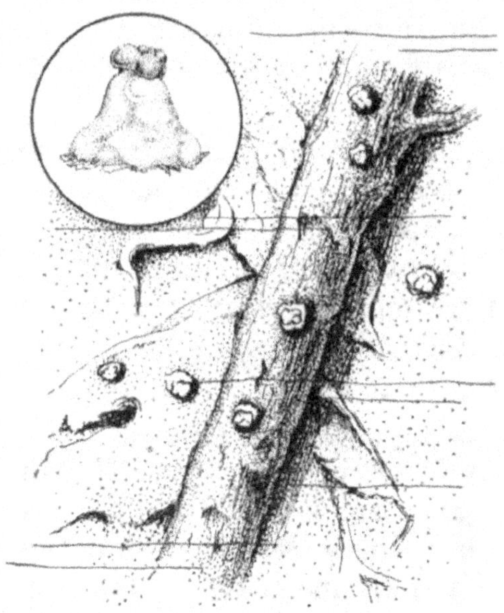

Fig. 7. Spermatophores of spotted salamander in situ on April 14.
Inset: A single one, greatly enlarged. After Bishop.

hour. A further but very gradual swelling of the globular
mass also takes place. Typical clusters are shown in
Figure 9. The number of eggs to a cluster varies from a
dozen or so to well over 200, but 100 may be considered
an average number. The egg itself is approximately $\frac{1}{8}$
of an inch in diameter, dark brown or gray at one pole,
dingy white or yellow at the other. It is surrounded by
three envelopes, the outer one with a diameter of about
$\frac{1}{4}$ of an inch. The outer envelopes lose their shape by
fusion with each other, and the cluster, which is thus so
firmly bound together that it may be lifted from the

water by the supporting stick or stem, appears to have a thick coating of more or less translucent and frequently greenish mucus.

The greenish hue is caused by a unicellular plant that commonly grows abundantly inside the egg envelopes of the spotted and Jefferson's salamanders. Gilbert presents evidence that the relationship between this alga and the eggs is a symbiotic one: The eggs develop more rapidly if the plant is there and the plant derives benefit from the carbon dioxide and nitrogenous wastes of the growing embryos.

As already stated, this species is aroused each spring by the first long thaw or warm rainy spell. Records indicate that, in the latitude of Chicago, mating takes place between the middle of March and the middle of April and precedes laying by a

FIG. 8. Spotted salamander seen from above. After Bishop.

week or less. The incubation period varies in length from thirty-one to fifty-four days, but its usual duration is six weeks. At room temperature, eggs hatch in eighteen to twenty-three days. Experiments have shown that normal larval development takes place in temperatures between 37° and 74° F. It is interesting that the larva has such a wide margin of safety as far as temperature is concerned.

Growth and Age.—The average hatchling is half an inch long and has a rod-like projection, the balancer, on either side below but a little farther back than the eye. The balancers usually persist from seven to ten days before dropping off. The gills of the mature larva are conspicuous, the head is broad, and the high tail crests or fins extend (on the upper side) some distance along the back. The larval period may last from two to three and a half months in the latitude of Chicago. Larvae usually metamorphose when 1¾ to 2 inches long but the total range of size at transformation is 1⅝ to 2⅞ inches. During the first year after metamorphosis the larvae reach a length of about 3¼ inches, but such half-grown individuals are rarely seen. The average adult male measures 6⅞ inches, the tail usually taking up slightly less than half of this. The maximum length is 7¾ inches.

One of these salamanders caught when already adult lived twenty-two years in captivity; another, captured as a larva in 1915 or 1916, was thriving in 1937. A longevity of at least twenty-four years has thus been proved.

Habits.—The spotted salamander is solitary and nocturnal, never congregating except to breed, and venturing abroad during the day only when the sky is heavily overcast. It burrows in loose soil and leaf mold or makes its home in a cavity under a log, a flat stone, or some other prone object. Not infrequently, individuals tumble into cellars where they cause considerable concern because of their "poisonous" colors. Needless to say, they are entirely harmless to man. The larval habits are like those of the marbled salamander.

Food.—The contents of about forty stomachs consisted of earthworms, centipeds, millipeds, snails, slugs, spiders, beetles, ants, crickets, other adult insects, and some insect larvae. The larval salamanders have been known to eat a waterbug, water-boatmen, and even tiny fish.

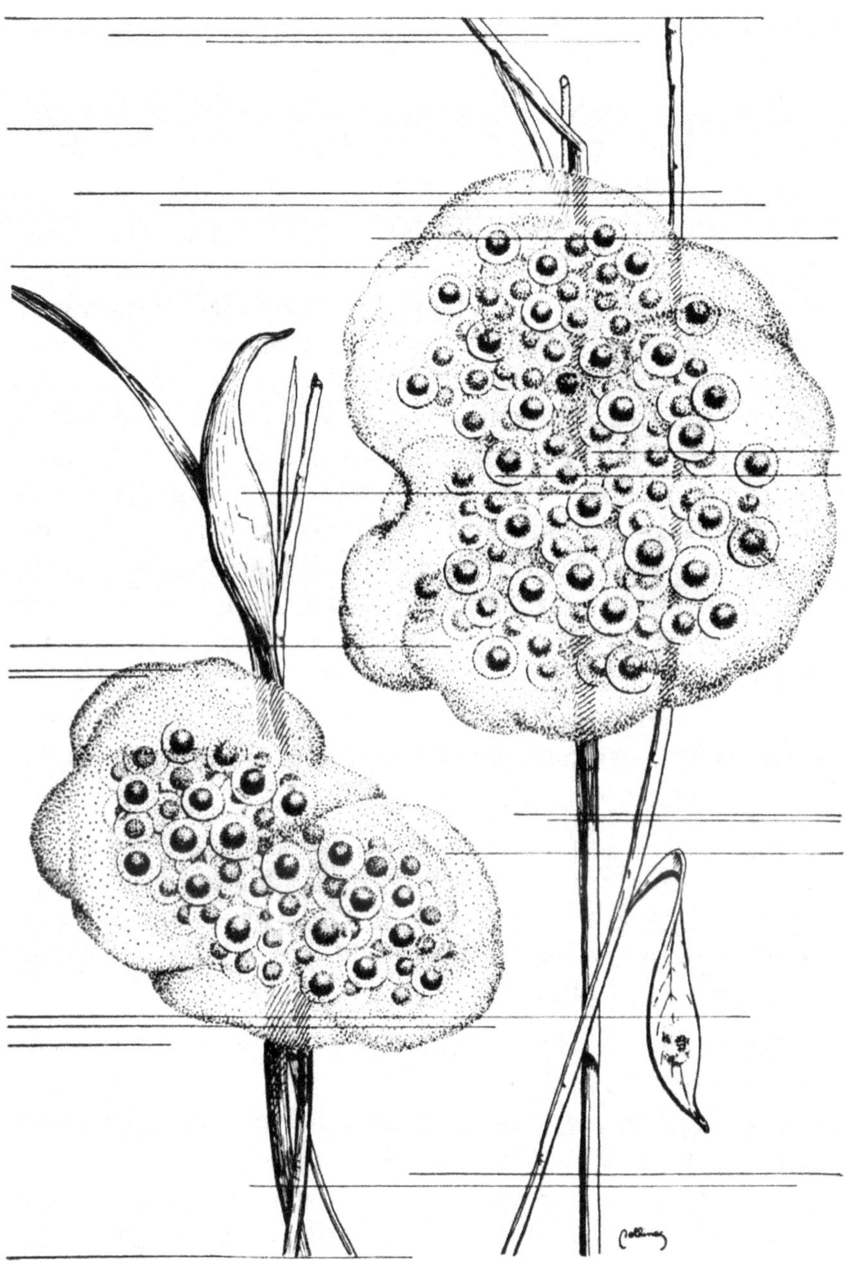

FIG. 9. Typical egg clusters of spotted salamander as they appeared on April 9. A spermatophore can be seen on leaf below larger cluster. After Bishop.

The empty stomachs found in certain migrating and mating individuals indicate that food is not taken until these activities have been concluded.

Economic Importance.—The larval spotted salamander has long been standard material for workers in embryology and other branches of zoology, thousands being sacrificed annually on the altar of experimental science. The number of technical publications in which the name of this species appears is astonishing and in them it is often referred to as *"punctatum"* instead of *"maculatum."* Development from cleavage of the egg to disappearance of the yolk was divided into forty-six stages by Harrison many years ago, and its exact rate at a constant temperature determined. Unfortunately, these stages have never been completely illustrated in print. Dempster, among others, has made detailed studies of embryonic and early larval growth under both natural and controlled conditions. The interesting results of his investigations lie beyond the scope of this work.

Habitat.—This is a woodland species most abundant in deciduous and mixed woods but also found in evergreen forests. Bishop has collected it in hillside meadows with stones and an occasional log affording the only cover, and in bottom lands along creeks.

Captivity.—Many laboratories raise great numbers of spotted salamander larvae for use in experimental zoology, as explained above. Brief directions for their care may be found in Rugh's *Experimental Embryology, A Manual of Techniques and Procedures,* published in 1941 by the New York University Press. Rugh also includes new drawings of most of Harrison's forty-six classic stages of development.

Occurrence.—Common in certain local areas; reported from Cook, Lake, and Will counties, Illinois; Porter County, Indiana; and Berrien County, Michigan. It is widely distributed in the eastern United States and adjacent Canada, ranging as far west as Wisconsin and Texas.

Reference.—The Salamanders of New York. By Sherman C. Bishop. New York State Museum Bulletin, No. 324, 1941. An excellent general account.

MARBLED SALAMANDER
Ambystoma opacum
Figures 5, 10, and 11

Recognition.—This is a black salamander with conspicuous light bands across the back. These bands are narrow along the middle of the back but often widen and join on the upper sides to enclose a series of black spots. Various other modifications occur, such as the failure of some or all of the light bands to meet on the back.

The Sexes.—The light markings of the male are white, those of the female grayish white, a difference that is most pronounced in the breeding season. There is a greater tendency for the legs of the female to be tinged with brown. In this sex the vent protrudes only during the breeding season and then but slightly, whereas the male's vent protrudes noticeably at all times, especially throughout the breeding season.

Reproduction.—In the autumn, males and females migrate to the nesting grounds, the former preceding by a few days. The males initiate a grotesque courtship that is chiefly a game of violent butting of females and other males by the more active males, the purpose being to force the snout under the opponent. Certain characteristic performances result. One of these was named "fencing" by Noble and Brady, who made extensive laboratory and field observations on the breeding of this species. In "fencing," each of two males tries at the same time to get his head under the other's chin, their movements attaining such a speed that the heads appear as a blur. The other performance, the "waltz," occurs when a male attempts to thrust his snout under a female's cloaca, and the female responds with similar efforts, the pair sometimes revolving about a common center for minutes on end (Fig. 5e).

Courtship ends when the males begin to deposit spermatophores (Fig. 5f). During deposition the body is elevated on stiff legs and the tail undulated. Subsequent gentle nosing of a female induces her to pass chin and belly over a spermatophore until the cloacal lips are in a position to receive it. A spermatophore is shown in Figure 10.

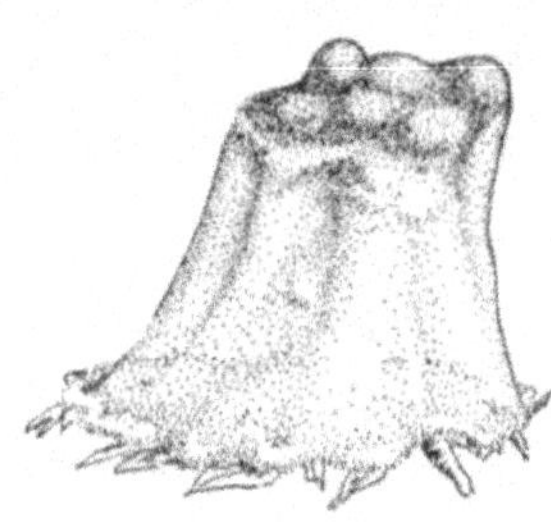

Fig. 10. Newly deposited spermatophore of marbled salamander. After Noble and Brady. Greatly enlarged.

Dry pond beds or other areas that will be flooded by winter and late autumn rains are chosen as temporary nesting sites. The female selects a depression or cavity concealed under moss, leaf mold, drift débris, or some object such as a log or stone and then shapes it by turning around in it. She next deposits singly about 100 eggs. The average number has been put as high as 150 and a clutch with 232 is on record. The eggs are brooded by the female for a few weeks (Fig. 11), the duration of brooding depending on the rainfall, since marbled salamanders drown readily. The eggs may be deserted even before they are flooded.

The egg measures barely $\frac{1}{8}$ of an inch in diameter and is encased in two envelopes that are separated by a layer of mucus. The outer envelope has a diameter of about $\frac{3}{16}$ of an inch. The eggs stick together somewhat when dry but lose their adhesiveness in water. They withstand desiccation well but shrink noticeably as they dry.

As hatching time arrives, a substance secreted by minute unicellular glands scattered over the head of the embryo weakens the egg capsules so much that they are easily ruptured by the struggling embryo. Until further studies have been made, it is impossible to say whether

FIG. 11. Brooding of eggs by female salamanders. Above: Red-backed salamander as found on July 16. Below: Marbled salamander as found in North Carolina on October 26. After Bishop.

an escape could be effected without aid of the head glands.
Similar glands are found in many amphibians but their
role in hatching has seldom been investigated.

The marbled salamander is unique among the local
species of the genus *Ambystoma* in being an autumn
instead of a spring breeder. At least in the northern part
of the range, the adults migrate to the breeding grounds in
September and laying takes place during the last half
of September or the first week of October.

When rains come promptly, incubation is hastened
and may be completed in a few weeks; dryness greatly
prolongs it and drought may delay hatching until spring.
Temperature is only a minor factor; however, experiments
have shown that eggs do not hatch at 35° F. although
they hatch well at 70° F.

Growth and Age.—Hatchlings are not uniform in size
and development because the time spent in the egg is so
variable; ¾ of an inch may be taken as the average total
length at hatching and 2½ to 3 inches as the length at
maturity and transformation. In southern New York,
metamorphosis occurs during June at an age of eight or
nine months. The hatchlings, like those of the two preceding species, have a rod-like projection, the balancer, on
either side, below but a little farther back than the eye.
The balancers usually persist for several days. The gills of
the mature larva are conspicuous, the head is broad, and
the high tail crests or fins extend (on the upper side)
forward almost to the head.

Exact information on size and age at sexual maturity
is not available, but Bishop calculates that in South
Carolina maturity is reached fifteen to seventeen months
after transformation. The average adult total length is
4 inches, the tail occupying a little more than a third;
4¾ inches is the maximum length. No one knows how
long this salamander lives.

Habits.—This inactive, nocturnal species lives nearer
the surface than most other members of the genus *Amby-*

stoma and often hides under exposed objects such as logs, bark, stones, and drift material. It is entirely inoffensive.

The sluggish, delicate larvae readily float at any level with no apparent effort and, where the water is deep, spend much of their time suspended in mid-water, ready to dart away when alarmed. In shallow pools they conceal themselves in bottom débris. Their limbs are weak but the high tail fins enable them to swim moderately well.

Food.—Earthworms, snails, slugs, and insects such as beetles and flies have been found in the few stomachs examined; the larvae eat crustaceans and snails. Further information on the feeding habits is badly needed.

Habitat.—In the northeastern states this species is usually recorded from dry woods and their vicinity, but in other parts of the range it frequents low or even swampy forests. More detailed studies are required to determine how real is this reported difference in habitat preference. Even in the northeast, young individuals tend to remain in damp areas near their site of metamorphosis. The larvae are wholly aquatic and occur in temporary or permanent ponds, flooded ditches, sluggish streams, or even the quieter sections of streams with current.

Captivity.—The marbled salamander does well in captivity, its unusual breeding behavior making it an interesting species to observe. A terrarium measuring fifteen by twenty inches is large enough for a dozen specimens. The courtship dance is best watched in a dim; red light such as that of a flashlight or a weak electric bulb covered with translucent red paper.

The larvae should be allowed to emerge in water because those that hatch on land are not well developed and presumably are weak. They will feed on minute invertebrates, which may be strained from stagnant pond water or bought at any large biological supply house. The small crustacean known as cyclops is commonly sold and is especially suitable for young larvae.

Occurrence.—In the Chicago area the marbled salamander has been found only in forests of La Porte County, Indiana, where large numbers exist. It is widely distributed over the eastern United States from the Mississippi Basin to the coast except in the north where a line through Chicago and Boston marks its approximate northern limits. The local Indiana population obviously lies near the northwestern extremity of its range.

References.—The Salamanders of New York. By Sherman C. Bishop. New York State Museum Bulletin, No. 324, 1941. An excellent general account.

Observations on the Life History of the Marbled Salamander, *Ambystoma opacum* Gravenhorst. By G. K. Noble and M. K. Brady. Zoologica, Vol. 11, pp. 89–132, 1933. A detailed, technical account of reproduction.

TIGER SALAMANDER
Ambystoma tigrinum tigrinum

Figures 2, 12, and 13

Recognition.—Numerous yellow spots irregular in size and shape adorn the body and are concentrated along the sides of the belly where the somewhat similar spotted salamander is never spotted. The ground color is black to deep brown. Size alone will often identify the tiger salamander since no other local kind except the mudpuppy and siren ever exceeds a total length of 7¾ inches; most adult tiger salamanders of our region are longer than this.

The Sexes.—The vent is longer in males and, during the breeding season, it is greatly swollen, whereas such a swelling is never evident in the female. Males are larger and their tails proportionately as well as actually longer. In a series of forty-five adults from Chicago collected at one place in early March, the tail is noticeably shorter than the body in the nine females; in the thirty-six males the tail is longer than the body in twenty-five, shorter in nine, and equal to it in two. The tail of only one male is shorter than the longest tail among the females. Judged by this lot, all mature tiger salamanders with tails longer than the body are males. Bishop finds that the hind legs are longer and stouter in this sex, but such differences, if present, are scarcely discernible in the series of forty-five.

Reproduction.—Breeding starts in early spring when the hibernating adults, aroused by warm rains, enter some woodland pond or pool, which may yet be partly ice-bound. Just how far from the breeding sites the adults hibernate is not known. Bishop writes of regular spring migrations on Long Island, New York, but at Lake Forest, Illinois, B. G. Smith built a zigzag burlap fence along one side of a breeding pond and failed to trap any specimens in pits dug at the angles on the landward side. A few adults had already entered when the fence was erected very early in the season but more should have been caught had there been a true migration to the pond. It is possible that at least in our area a movement to the immediate vicinity of the breeding sites takes place in the autumn. Additional traps should be made in late February around favorite breeding sites.

FIG. 12. Tiger salamander, seen from above. From Du Page County, Illinois.

Courtship under natural conditions has never been observed but Kumpf watched it in a tank and her account may be summarized as follows: At first the salamanders walk and swim around a great deal. After a time, both sexes begin to nose and push each other about, the males paying more attention to the females. When a well-aroused male succeeds in lifting a female on his snout he swims around supporting her and shifts his head along her belly in either direction. This procedure always ends with his vigorously butting her cloaca until he is ready to stalk ahead and deposit a spermatophore. In doing this the male assumes a characteristic posture: The rigidly outstretched feet are raised and the tail is elevated at right angles to the body. As the spermatophore is extruded, the body is convulsed, the tail violently undulated, and the cloaca rubbed on the bottom. The female, having followed her mate with her snout closely applied to his cloacal region, now advances and picks up the head of the spermatophore, assuming as she does so the same sprawling posture. In no other species of the genus do both sexes hold themselves in such a position at the climax of courtship, although in Jefferson's salamander the males behave in much the same way. Male tiger salamanders sometimes deposit spermatophores when not actually courting, but these are ignored by the females.

The egg clusters are usually attached to twigs, or stems a foot or more below the surface of the water. When first deposited they are less than an inch in diameter but the protective mucus surrounding them swells so rapidly by absorption of water that the diameter of a cluster increases four or five fold in about an hour. After this, a gradual swelling takes place and the clusters, though at first smaller than those of the spotted salamander, are often larger about the time of hatching. The fused outer envelopes do not hold the cluster together firmly enough to prevent slipping when it is lifted from the water by the supporting twig or stem. The average cluster measures about 2¼ by 2¾ inches. The number of eggs in one cluster varies from 23 to 110 and averages 52, clusters with more than 76 being rare. The egg itself is approximately ⅛ of an inch in diameter, light to dark brown at one pole, pale cream to buff at the other. It is surrounded by three envelopes, the outermost having a diameter of about 5⁄16 of an inch, which increases another ⅛ of an inch by hatching time.

As already stated, this species is aroused each spring by warm rains. Exact dates of first appearance have not been recorded for the Chicago region but it presumably takes place about the middle of March; on Long Island,

FIG. 13. Mature larva of tiger salamander. Specimen from Cook County, Illinois, killed July 12.

New York, it has been known to occur ten days earlier. Eggs are numerous by the end of March and the laying period probably lasts from two to four weeks, depending on weather conditions. The exact duration of incubation has not been ascertained, but it is approximately twenty-eight days. At room temperature eggs hatch in twelve to eighteen days.

Growth and Age.—The average hatchling is 9⁄16 of an inch long and lacks the balancers developed by the three preceding species. The length of the larval period has not been accurately determined, although Bishop records one case in which metamorphosis seems to have occurred seventy-three to seventy-five days after hatching. Confined larvae metamorphose in about four months. Twenty-one mature larvae from Long Island, New York, varied in length from 3⁄16 to 4⅞ inches and averaged 4³⁄16 inches. Figure 13 shows a large larva from Cook County, Illinois.

Sexual maturity may be reached in the spring following transformation.

The size of the species in our area is indicated by measurements of the series of forty-five breeding adults collected at one time and place in Chicago. The thirty-six males varied in length from $7\frac{5}{16}$ to 10 inches, averaging $8\frac{3}{4}$; the nine females from $6\frac{5}{16}$ to $8\frac{7}{16}$, averaging $7\frac{5}{8}$. The longest wild-caught specimen recorded in the literature is from Racine, Wisconsin, and measured 10 inches, so apparently the subspecies attains its maximum size in the Chicago region.

A tiger salamander that hatched in an aquarium at the University of Michigan and lived there for eleven years was $10\frac{1}{4}$ inches long at the age of three years. Another thrived in the same aquarium seven years after its capture as an adult. These figures give a fair idea of the longevity of the species. In some parts of its range this salamander fails to metamorphose, reproducing while in a larval state, like certain other species of *Ambystoma*. Such neotenic larvae are known as "axolotls" and have long been popular in zoological gardens. Flower gives a record of one identified as *Ambystoma tigrinum* that lived in captivity more than twenty-five years. Since axolotls do not occur in the Chicago area and are at best hard to identify, it is safer to regard the University of Michigan specimens as holding the longevity record for the local form of tiger salamander.

Habits.—The tiger salamander is nocturnal and much given to burrowing deeply in loose soil or leaf mold or living in abandoned mammal runways. Farmers often find it under piles of débris or manure or in drains that are readily followed for some distance. The discovery of this large but harmless creature in cellars or window wells sometimes causes needless concern. It is most frequently trapped in such places during the autumn when in search of a hibernation site or possibly when migrating toward

Photograph by Charles E. Mohr

EGGS OF MUDPUPPY (*Necturus maculosus maculosus*)

A TYPICAL HOME OF THE MUDPUPPY IN THE CHICAGO AREA

the breeding ponds as discussed above. The larval habits are like those of the marbled salamander.

Food.—Although no one has ever examined numbers of stomachs, captive specimens are well known to devour almost any animal small enough to be swallowed whole. Earthworms, mollusks, insects, fish, frogs, other salamanders, and even baby mice are accepted.

Economic Importance.—Like the spotted salamander, this species has long been standard material for workers in experimental zoology, and thousands are raised annually in scientific laboratories.

Habitat.—This amphibian inhabits almost any type of woodland and thrives in varied degrees of humidity. Subterranean habits no doubt enable it to survive beneath a variety of surface conditions. It is not infrequently dug up in garden soil.

Captivity.—As already mentioned, many laboratories raise great numbers of tiger salamander larvae for use in experimental zoology and a reference to Rugh's directions for taking care of *Ambystoma* larvae is given (see SPOTTED SALAMANDER). Larval tiger salamanders are especially voracious and mutilate or kill one another if confined together. The adults make interesting and hardy pets in a terrarium with moss or decayed wood in which to hide. They will feed voraciously on living meal worms, earthworms, or any other animals small enough to be swallowed whole. Pieces of raw beef supported on the point of a slender stick and moved back and forth at the side rather than in front of the head will be snapped up by individuals that have become used to captivity.

Occurrence.—This is the most familiar salamander of the Chicago area, throughout which it is found in suitable habitats.

Ambystoma tigrinum is widely distributed over the United States, adjacent Canada, and the plateau of Mexico to the coastal plain of Vera Cruz. Dunn has recently divided it into seven subspecies on the basis of color differences. The local subspecies occurs over much of the eastern third of this country; no tiger salamanders are found in the greater part of the Appalachian uplands, and the status of the population living in the region that includes Kentucky, eastern Texas, and intervening territory has not been determined.

Reference.—The Salamanders of New York. By Sherman C. Bishop. New York State Museum Bulletin, No. 324, 1941. An excellent general account.

RED-BACKED SALAMANDER

Plethodon cinereus

Plate 4 and Figures 2 and 11

Recognition.—A naso-labial groove (evident under a lens as a fine line from the nostril to the mouth; Fig. 2) and five toes on the hind limb distinguish this species from other local kinds except the two-lined salamander. The tongue of the latter is set on an extensible stalk, whereas in the red-backed salamander it is attached to the floor of the mouth. Since two of these points are hard to determine, certain additional facts may prove helpful. The slender red-backed salamander is never bigger around than a lead pencil (diameter $\frac{1}{4}$ inch) and is rarely 4 inches long. In contrast to the two-lined salamander, it is wholly terrestrial and the external gills are lost before it has reached a length of an inch. This tiny gilled stage is rarely seen because it persists only a few days.

Two phases, one with back and upper sides of approximately the same color, the other with a strongly contrasting red back (Plate 4), commonly occur together, although in certain regions only one has been seen. The phases are usually found in about equal numbers but either may predominate.

The Sexes.—The snouts of the males are swollen around the naso-labial grooves and the females average $\frac{1}{8}$ of an inch longer than the males. There are other still more obscure differences.

Reproduction.—Courtship, mating, and laying have never been observed under natural conditions, but laboratory studies of courtship have determined that it follows the general pattern described for the four-toed salamander. Fertilization is accomplished by means of spermatophores.

A captive female was seen to keep the body in one place while laying, so that the eggs formed a compact cluster. An egg was forced out in twenty seconds, five to ten seconds elapsing between extrusions. The cluster is usually suspended by a single mucous cable from the top of a small cavity in a well-decayed log or stump and attended by a female who maintains actual contact with it (Fig. 11).

Most clusters contain from seven to ten eggs although a clutch with fourteen has been recorded. Eggs vary in diameter from ⅛ to 3/16 of an inch and are light yellow in color. They are readily confused with slug eggs, which differ in being translucent and having brittle shells.

In southern Michigan, mating begins late in October and is resumed in the spring for a few weeks. The incubation period has not been determined but, in the latitude of Chicago, laying takes place from mid-June to mid-July, hatching through most of August and in early September. High temperatures undoubtedly hasten development.

Growth and Age.—Newly hatched larvae average ¾ of an inch from tip to tip and have flat, colorless gills that disappear in a few days. Only the gills distinguish them in general appearance from the adult. Breeding age is reached two years after hatching when the body is barely 1 3/16 inches long. The average adult length is 1⅝ or 1¾ inches. The tail is slightly shorter than the body and the maximum total length very rarely exceeds

4 inches.   A specimen recently found on Staten Island, New York, has the astonishing record length of 4¾ inches. No one knows how long these salamanders live.

Habits.—This timid, secretive amphibian is seldom seen abroad during the day but must be sought in rotten logs or stumps or under other objects of forest or woodland floor. Droughts cause it to disappear from its usual haunts; presumably it descends to lower levels in search of moisture.

It jumps with agility, using the tail rather than the limbs in doing so, and it climbs well in spite of having such short legs. The skin is shed at undetermined intervals and eaten, the first shedding taking place a few days after hatching. The tail is readily thrown off, a provision that facilitates escape. If the tail is seized the body quickly escapes, and if the body is seized the wriggling tail with its raw end tempts the enemy to release the body and pursue the tail.

Food.—Larval and mature insects, chiefly beetles and ants, constitute about half the food, but many other small animals such as spiders, snails, and worms are eaten. Hundreds of stomachs have been examined to determine this.

Habitat.—Frequenting forest and woodland floor, the red-backed salamander is the only wholly terrestrial amphibian of the Chicago region. In spite of this it requires moisture and is most abundant in damp situations such as low ground bordering streams.

Captivity.—Preparing a terrarium for such a small creature is a simple matter but collecting animals small enough to satisfy its appetite requires persistence. It is especially interesting as one of the few amphibians that have become entirely free of the bondage of water and thus advanced to the stage first attained by reptiles as a group.

Occurrence.—Common in the northwest corner of Indiana but rare in Illinois north of Chicago. There is no reasonable explanation of its scarcity in this part of our area, since it is well known throughout Wisconsin and Michigan. The species is also widely distributed in the eastern third of the United States and is found in adjacent parts of Canada.

Reference.—The Salamanders of New York. By Sherman C. Bishop. New York State Museum Bulletin, No. 324, 1941. An excellent general account.

FOUR-TOED SALAMANDER
Hemidactylium scutatum
Plate 4 and Figure 6

Recognition.—The four-toed salamander and the mud-puppy are the only local salamanders with four instead of five toes on the hind limb. The small four-toed sala-mander never exceeds a total length of 4 inches and loses its slender external gills when it is less than an inch long, whereas the robust mudpuppy reaches a length of more than a foot and retains its bushy external gills throughout life.

The Sexes.—The average total length of the more slender male is ⅜ of an inch less than that of the stouter female, but the tail of the male is relatively longer. The male's snout is swollen on either side below the nasal openings and a few upper front teeth pierce the lip. There are minor differences in color.

Reproduction.—Courtship has been observed only in captive specimens. The male rubs his lips and adjacent head parts or even the side of the body against the snout of his mate. After becoming aroused, the female follows him about, keeping her chin pressed against the base of his tail, which is slowly undulated. The female picks up the spermatophores deposited by the male, but details of this procedure are unknown.

The females migrate in early spring from their winter quarters to the nesting grounds, a journey that the males do not seem to make. The nesting sites are in rather open bogs, at shaded woodland pools, or along streams meandering through swamps. The nests are simple cavities in decayed wood, sphagnum moss, grass roots, or moss rhizoids. Some nests seem to have been formed or at least shaped by movements of the female. They are never more than a few inches from water; usually they are just above it.

On one occasion at noon and on another at three o'clock in the afternoon, Bishop actually watched females lay. The belly was turned up, as shown in Figure 6, while the eggs were slowly forced out one at a time. A clutch usually consists of some thirty eggs in a compact mass. The egg, about ⅛ of an inch in diameter, is yellow below and lightly pigmented above; the outer of its two mucous envelopes has a diameter twice that of the egg.

The long mating season comes in the autumn and late summer, the laying time in early spring. In southern Michigan, incubation requires from six to eight weeks, high temperatures speeding development.

Growth and Age.—Hatchling four-toed salamanders are barely ½ of an inch long, mature larvae approximately ¼ of an inch longer. The aquatic larval period has been estimated to last six weeks in southern Michigan. Sexual maturity is reached twenty-eight months after hatching. Most mature females measure from 3 to 3¼ inches from tip to tip, the tail as a rule being noticeably longer than the body. The maximum length is 3½ inches. Nothing is known about the longevity of this salamander.

Habits.—Such a small, secretive species escapes notice except where it is abundant or when it is migrating to the nesting sites in the spring. During the day it hides under objects on the ground such as stones, logs, and stumps, but it is sometimes seen abroad at night. The larvae are thoroughly aquatic, and even the adults can swim. The habit of coiling when disturbed is characteristic of the species.

The tail is readily thrown off, a constriction at its base marking the point of detachment. The wound is protected, since the break in the skin is beyond that in the trunk of the tail. The value of such a habit has been discussed (see p. 54).

Food.—No one has made a detailed study of the food habits. One stomach was found to contain spiders, springtails, drosophilid flies, and homopterous bugs; another, remains of staphylinid beetles and moth larvae.

Habitat.—Open or grassy woodland near a site suitable for breeding is the preferred habitat. Meadows and grassy hillsides with flat stones or numerous logs and stumps in advanced stages of decay are also frequented in some parts of the range but not in the local region. The larvae live in the water near which the eggs were laid.

Occurrence.—The few specimens taken locally were found in Cook and Lake counties, Illinois, and in Porter County, Indiana. Although rare around Chicago, this salamander is widely distributed over the eastern third of the United States.

Reference.—The Salamanders of New York. By Sherman C. Bishop. New York State Museum Bulletin, No. 324, 1941. An excellent general account.

Two-lined Salamander
Eurycea bislineata bislineata

Figures 3 and 5

Recognition.—A naso-labial groove (evident under a lens as a fine line from the nostril to the mouth) and five toes on the hind limb distinguish this species from other local kinds except the red-backed salamander. The tongue of the latter is attached to the floor of the mouth, whereas in the two-lined salamander it is set on an extensible stalk (Fig. 3).

Since two of these points are hard to determine, certain additional facts may prove helpful. The slender two-lined salamander is never bigger around than a lead pencil (¼ of an inch in diameter) and is rarely 4 inches long. In contrast to the red-backed salamander, it is a frequenter of streams, springs, and bogs, rarely leaving the immediate vicinity of water.

The Sexes.—The upper front teeth of the male are bicuspid during part of the year and larger and longer than those of the female, whose teeth always have a single cusp or point. Differences in body plus tail length are not marked although the longest individuals seem to be males. There are also other obscure sexual differences.

Reproduction.—Captive two-lined salamanders have been seen to perform an elaborate evening courtship dance. This performance is begun by the male, who pushes the female about with his snout. Being thus aroused, the female rubs snouts and cheeks with her mate, who frequently bends his head around her snout (Fig. 5*b*). After an hour or more of these preliminaries, the female straddles the male with her fore limbs, pressing her chin just behind the highest point of his tail (Fig. 5*a*). The male at once walks forward, wagging the base of his tail, while the female keeps pace, continually turning her head sharply in a direction opposite to the bend in his tail.

Although spermatophores have been deposited by captive males and taken from females, nobody has ever found one deposited under natural conditions.

When ready to lay, the female turns her belly up, arches the back and tail, and sticks the eggs one at a time to the surface above her. The time required for the laying of each egg is from two to three minutes, an hour or more for the entire clutch. This process has been observed only in captive individuals artificially induced to lay.

Many lots of eggs have been found in their natural surroundings. They are always attached to the lower surface of a stone or other object and at least sometimes guarded by the female. No nest is made, but the site of

JEFFERSON'S SALAMANDER
(*Ambystoma jeffersonianum*)
Seen from above

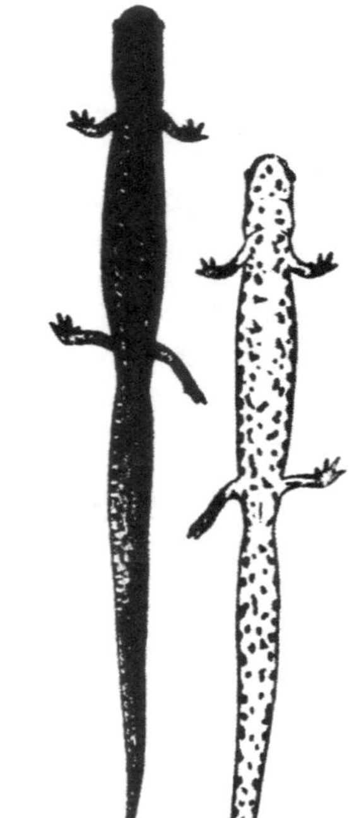

FOUR-TOED SALAMANDER
(*Hemidactylium scutatum*)
Seen from above and below

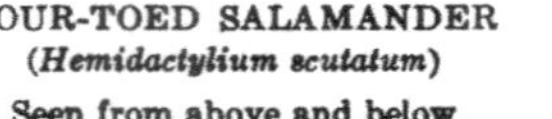

RED-BACKED SALAMANDER
(*Plethodon cinereus*)
Gray and red phases

attachment is bathed by running water and may be just beneath its surface or submerged several inches. The white or pale yellow eggs, usually twenty or thirty in number, form a single layer and, for the most part, lie close to one another, the area covered being from three to six inches across. Often the outermost eggs are slightly scattered. Clusters containing the mixed complements of several females are sometimes found. Each egg measures about $\frac{1}{8}$ of an inch in diameter and is enclosed in two mucous envelopes.

The extensive laying season commences in April or even late March and ends with June. Hatching begins a month before laying ceases and continues through August. Wilder states that the incubation period is about one month long but in some cases it must be considerably longer, the eggs laid early in the season or in cold water developing more slowly. Exact information on this subject is badly needed.

Growth and Age.—Larvae hatch when approximately $\frac{1}{2}$ of an inch long and reach a maximum total length of $2\frac{11}{16}$ inches, but the average length of metamorphosing individuals is only $2\frac{1}{16}$ inches. Adults average 3 inches, although this figure would be low for individuals from the northeastern extremity of the range, where the species attains its greatest size and may even exceed the usual 4-inch maximum. In specimens of moderate size, the tail is about as long as the body, but it is slightly longer in large individuals.

The larvae begin to metamorphose about a year after hatching and continue to transform through another year or even two. Sexual maturity is attained in the autumn following the summer of completed metamorphosis and eggs are laid the subsequent spring. The length of life has not been determined. At metamorphosis the high tail fin of the larva is lost, along with the gills, the lip folds, and the row of light spots on the side.

Habits.—This agile salamander can escape into crevices with surprising speed. When pursued it sometimes alternately bends and straightens the body in a spring-like manner that propels it at an astonishing rate. It is seldom seen abroad during the day. The larva is wholly aquatic, the adult at home either on land or in the water.

Both adult and larva remain active during the winter months, their secretive, aquatic habits enabling them to avoid exposure to the low air temperatures of the surface and take refuge in warm spring water or the temperate air of deep crevices.

Food and Feeding Habits.—Hamilton analyzed the contents of forty-seven stomachs, using the percentage-by-bulk method. The following six items (given with their percentages) comprised three-fourths of the food: beetles and their larvae (16.2), spiders (14), sowbugs (13.7), mayflies (10.5), flies (10), and annelid worms (9.8). Several individuals collected in January were feeding in spite of freezing surface temperatures.

Habitat.—Moderately swift, clear streams with rocky beds affording innumerable crevices are the preferred habitat. Here these salamanders hide under flat stones and other objects of the stream bed or bank and even wander scores of yards from water after rains. Springs and bogs are also frequented.

Occurrence.—The two-lined salamander reaches the extreme western limit of its distribution in the Chicago area, where it has been found only at Custer Park, Will County, Illinois. From Indiana it ranges eastward and northeastward over the middle Atlantic and northeastern states. A population of large individuals inhabiting southern Quebec recently has been set off as a subspecies, *E. bislineata major.*

Reference.—The Salamanders of New York. By Sherman C. Bishop. New York State Museum Bulletin, No. 324, 1941. An excellent general account.

SIREN

Siren intermedia nettingi

Figure 14

Recognition.—The absence of hind limbs identifies this eel-shaped salamander at a glance. The small fore limbs lie just behind the conspicuous external gills, which persist throughout life.

The Sexes.—The average total length of males is a little greater than that of females. Cagle and Smith measured a series (forty-seven males and forty-six females) that included a good number of mature individuals of both sexes and was taken from a single Illinois winter aggregation. Nearly all of the mature females measured from $9\frac{1}{2}$ to $11\frac{1}{4}$ inches, whereas the great majority of the corresponding age group of males were from $10\frac{3}{4}$ to $12\frac{7}{8}$ inches long.

Reproduction.—Noble and Marshall studied this subspecies in northeastern Arkansas and found during the second week of April two lots of eggs in hollows in the mucky bottoms of shallow ponds. In one case, 555 eggs adhered in a clump, in the other only 260, but there was no way of telling whether any eggs had been lost from either. A siren that swam away as the larger lot was lifted from the water may have been a guarding adult.

These investigators dissected 299 eggs from a female, and 224 and 706 were found by Cagle and Smith in two hibernating Illinois specimens. It is apparent that siren produce highly variable numbers of eggs. The individual egg is pigmented at one pole and is about $\frac{1}{8}$ of an inch in diameter. The outermost of its three capsules measures at first $\frac{3}{16}$ of an inch in diameter but swells a little as time goes on. It is opaque.

Growth and Age.—The hatchling is barely $\frac{1}{2}$ of an inch long and has well-developed gills but a mere stub of a tail. A thick fold extends along the middle of the back

almost to the head and is bordered on either side by a dark
stripe.   This fold develops into a high dorsal fin that
attains its maximum development when the hatchling is
about twenty-five days old, begins to disappear three or
four weeks later, and reaches its final stage of reduction,
in which it is confined to the distal four-fifths of the tail,

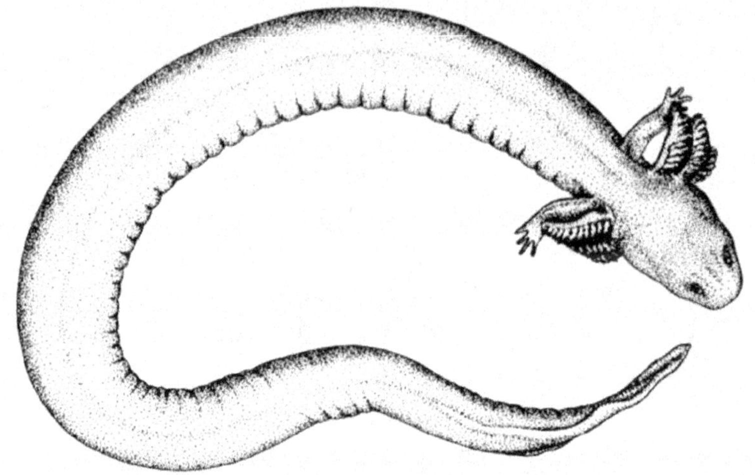

Fig. 14. Adult siren, seen from above.

seven months thereafter.   The limbs are not fully developed until two months after hatching.

Judging by the measurements of Cagle and Smith's
Illinois series, siren from 6 to 8¾ inches long have lived
through one growing season, those measuring more than
9 inches, through at least two.   Sexual maturity is attained
by the females, and probably by the males, during their
second summer or fall.   The adult's tail is a little less than
half as long as its body and the maximum total length is
15.6 inches.

The unfortunate confusion that long existed between
the two species of the genus *Siren* makes it impossible to
say which of the two lived twenty-four years in the Jardin
des Plantes, Paris.   It might have been *intermedia*, and,
since other siren have survived eight and nine years of

captivity, it is safe to assume that our local kind attains a respectable age.

Habits.—This nocturnal amphibian is fond of burrowing in bottom débris and can swim with considerable speed for short distances. The sound made by it on rare occasions has been described as a "whistling hiss." Carr heard *Siren lacertina* imprisoned under a crust of dried peat emit "plaintive yelps."

Although thoroughly aquatic, *nettingi* is able to survive drought by descending into mud. This ability also enables it to live in areas that are dry for part of every year. A number of specimens that had followed crayfish burrows to depths varying from eighteen to forty inches in Franklin County, Illinois, late in December, were active enough to try to escape when handled. Their home had been drained of its shallow water since midsummer, so they had circumvented cold as well as dryness by entering mud. The Cagle and Smith series twice mentioned above was part of a hibernating aggregate found on New Year's Day in the protected, ice-free water of a culvert. The siren were resting on a thin layer of mud-covered cinders in only seven inches of water.

The gills of mud-encased individuals are mere stubs with the reduced filaments covered by skin. When put in water, such specimens rise to the surface to breathe, as did, according to Cope, an individual that had accidentally lost its gills. It would be interesting to know whether the young siren is as versatile, since its skin has not yet thickened and acquired the cornified layer that develops at metamorphosis and resists the drying effect of air. In the genus *Siren*, the skin metamorphoses, whereas the animal for the most part remains in a larval state.

Food.—No food was found in adult siren dissected by Cagle and Smith, but Noble and Marshall's specimens expelled fragments of mollusks and crustaceans along with large quantities of algae. Hurter caught siren on

hooks baited with worms and states that they eat minnows. Carr's account of the trouble that allied *Siren
lacertina* has in capturing shrimp makes one question
Hurter's statement. Carr examined twelve stomachs of
young *Siren intermedia intermedia*, which is very closely
related to our local siren, and found in them plankton,
amphipods, lumbriculid worms, and cranefly larvae and
pupae.

Habitat.—Marshes, swamps, sloughs, ponds, drainage
ditches, and sluggish streams are the haunts of this
amphibian. It prefers a mucky, plant-grown bottom and,
as already explained, thrives in water that is by no means
permanent. The young are said to prefer shallower water
than do the adults.

Captivity.—The eel-like form, scarcely noticeable
limbs, and larval state of the siren make it an interesting
amphibian in any collection. Captive individuals will
eat raw meat as well as small live animals. If one is kept
in water with an insufficient supply of oxygen, the gills
will dwindle but the animal will not suffocate.

Occurrence.—The single record for the Chicago area
is based on a small specimen from Hebron, Porter County,
Indiana, and marks the northernmost point reached by
this subspecies, which ranges southward through Louisiana and eastern Texas to the northeastern corner of
Mexico. It has long been confused with *Siren lacertina*
of the southeastern Atlantic coastal plain and certain
records of both forms cannot be allocated with certainty.

Reference.—The Validity of *Siren intermedia* Le Conte, with Observations on Its Life History. By G. K. Noble and B. C. Marshall.
American Museum Novitates, No. 532, 1932. Contains nearly all
the available information on reproduction.

The frog begins life in water as a tadpole, breathing like a fish, but later changes its structure so completely that it leaves the water and spends its adult life on land, or at least as an air-breathing animal. This change, called metamorphosis, is of more than casual interest because, in transforming, each individual repeats the history of the evolution of the higher animals from an aquatic to a terrestrial environment. Salamanders also metamorphose, but their change has escaped emphasis because the tail is not lost and, to the untrained eye, adult and larva look alike. The metamorphosis of the frog has been explained and illustrated in every popular book on backboned animals and every textbook of zoology. The following pages will show that there are many other interesting facts about the life of the frog. One of these, not considered below because every local kind does have its tadpole, is that some tropical species skip the larval stage and hatch as tiny but perfect frogs.

A frog is built for hopping and jumping. A cricket frog can leap a distance equal to forty times its head-and-body length, and I have seen a small Chinese frog jump seventy-five times its length. The long, powerful hind limbs give the push, while the fore limbs merely support the body. In man, too, the front and hind limbs differ greatly in size and use. Webs between the toes enable any frog to swim well; diving is even more easily added to its accomplishments. Burrowing species dig with the hind limbs, and tree frogs cling to vertical surfaces largely by means of disks on the tips of the toes.

To the scientist, the frogs comprise the Order Salientia (formerly Anura) of the Class Amphibia. The word "frog," as commonly used, does not include the toads, but this is unfortunate, since no line can be drawn between frogs and toads. Ambiguity might be avoided by referring to toads as "toad frogs."

The Frog Book, by Mary C. Dickerson, was published in 1906 and reprinted without change years later after the author's death. This work is one of the finest accounts of a group of American animals ever published. *Handbook of Frogs and Toads*, by Anna and Albert Wright, is a briefer recent (1933) account. A general and highly technical treatment of frogs will be found in G. Kingsley Noble's *The Biology of the Amphibia* (1931).

Careful examination of the feet of frogs facilitates identification; the more mature tadpoles can also be recognized by their feet. Tadpoles in early stages of growth are hard to identify, but consideration of the habitat and search for remnants of the egg mass may give a clue. As the first group of backboned animals to become fully vocal, frogs deserve special notice. The males are able to sing loudly because they have resonating chambers or "vocal sacs" under the head. When the lungs force air into these they expand like toy balloons and set up vibrations audible at great distances. The two openings in the floor of the mouth (Fig. 26) that let air into the vocal sacs help in sex recognition and, by their round or slit-like form, also are of assistance in identifying the species. The sacs themselves differ from species to species in shape and position and are even more useful in identification.

Skin dry and warty; a large oblong gland on shoulder.
Dark spots on back usually enclosing a single wart.
American Toad, p. 69
Dark spots on back usually enclosing several warts.
Fowler's Toad, p. 81
Skin moist; warts and shoulder gland lacking.
A dark X on back; head and body never longer than 1⅜ inches; tips of toes with small but distinct disks.
Spring Peeper, p. 95
Back without dark cross.
Back with dark stripes; hind feet not webbed.
Swamp Tree Frog, p. 90
Back without stripes; hind feet webbed.
A dark mark between eyes, and an oblique stripe on side of body; head and body not longer than 1⅜ inches................................Cricket Frog, p. 86
No such markings present.
Tips of toes with large disks; found on trees and bushes...........................Tree Frog, p. 100
Toes tapering to a point; not arboreal.
Back and sides without green; a black patch behind eye.....................Wood Frog, p. 105
Back and sides largely green.
A ridge of skin along side of back; head and body not longer than 4 inches.
Back with bold, crowded spots.
Concealed parts of thighs and adjacent belly orange-yellow.....Pickerel Frog, p. 127
No orange-yellow on thighs and belly.
Leopard Frog, p. 133
Back without bold, crowded spots.
Green Frog, p. 121
No ridge of skin on back; head and body often more than 4 inches long..........Bullfrog, p. 111

AMERICAN TOAD
Bufo americanus americanus
Figures 15–17

Recognition.—Most people identify the toad at a glance by its dry, warty, yellowish-brown back and sides. A conspicuous, oblong gland on either shoulder is a sure sign of a toad. The differences between the American and Fowler's toads are given in the account of the latter.

The Sexes.—In the breeding season, males are easily recognized by the black or brown growths on the inner side of the thumb, on the tubercle at its base, and on one or two fingers. At this time, the median, unpaired vocal sac is covered with skin like that of the belly in texture but black in color; this resonating chamber is connected with the mouth by two slit-like openings. Females are noticeably larger than males. A female measuring 5½ inches from snout to vent is on record but such giants are rare; a 4½-inch one is exceptional and 3½ inches may be taken as the usual size of fully grown specimens. The largest males measure but 3½ inches, whereas most males are between 2½ and 3 inches long. There is a slight sexual difference in coloration, and the males are said to be more spiny and have blunter snouts.

Reproduction.—American toads usually select shallow, weed- or débris-choked ponds and lake borders as breeding sites, although almost any quiet water will satisfy them. Being terrestrial, they have little ability to distinguish between temporary and permanent bodies of water but they do prefer shallows and avoid all but the weakest currents.

Soon after emerging from hibernation, toads travel to the breeding sites in large numbers, aggregates of a thousand individuals being common. Movement is most active at night though it also occurs in broad daylight, especially during rainy weather. The males reach the ponds in greater number at first but later the sexes arrive together, an occasional female even bearing her mate. Miller found that there were always a great many more males than females in a breeding aggregation and explained it by the assumption that the females left after spawning, whereas the males lingered to mate repeatedly. The study of one pond by Piatt refutes this assumption, since only one among 258 marked individuals (including 120 pairs) was discovered mating a second time and that one was female; Piatt says nothing about early arrival of males. In still another pond, on April 21, Maynard found 218 males to 39 females; on April 30, only 53 males to 267 females. Obviously, this problem of order of arrival and proportion of the sexes calls for further investigation.

Just how a breeding site is chosen has not been determined. Presumably, a few males reach water more or less by chance and attract others by their calls. The concentration of individuals in a small area often not more than fifteen feet in diameter is a characteristic condition that substantiates this explanation. On the other hand, an observation by Maynard is good evidence that the selection of and aggregation at a site are not merely a question of one toad stumbling on water and others following his call. This observer saw toads that floated more than two miles down a stream, swam to shore at a point between two suitable ponds, and, with only seventeen exceptions (among hundreds), went to the same pond. The removal one night of all the toads from this preferred pond did not affect the movement toward it. Maynard believes that similar migrations were made year after year.

The aroused male surrounded by other toads ready to breed cannot recognize a female but merely grasps the nearest individual or pair. If the toad seized happens to be a male (when a pair is involved, contact is nearly always made with the male) he vibrates the back sharply and is promptly released. This "warning vibration" is accompanied by a dull sound audible at only a few inches. If a lone female has been mounted, she remains silent and the male perfects his grasp by sinking his fists into her armpits.

Actual laying begins soon after, the male having drawn his legs up and placed his feet upon her thighs. The female straightens the body, raises the head, and extends the hind limbs, while her mate hooks his feet between her legs and arches his back. She now deposits from 200 to 300 eggs in the area enclosed by the legs and bodies of the pair, and these are immediately fertilized. Only a few seconds are required for these co-ordinated movements, which are followed by a period from one to three minutes long during which the pair holds its position before advancing a short distance. About fifteen minutes of rest now intervene before the cycle is begun again. Laying requires, according to Miller, from six to eighteen hours. This is not surprising, since a complement commonly contains from 4,000 to 15,000 eggs. Small females may lay as few as 2,000; large, unusually prolific ones lay up to 20,600. A spent female escapes from her mate by bending the back sharply downward.

In the Chicago area, toad eggs are unique in being held by long, transparent cables of mucus $\frac{1}{8}$ to $\frac{5}{32}$ of an inch in diameter (Fig. 15, left), which are expelled in pairs; each cable, the product of a single ovary, measures from 20 to 72 feet. A large complement, after the mucus has absorbed water, may weigh $5\frac{1}{2}$ times as much as the toad that laid it. Occasionally, four cables or strings come out at once. The eggs of a cable are in single file separated from one another by spaces about equal to egg diameters; or they are crowded, even to the extent of being in double or, rarely, triple rows. Close examination will reveal an inner cable with partitions between the individual eggs. The eggs are black at one pole and white at the other; they measure between $\frac{1}{32}$ and $\frac{1}{16}$ of an inch in diameter.

Three intensive studies of breeding have been made in about the same latitude: the first at Worcester, Massachusetts, by Miller; the second at Ithaca, New York, by Wright; the third in Albany County, New York, by Piatt. These give a good picture and allow us to draw certain conclusions. Toads breed from the first part of April through May with stragglers entering the ponds through June and, rarely, in July. An early season brings toads out to linger before beginning to mate, whereas a late one causes them to enter the water almost immediately. The height of the season comes during the last week of April or the first half of May after the water surface temperature has climbed to 65° F. and that of the air is five or more degrees warmer.

In the pond studied by Piatt, the toads bred at four well-separated sites, each aggregate succeeding the other at fairly regular intervals, the first beginning April 20, the last May 21. The individuals of one aggregation (with the exception of a female that laid twice) did not intermingle with those of another. The water temperatures, taken at the beginning of each wave, were rather high, ranging from 73° F. to 78° F. Mating at one site was nearly (one case) or entirely completed before it was begun at another; the toads left the ponds promptly after laying. Miller's observations of one year involved five different ponds. He recorded maximum activity at ponds 1 and 2 on April 29, ponds 3, 4, and 5 on May 1, 14, and 18, respectively. Wright determined that all the mass spawning is over by May 20. It is interesting to speculate on the cause of this laying in waves. Fluctuations in temperature are no doubt influential, and difference in time of emergence from hibernation must also be a factor. Late stragglers present another problem; are they "repeaters" or merely individuals that spent the winter at greater depths or on northern exposures, and emerged tardily?

When subjected to temperatures of 70° F. or higher, the eggs hatch in from two to five days, whereas, at 55° F. to 65° F., from eight to twelve days are required. Devel-

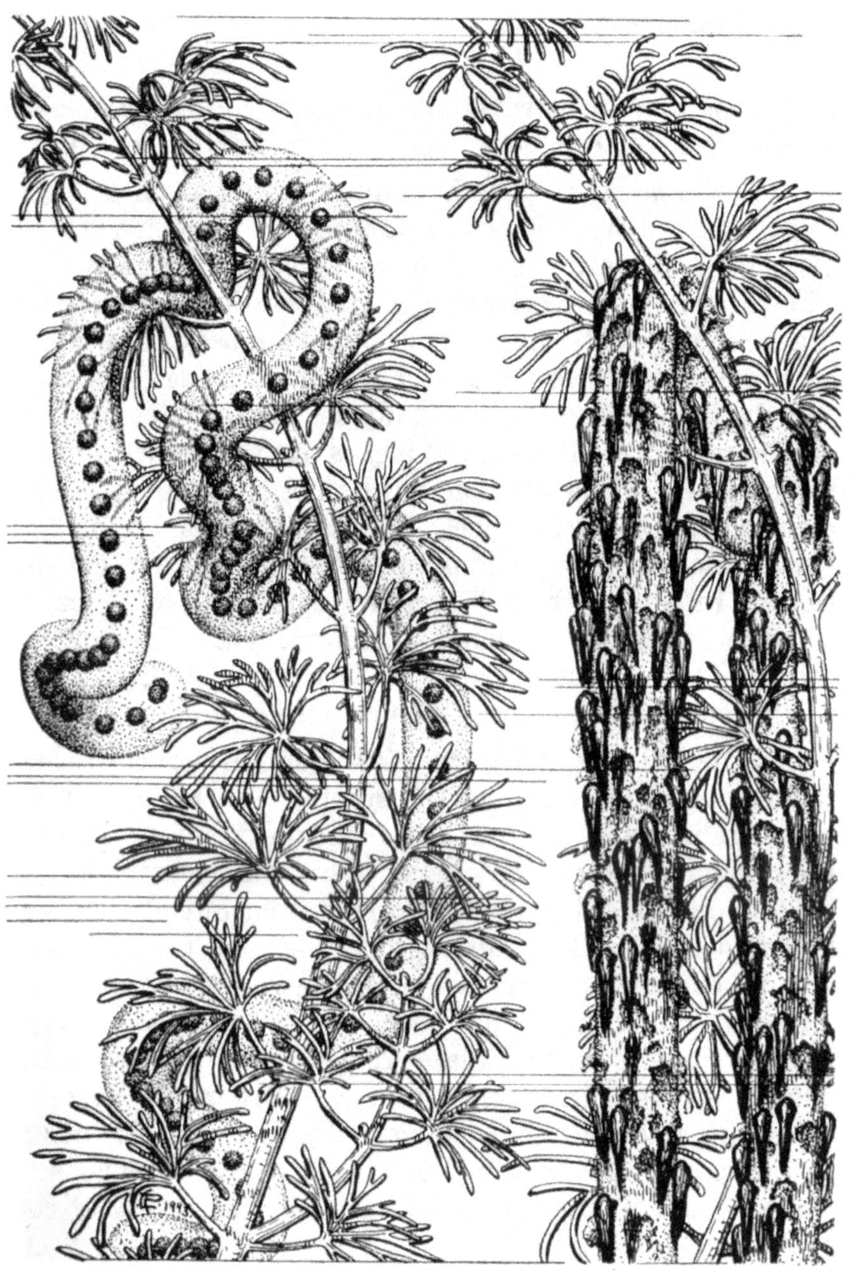

FIG. 15. Left: Egg cables of American toad twenty-four hours after they were laid. Right: Same cables three days later, showing newly hatched larvae. After Dickerson.

opment is normal between 50° F. and 86° F. The actual escape from the egg takes from twenty to sixty minutes.

Growth and Age.—The hatchling is ⅛ of an inch long. Eggs watched by Dickerson hatched in four days (Fig. 15, right), so presumably they were kept at about 70° F. The external gills reached their greatest development on the second day after hatching and had almost disappeared on the fourth. Two days later the mouths were evident, and the well-formed but tiny tadpoles began to feed. The maximum larval length is 1⅛ inches but the snout-to-vent measurement of the average newly metamorphosed specimen is only ⅜ of an inch. The duration of larval life varies considerably with temperature and other conditions. In the northern states, from forty to sixty days elapse between hatching and transformation. This means that there the vast majority of toads transform during the latter half of June and the first part of July.

In the latitude of Ithaca, New York, American toads remain immature through the summer following that of their transformation and breed the next spring at the approximate age of two years. This was clearly shown by four individuals marked by Hamilton but allowed to live under natural conditions. These four toads, when first taken, measured from 1¼ to 1⁷⁄₁₆ inches and at least doubled their length in 97 to 121 days from dates in May or early June to others in late August or early September. This means that they were more than 2½ inches long by the spring following these periods of growth; Miller found that even females 2⅜ inches long are sexually mature. The question of the age when marked remains to be settled. Dickerson gives the length at six weeks as about one inch, so Hamilton's four toads could not have been more than a year old when 1¼ to 1⅜ inches long. That rapid growth of females does not cease at maturity is suggested by his 3⅛-inch specimen that increased 1¹⁄₁₆ of an inch in fifteen days. Growth is decidedly more rapid in June and July than in August and September.

Dickerson is often quoted as authority for the statement that this toad has been known to live thirty-six
years; actually she was referring to a European species
of *Bufo*. There is no reliable record of the length of life of
Bufo americanus.

Habits.—The mating call of this species is a high-
pitched, musical trill sustained for about ten seconds and
plainly audible for a quarter of a mile. It has a dual
character suggesting the combination of a high whistle
and a low drone. Air and water temperatures of 60° F.
and 55° F., respectively, are required to initiate the call,
but, once begun, it may be continued after the air has
dropped even to 39° F. A rise to 70° F. is needed to
produce a maximum chorus. A warm rain will occasionally induce a few males to call weakly in late summer,
long after the breeding season. The female is mute. The
function of the gentle chirping notes uttered when one
picks up a breeding toad is not known.

This solitary creature spends most of its time in a
shallow burrow that it digs through damp soil with the
hind limbs, and always backs into. A hideout is generally
well concealed by vegetation or débris and used repeatedly. When night begins to fall or heavy clouds obscure
the sky, the toad emerges for a few hours to devour
insects. Higginbotham's experiments indicate that,
although an occasional adult may be diurnal, the species
exhibits an inherent nocturnal rhythm that is poorly
developed in young individuals.

Humidity no doubt greatly influences this behavior
pattern for, in spite of its dry skin, the toad, like other
amphibians, has limited ability to conserve water. Con-
versely, it absorbs this element rapidly; one weighing
forty grams increased ten grams in weight when placed
for three hours in water a quarter of an inch deep. The
newly metamorphosed individuals are especially suscep-
tible to drying up; during droughts, they hide in the
damp, shady borders of the breeding sites. If, after a

large number has been, so to speak, held back, a rain breaks the drought, countless thousands of toadlets take advantage of the moist condition to swarm over the land. Such a phenomenon is often noted with astonishment and described as a "rain of toads," most observers believing that the little amphibians fell with the rain.

The toad is relatively slow and deliberate. When greatly alarmed, it jumps rapidly and thus travels with surprising speed for a short distance. It can walk as well as hop but its swimming is poor in comparison with the truly aquatic frogs of the genus *Rana*.

The homing ability of *Bufo americanus* has never been studied; popular belief based on accumulated casual observations credit it with the habit of residing in one place for many successive years and being able to return to its home if taken away. Young individuals released by Hamilton four miles from the point of capture remained at the site of release. This distance is relatively great, even for an adult, so no conclusion can be drawn from his test, which was only incidental to marking experiments.

In order to escape the rigors of winter, toads back their way into loose soil to a point a little below the frost line. This may be from a few inches to as much as three or four feet below the surface. Banks and piles of débris are also used. The toad descends deeper and deeper as autumn advances and winter sets in. The hole above him closes and he assumes a characteristic posture, the hind legs drawn snugly up and the front ones pressed against the side of the depressed head, allowing the hands to meet over the snout.

Some specimens molt with surprising frequency; one of Miller's captive females weighing 48 grams (1.7 ounces) and certainly sexually mature, molted every seventh to eleventh day from October 23 to April 8. Others shed with less regularity, some apparently not doing so for four weeks. Frost's data indicate a frequency of two to three times a month, and he seems to have worked with adults. The very young toads must shed much more often; no observations have been made on them.

A molting toad is a ludicrous sight not often seen because the act is accomplished in such a short time—from two to five minutes. The toad assumes a position with the back greatly humped, the head lowered, and the legs

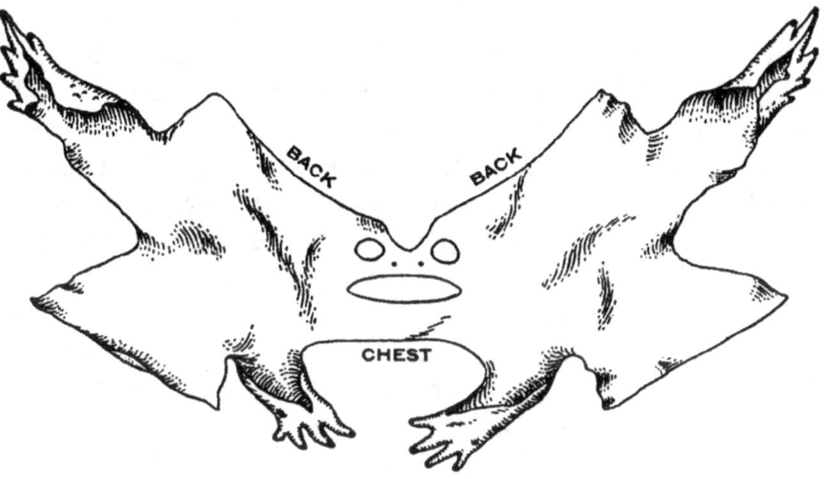

FIG. 16. Slough of American toad.

doubled up. First, the skin splits down back and belly, across breast and lower back. Next, by repeatedly opening the mouth and expanding the body, the toad works its skin forward. The hind legs are freed by rubbing them against the body after their skin has split to the tips of the longest toes. The cleft crossing the breast continues to the base of each first finger and initiates the final stage. The skin of hands and feet may be turned wrong side out. If it does not go down the throat as it comes off, the slough is swallowed with convulsive effort, the mouth being slowly opened and closed while even the eyeballs seem to help in forcing the black lump down. The new but wet skin now dries, its colors darken, and its owner regains composure. A slough that has been retrieved and spread out is shown in Figure 16.

Food and Feeding Habits.—Enough has been written about the feeding habits of the American toad to fill a book. The hundreds of stomachs examined prove that this useful animal eats chiefly insects but also takes many other small invertebrates, among them spiders, slugs, and earthworms. Size of the prey is the main limiting factor, for the variety of insects devoured is great. Miller dissected stomachs and conducted careful experiments that led him to conclusions some of which are contrary to certain often-repeated statements. A toad of ordinary size (36 grams in weight) will eat insects at the rate of 26 a day, consuming from May through August 3,200 of them weighing 134 grams (4.7 ounces). The specimens tested by him refused to eat 36 per cent of the days, so the free individual probably does not feed daily. Examinations of stomachs convinced Miller that digestion is too slow to permit filling of the stomach more than once in twenty-four hours. A large specimen will readily take three or four score insects of moderate size at a sitting. Counting the number lapped up by toads gathered under a street light, a favorite feeding site, is an amusement often indulged in by naturalists.

Two tadpoles dissected had consumed diatoms, algae, flagellates, and eggs of crustaceans. Hamilton examined the stomachs of 400 newly transformed individuals and reported that flies, mites, ants, beetles (mostly in larval form), and thrips made up, respectively, 22, 15, 13, 12, and 10 per cent of the contents by bulk. In spite of their low percentage, thrips appeared in nearly every stomach. Munz found no aquatic animals in the tiny toads studied by him.

Toads often approach their prey stealthily before the lightning-like action of the sticky, elastic tongue makes it vanish as if by magic. A forward lunge co-ordinated with a two-inch reach of the tongue can do the job at a surprising distance. Long wings and bodies introduce difficulties readily overcome by skilful use of the hands after tongue and jaws have made a good start. A motionless animal is seldom noticed, and unsuitable objects in motion are often slapped with the tongue in vain. Two specimens kept by me get into ridiculous complications when fed together, for one, apparently attracted by the movement of the other's nostrils, gives her a violent lick in the face that spoils her appetite. One might almost conclude that the act is intentional, since it allows the aggressor to get all the food.

In spite of its nocturnal habits, a toad cannot eat in pitch darkness.

Enemies.—Although no toad hopping about at dusk is adept at escaping by flight from so active an enemy as a mammal or a bird of prey, the American toad holds its own astonishingly well. Somber colors combined with secretive habits are important survival factors. A toad has four means of active defense: It may inflate the body, feign death, eject urine, or exude a milky poison over its skin. The first is used against snakes, since they must swallow their food whole; the second is of somewhat questionable or at least undetermined value; the third probably annoys mammals (the urine has no especially unpleasant qualities); the fourth doubtless saves more toad life than all the others combined.

The poison of the toad comes from glands that lie in the skin of both back and belly but are most numerous in the back, where groups of them form the conspicuous warts. Muscle fibers lying in the walls of each gland expel the venom in such quantities that it often stands out in drops on the pair of conspicuous swellings of the shoulders. The human skin is not sensitive to this substance, but the eyes and lining of the mouth are acutely irritated by it. Neither this substance nor the urine produces warts on man, popular belief notwithstanding.

A surprising number of animals prey on toads in spite of the unpalatable skin. Sixteen of 145 food-containing stomachs of the broad-winged hawk held remains of undetermined species of toads; other bird enemies are owls, herons, and bitterns. Hog-nosed snakes virtually specialize on a diet of toads, whereas garter as well as water snakes are very fond of them. Tiny toads migrating from their breeding site are relished by domestic fowl of various kinds, and the tadpoles are preyed on by innumerable insect larvae, fish, and even salamanders.

Economic Importance.—The value of a single toad to the farmer has been estimated as anywhere from five to twenty dollars per year, but Miller concludes that the lower figure is nearer the truth. Obviously, the number of noxious insects destroyed would vary from place to place and from season to season. The ability of the toad to survive in cultivated areas is strongly in its favor and it should be regarded as a welcome inhabitant of every farm and garden.

Habitat.—These amphibians are likely to be encountered in almost any area that offers damp soil or débris for concealment. Town and city gardens are frequently inhabited. Altitudes of 3,500 and 5,800 feet are reached in New Hampshire and at the Tennessee–North Carolina boundary, respectively. Where competition with Fowler's toad is keen, *Bufo fowleri* prefers the valleys, *Bufo americanus* the higher country.

Captivity.—No amphibian pet is more quaint and interesting than a toad. After receiving a little gentle handling, all shyness disappears and the confined toad makes himself thoroughly at home. Any shaded terrarium with loose, damp soil or other soft material is suitable, and drinking water need not be provided. Meal worms purchased at pet or bird stores may be used for food when insects and earthworms are not available.

Occurrence.—The American toad is found throughout the northeastern United States and southern Ontario, its range joining, in an undetermined region, that of *Bufo americanus copei* of northern Ontario and Quebec. To the west, it occurs throughout the tier of states immediately west of the Mississippi River, but it is lacking in the low-lands of the Gulf and other southeastern states. Locally, the American toad is generally distributed. There are records for the single Michigan, two Wisconsin, four Illinois, and two Indiana counties of the Chicago area; the ten counties lacking records are those in which relatively little collecting has been done.

References.—The American Toad (*Bufo lentiginosus americanus* Le Conte). By Newton Miller. The American Naturalist, vol. 43, pp. 641–668, 730–745, 1909.

The Frog Book. By Mary C. Dickerson. Doubleday, Doran & Company, New York, 1931. Both Miller and Dickerson give good general accounts, now somewhat out-of-date.

The Sexual Behavior of Anura, 6. The Mating Pattern of *Bufo americanus*, *Bufo fowleri*, and *Bufo terrestris*. By Lester R. Aronson. American Museum Novitates, No. 1250, 1944.

FOWLER'S TOAD
Bufo woodhousii fowleri
Figures 17 and 18

Recognition.—Fowler's toad can be distinguished from the American toad by close examination only. Most of the dark spots on the back of Fowler's toad enclose a group of warts, whereas in the other species the dorsal spots usually enclose a single wart, less frequently two or three. The bony ridge crossing the head just behind the eye is in broad contact with the end of the conspicuous shoulder gland in Fowler's toad; gland and ridge are well separated in the American toad, although a spur from the outer end of the ridge may extend backward to the gland.

The Sexes.—No thorough study of sexual differences in this species has ever been made, but accumulated observations indicate that breeding males, like those of *Bufo americanus*, have dark throats and black growths on the thumb and adjacent parts of the hand. The vocal sac is larger in Fowler's toad and is described as "external," which means that the modification of the skin over it is marked enough to be noticeable from the outside. This resonating chamber is connected with the mouth by two slit-like openings. Females are larger and usually lighter in color but, according to Dickerson, have slightly shorter legs.

Reproduction.—Surprisingly little has been written about the life history of this amphibian because nearly all of the early interest in it was directed toward a comparison of it with the superficially similar but amply distinct American toad. Although the reproductive habits of these two are much alike, and Aronson reports that the egg-laying behavior of the two species is similar, further studies will certainly bring to light minor differences. Wright, for example, finds that egg strings of Fowler's toad lack the inner cable with its partitions between individual eggs.

Recently, Blair has made a highly significant study of the factors that enable the American and Fowler's toads to retain their identity in spite of being closely associated in many places and freely interbreeding when given the opportunity. These factors, or "isolating mechanisms," prove to be largely of a reproductive nature, although contrasting habitat preferences tend to keep the populations of the two toads apart in some areas. The most important isolating mechanism is a difference in breeding season: The American toad appears first, reaches a laying climax two or three weeks sooner, and stops mating earlier in the summer. This mechanism occasionally fails to keep the two kinds from actually spawning at the same time and place, or even hybridizing. Mechanisms of less importance are differences in size, call, and choice of breeding site. The first and second of these have been but poorly investigated and the third is known to be of little consequence.

The ability of sexually aroused males to make their way back to a breeding aggregation was investigated by the Breders and Redmond, who took, on the evening of

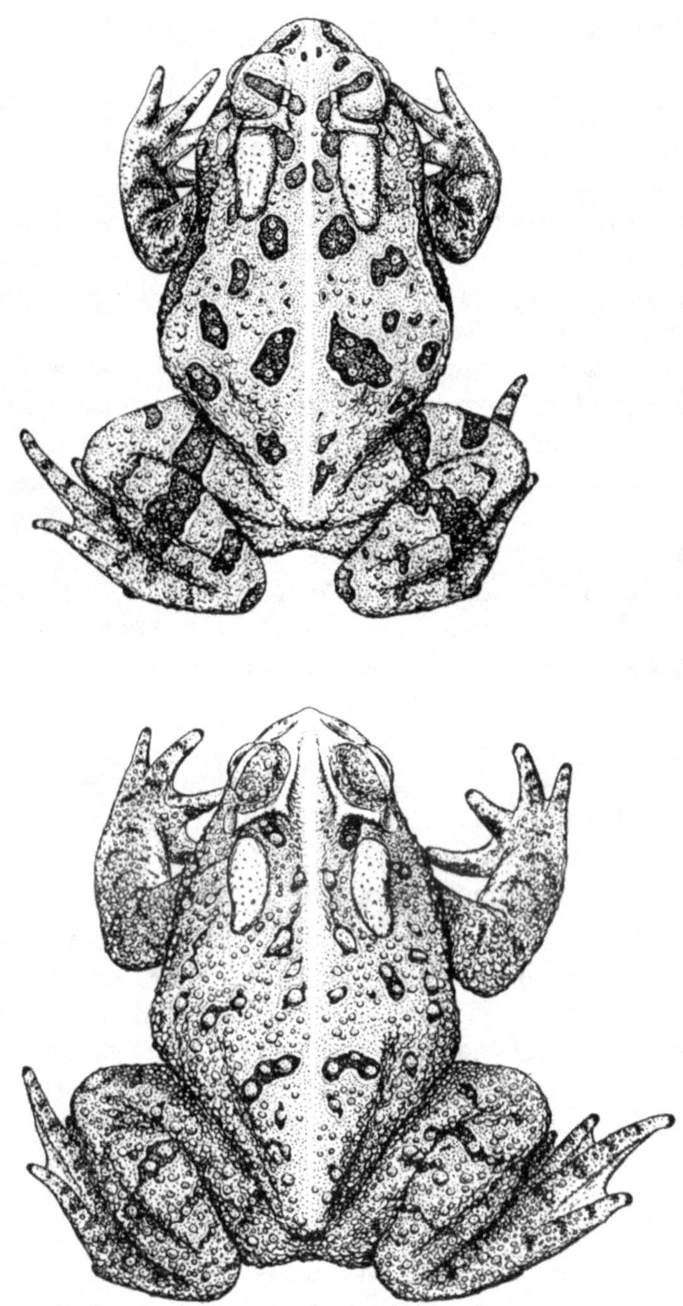

Fig. 17. Above: Fowler's toad, seen from above. Below: American toad, seen from above.

June 13, eleven calling males from a pond and released them at a point 1,000 feet away and nearer to another noisy aggregation than to their own. At sunset of June 14, two were recovered from the home pond and three days later two more turned up there. In returning, these toads had probably gone over three broad highways (crowded day and night with motor traffic) as well as a triple-tracked railroad bed on an embankment covered with cinders. An alternative but circuitous route would have entailed the crossing of two highways and a bridge over the railroad; during this longer journey they would have been exposed to much greater danger from motor vehicles. The remaining seven specimens were never seen away from the point of release. This investigation provides supplementary evidence of the complexity of the aggregation and homing reactions of toads in general, a subject treated at greater length in the discussion of the American toad (see p. 69).

Growth and Age.—Fowler's toad is a little smaller than the other local one. This difference is reflected in the tadpoles as well as in newly transformed individuals. The rate of development is probably similar.

Habits.—The mating call is a weird, metallic drone that lacks the pleasing quality of the American toad's musical trill. The call of Fowler's toad may start on a relatively high note but a descent invariably gives it a doleful character. The carrying power is great; I once plainly heard a lone male at a distance of 900 feet. Harper found that at 66° F. a male began a call every 9.4 seconds (average of twenty consecutive calls), whereas at 77° F. another male called every 6.2 seconds (average of eleven). More elaborate tests would be required to prove that temperature was actually responsible for this difference in rate. The single call lasts about 1.5 seconds.

Fowler's toad is more active and alert but less hardy than the American toad. This difference in hardiness is shown by the earlier retirement of the former in the autumn and its later spring emergence. When roughly handled these amphibians often feign death, as shown in Figure 18.

Food.—Few stomachs have been examined. The little information available indicates that Fowler's toad eats chiefly insects but does not refuse other small invertebrates. It is less fond of earthworms than is the American toad.

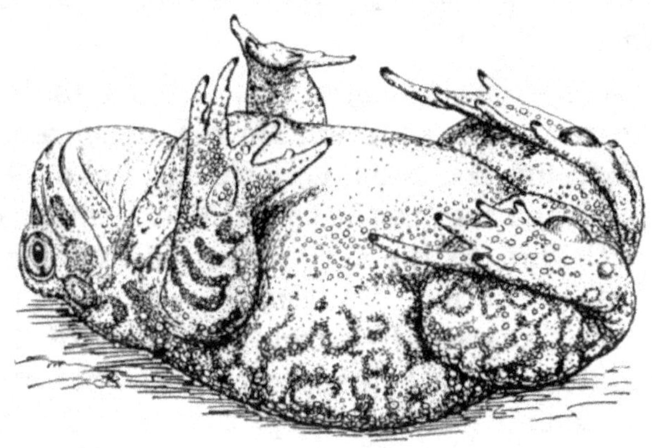

FIG. 18. Fowler's toad feigning death. After Dickerson.

Economic Importance.—Approximately as useful as *Bufo americanus.*

Habitat.—Where competition exists, this toad inhabits the warmer, sandy lowlands of river bank or lake shore, leaving the cooler, higher areas to its larger, more robust rival. This difference in habitat preference is noticeable in the Great Lakes region, where *Bufo woodhousii fowleri* frequents the dune areas. Lack of robustness is also reflected in the presence of Fowler's toad on certain coastal islands such as Long Island, New York, to the exclusion of the other, and the corresponding absence of the smaller kind in the higher altitudes of mountainous regions. In New Hampshire, it ascends only to 380 feet (against 3,500), in the southern Appalachian Highlands to 4,250 feet (against 5,800).

Captivity.—Blair raised his experimental toad tadpoles of this and other forms in shallow enamel pans containing aquatic plants that apparently played the dual role of supplying oxygen and serving as food. These plants are sold under the names "Elodea" and "Cabomba" at biological supply houses. He supplemented the diet with small amounts of dog biscuit, boiled egg-yolk, and peanut butter. The very young toads were fed fruit flies with vestigial wings, and aphids, and the larger ones were fed earthworms.

Occurrence.—The northern and western limits of distribution extend from southern New Hampshire westward through extreme southern Ontario to Lake Michigan; from the Chicago area to the southeastern corner of Iowa, thence southward to the Gulf Coast of extreme eastern Texas. Intergradation with *Bufo woodhousii woodhousii* takes place at the southwestern extremity of the range. In the Middle Atlantic and adjacent states, the occurrence of Fowler's toad is general, except that it does not inhabit the coastal plain from South Carolina to Alabama.

Locally, *Bufo w. fowleri* is probably confined to sandy areas along Lake Michigan and south of the Kankakee River. There are records for Lake, Cook, and Kankakee counties of Illinois; Lake, Porter, La Porte, and Starke counties of Indiana; and Berrien County in Michigan.

Reference.—The Frog Book. By Mary C. Dickerson. Doubleday, Doran & Company, New York, 1931. A good general account, somewhat out-of-date.

CRICKET FROG
Acris gryllus
Figure 19

Recognition.—The head and body of this midget never measure more than $1\frac{5}{16}$ inches, and the toes of the hind limbs are webbed. The colors are variable, but a triangular mark between the eyes and a dark oblique stripe on the side of the body make identification easy. The tips of the toes are expanded into very small disks.

The Sexes.—In breeding specimens, the male's thumb has an inconspicuous pad on its inner side, the loose skin of chin and throat (covering the vocal sac) is grayish

FIG. 19. Cricket frog, seen from above.

black and yellow, and there is a pair of slit-like openings in the floor of the mouth leading to the vocal sac; these modifications are lacking in the female, which is larger and, according to Smith, has longer fingers.

Reproduction.—Breeding commonly takes place in the shallow, quiet, plant-grown water of the ordinary habitat, but temporary roadside and pasture pools are also used.

Greenberg confined large numbers of sexually excited individuals from Iowa in glass tanks containing plants and stones simulating the natural environment. According to him, the call of a male excites other males so that one often seizes another and holds on until the victim itself calls. Females approach calling males and, once seized, are not turned loose, because they remain silent. The voice is thus shown to be of primary importance in sex recognition. Greenberg suggests that the male's conspicuous yellow and black vocal sac may, when expanded, also attract the female from a distance. The grip of the male is axillary; that is, the female is held just behind the arms. Actual laying has not been observed.

The eggs are laid singly and attached to submerged stems and twigs. A confined individual from northeastern Kansas laid 248 eggs on May 10. Greenberg found the breeding season at its height in southeastern Iowa on June 2. In the approximate latitude of Chicago, breeding apparently begins in May and extends into July. Additional records are much needed.

Growth and Age.—Little information on the tadpoles is available, but from data given by Boyer and Heinze on a specimen taken in Missouri near St. Louis, some idea of size at transformation can be gained. During a $40\frac{3}{4}$-hour period beginning August 9, this individual reduced its body and tail length, respectively, from $\frac{19}{32}$ and $1\frac{1}{4}$ to $\frac{9}{16}$ and $\frac{1}{16}$ of an inch; in other words, a tail that must have been near its maximum size all but disappeared while the body scarcely changed in length. Transformation of the colony to which this tadpole belonged was about over by September 18. Metamorphosing specimens were seen at the Indiana Dunes of Lake County, on September 23.

Males apparently mature sexually when head and body measure between $\frac{3}{4}$ and $\frac{7}{8}$ of an inch, and attain a maximum size of $1\frac{1}{8}$ inches; females are larger, their greatest length being $1\frac{5}{16}$ inches. This sexual difference is well illustrated by two series taken in southeastern Iowa at the height of the breeding season: fourteen males had an average length of only 1 inch, ten females of $1\frac{3}{16}$ inches.

Habits.—The call is a series of thirty to forty sharp clicks like two pebbles or marbles being struck together, at first slowly and then more rapidly; a full chorus is a lively, rattling sound without great carrying power. One that has been silenced through fright quickly revives if two pebbles are knocked together by a concealed observer. Strong choruses are heard night and day during the height of the breeding season. In late summer, the frogs are silent, but they call weakly in autumn warm spells.

Although it belongs to a family of tree frogs, this tiny amphibian never climbs. A good swimmer, its time is spent at the water's edge. When slightly alarmed, it plunges into this element but promptly swims back to land; if really frightened, it dives deep enough to hide on the bottom. As a jumper, the cricket frog has astonishing proficiency, making leaps of three or four feet. This no doubt accounts for its ability during a drought to migrate from a vanishing aquatic site to a more permanent one. In spite of being a late breeder, it emerges early in the spring and retires late in the autumn. Hibernating individuals have been found among "leaves and water weeds near shore" as well as "under logs in the vicinity of a creek"; apparently the winter is spent either in or out of water.

Food.—Dissection of two small series indicates that a variety of terrestrial insects forms the bulk of the diet. A spider and a crayfish were found in stomachs of cricket frogs from Kansas.

Enemies.—Being active by day as well as by night and living on land but frequently entering water makes this toothsome morsel of a frog available to a great variety of enemies. One Missouri ribbon snake disgorged three cricket frogs.

Habitat.—The preferred haunts are along the open, marshy borders of pond, lake, and stream. Other plant-grown, aquatic situations such as grassy ditches, river-overflow pools, bogs, and swamps are likewise frequented.

This prairie frog has been taken in a wooded area of extreme western Tennessee. Schmidt has noticed at Homewood, Cook County, Illinois, that the swamp tree frog lives in shallow cat-tail marshes, the cricket frog in deeper gravel-pit ponds near-by. No one has determined if such an ecological segregation is evident elsewhere.

Occurrence.—The genus *Acris* is just now receiving close attention, the general opinion being that it comprises four subspecies of the one species, *Acris gryllus*. According to Francis Harper, who is monographing the group, one of the four forms occurs from southwestern Michigan to South Dakota, thence southward through Texas and New Mexico. The foregoing account is based entirely on material from this area.

The general local distribution is shown by records for fourteen of the nineteen counties of the Chicago area, including Berrien County, Michigan, as well as the three Wisconsin counties.

Reference.—The Amphibians of Kansas. By Hobart M. Smith. The American Midland Naturalist, vol. 15, pp. 377–528, 1934. A good general account.

SWAMP TREE FROG
Pseudacris nigrita triseriata
Figures 20 and 21

Recognition.—The three broad, dark stripes that extend down the back of this form make it recognizable at a glance. The head and body never measure more than $1\frac{1}{2}$ inches, and the tips of the toes are expanded into very small disks.

The Sexes.—In breeding specimens, the male's thumb bears a pad on its inner side, the skin of chin and throat (covering the vocal sac) is loose sand dark, and there is a pair of slit-like openings in the floor of the mouth leading to the vocal sac; these modifications are lacking in the female, which is larger than the male.

Reproduction.—Almost any quiet, shallow water with some low vegetation growing in it will satisfy the requirements of breeding aggregations. The temporary water of ditches, flooded fields, and marshy areas is most often used, but this frog also congregates in permanent water such as that at the edges of lakes. Strong choruses are often heard through sunny days as well as in the night.

FIG. 20. Swamp tree frog, seen from above.

Figure 21 shows a female approaching a calling male. After such preliminaries, the male mounts his mate, sinking his hands in her armpits. The pair apparently lay while under water, the female clinging with her fore limbs to a blade of grass or some similar object. One forenoon in early April, Wright and Allen watched a confined pair from Buffalo, New York, lay from 500 to 600 eggs in 2½ hours. Just before extruding eggs the female raised her rear end as the male stretched his downward to meet hers. A cluster containing from twenty to seventy eggs was laid in lots of two to ten during each of sixteen periods of activity. The duration of these periods varied from two to seven minutes, the pair resting a few minutes and rising to the surface between periods.

Judging by reports from different parts of the range, a female may lay from 500 to 1,500 eggs. The data on the number in a single cluster are conflicting, one statement putting it as low as from five to twenty, another as high as from 110 to 300 (mode about 140). Further observations are needed to explain this puzzling dis-

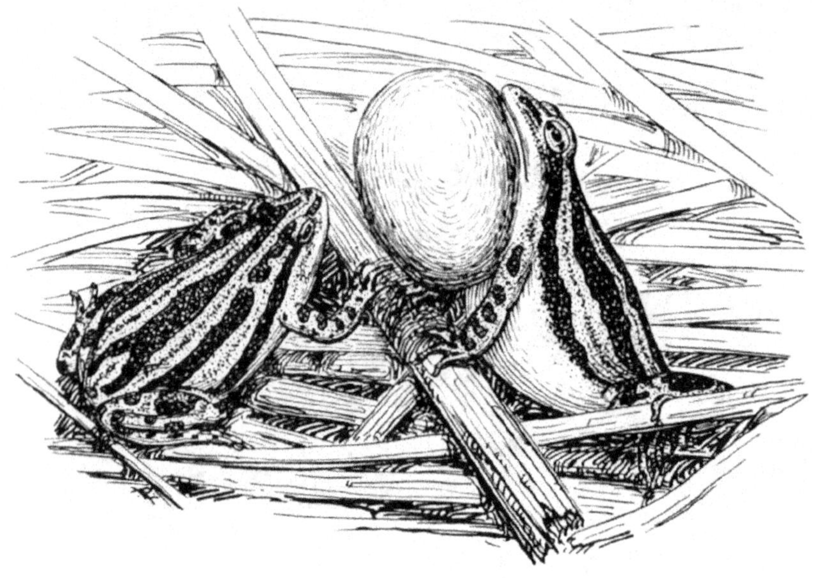

Fig. 21. Female swamp tree frog approaching a calling male. Drawn from flashlight photograph taken in Homewood, Illinois, by C. J. Albrecht.

agreement that may involve a geographical correlation, the larger clusters being produced in the west.

The egg is one-twentieth of an inch or a little less in diameter, brown or black at one pole, white at the other. In New York material, Wright finds that each egg is enclosed in one transparent capsule $\frac{3}{16}$ to $\frac{5}{16}$ (rarely $\frac{1}{8}$) of an inch in diameter, whereas, according to Smith, Kansas eggs have two capsules, the outer only $\frac{1}{8}$ of an inch in diameter.

The recorded dates of breeding activities are based on frogs from such widely scattered localities that collation is most difficult; moreover, temperature data are lacking. Walker, working in Hocking County, southern Ohio, observed eggs from March 14 to April 16; from this we may get an idea of the season and duration of breeding. Two clusters from Du Page County, Illinois, preserved in the Chicago Natural History Museum, are dated April 22 and contain elongate embryos. The embryos escape from the egg capsules in three to five days, notwithstanding statements that two weeks are required.

The fact that this species and the spring peeper sometimes breed at the same time in a single site and resemble each other in general appearance led Blair to cross the two in the laboratory. No normal tadpoles resulted from crossing female spring peepers with male swamp tree frogs, whereas the reciprocal cross produced forty-three tadpoles, three of which transformed and lived more than a year. This high mortality was apparently due to inadequate rearing technique rather than to lack of vitality. Whether such crosses occur in nature is not known.

Growth and Age.—The hatchling is only $\frac{3}{16}$ of an inch ($\frac{5}{16}$ in the west), the mature tadpole 1 to $1\frac{1}{4}$ inches long. Larval life lasts from forty to ninety days. The newly transformed individual measures from $\frac{5}{16}$ to $\frac{1}{2}$ of an inch. The maximum lengths of males and females are, respectively, $1\frac{1}{4}$ and $1\frac{1}{2}$ inches.

Habits.—The call is a low-pitched, somewhat musical rattle not easily described. It is seldom heard except during spring, when great numbers of males call incessantly from the breeding sites. Loud choruses can be heard for half a mile or more.

Although the approach of a person produces a sudden silence, the calling of a single frog will incite the rest to start again. The collector has only to secure one or two males, put them in a bag or closed receptacle and carry them around; their calling will keep the chorus alive in his vicinity.

This frog is a poor climber and swimmer. In marshes it dives to escape danger and either remains for some time hidden on the bottom or, after swimming a short distance, comes to the surface in a bunch of grass or other cover. On November 9, in woods of southern Michigan, Blanchard found eighty-eight specimens "in small depressions or cavities in the ground under leaves" where they were presumably ready to hibernate. Much remains to be learned about this interesting amphibian.

Food.—Various insects, including their aquatic larvae, and many spiders have been found in the stomachs of adults. Four very young individuals contained ants and algae.

Enemies.—Garter and ribbon snakes no doubt devour countless numbers of swamp tree frogs; there are two definite records of one having fallen victim to *Thamnophis sirtalis sirtalis*, and Gloyd saw specimens of *Thamnophis sauritus proximus* eating them in Kansas. He also took one from the mouth of a leopard frog. The tadpoles become less and less able to avoid their enemies as the temporary water of the breeding sites dries up. There are disadvantages as well as advantages in being able to breed in almost any pool formed by spring rains.

Habitat.—The swamp tree frog frequents damp woods, where it hides under dead leaves, logs, and the like. It also occurs in marshy areas. Occasional individuals are found in drier situations some distance from water. An altitude of 11,000 feet is reached in Utah. More detailed observations on the exact habitat preference of this widespread species are needed.

Occurrence.—*Pseudacris nigrita* is widely distributed over the United States (except New England) and adjacent Canada from the Atlantic Coast westward to Arizona, Utah, Idaho, and Alberta; in western Canada, it is found northward to Great Bear Lake. Several subspecies have been named but not in every case clearly defined. I consider *Pseudacris nigrita triseriata* as ranging from extreme western Pennsylvania and New York to the western limits of the range of *nigrita* in this country.

The numerous records in the Chicago area prove its presence in twelve of the nineteen local counties from Walworth County, Wisconsin, to Berrien County, Michigan.

Reference.—The Amphibians of Kansas. By Hobart M. Smith. The American Midland Naturalist, vol. 15, pp. 377–528, 1934. A good general account.

SPRING PEEPER
Hyla crucifer crucifer
Figures 22 and 23

Recognition.—The large, dark X on the back of this frog distinguishes it from all other local species. The tiny head and body are never more than 1⅜ inches long, and the tips of the toes are expanded into small but distinct disks that facilitate clinging to smooth surfaces.

The Sexes.—In breeding specimens, the male's thumb bears a pad on its inner side, the skin of chin and throat (covering the vocal sac) is loose and dark, and in the floor of the mouth there is a pair of slit-like openings leading to the vocal sac; these modifications are lacking in the female, which is noticeably larger than the male. The adult female has been described both as being usually and as being always lighter than the male. Since the individual's shade of brown is affected somewhat by changes in the environment, this slight sexual difference in color would presumably be most apparent in specimens that have spent some hours in the same surroundings.

Reproduction.—Spring peepers gather in great numbers wherever they find a combination of quiet, shallow water and low vegetation. Their shrill notes issue from the depths of forest swamp or pool, from open marsh-land, or from fields temporarily flooded by spring rains or overflowing streams. In the spring, one may drive for miles through flooded country that is alive with these vociferous midgets. Although their greatest activity takes place at night, they often call loudly throughout sunny days, especially in high, dense grass or shaded forest pool. Wright believes that the males migrate to the breeding sites more actively by night than by day and arrive in advance of the females.

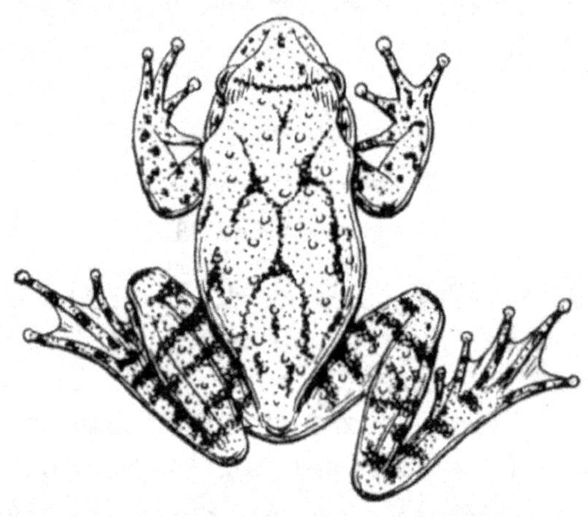

FIG. 22. Spring peeper, seen from above.

Upon finding a mate, the male mounts her and takes a tight grip with his arms so that his hands sink in her armpits. The female, clinging to some submerged stem or leaf with her fore limbs, soon turns her cloaca upward, as an egg (rarely two) appears at its orifice. The male now lowers his rear end, which, upon meeting hers, emits spermatozoa. The female next bends her body downward and away from her mate, sticking the egg to the supporting object. After each deposition, the female usually shifts her position if only slightly; the eggs normally become distributed along the support, each adjacent to its neighbor like beads on a string (Fig. 23). At the height of activity, an egg may be laid every five seconds, but deposition often progresses at a slower rate and is interrupted by trips to the surface and periods of rest.

Since a complement contains from 750 to 1,300 eggs, the entire laying process lasts for hours; Wright watched one pair that continued to lay for more than thirty hours and lingered in embrace four or five afterward.

The egg, approximately $\frac{1}{25}$ of an inch in diameter, varies in shade from white to cream at one pole, from black to brown at the other. Wright describes it as

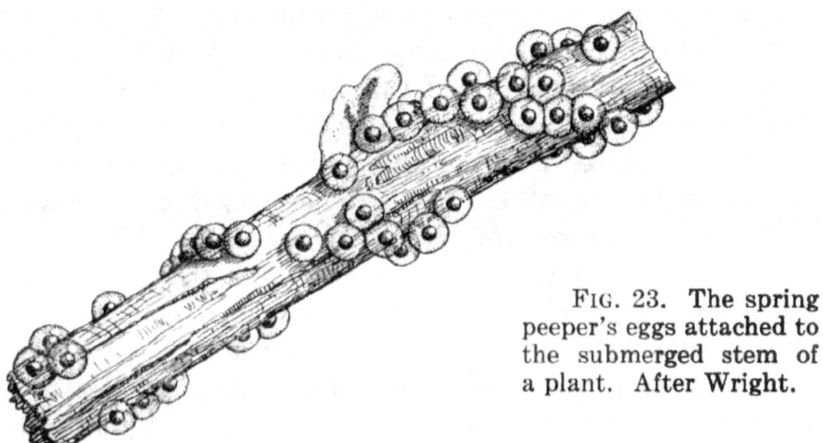

FIG. 23. The spring peeper's eggs attached to the submerged stem of a plant. After Wright.

enclosed in one mucous capsule about $\frac{1}{16}$ of an inch in diameter, whereas Noble maintained that there are two.

This species, one of the hardiest of frogs, emerges from hibernation when the air temperature first exceeds 40° F. The earliest choruses are heard when warm weather sends the mercury to 52° F. or higher but an individual caught in the descending temperature of a cold snap has been known to sing until the mercury dropped to 30° F. In the latitude of Chicago, emergence generally occurs during the last of March, good choruses are heard a week or two later; laying begins in early April, maintains great intensity from the middle of April to the middle of May, and slowly declines thereafter. It must be remembered that considerable variation is to be expected from year to year. In such a hardy breeder the length of time spent in the egg envelopes is variable in correlation with early spring weather; from six to fifteen days is given as its range, but eggs kept relatively warm in the laboratory hatch in four. Moore determined that development proceeds normally between 42° and 83° F.

Growth and Age.—The hatchling is only ⅜₆ of an inch long; the external gills develop and disappear during the first week, and the adhesive organs vanish by the end of the tenth day. The tadpoles, which are quick in their movements and non-gregarious, attain maturity in six or seven weeks, when they may measure as much as 1⅝₆ inches. Wright determined the duration of larval life at Ithaca, New York, as ranging from 90 to 100 days, whereas others have stated that metamorphosis may take place at the end of two months. The average length of head and body at transformation is ⅞₆ of an inch. The male becomes sexually mature at a little less than ¾ of an inch, the female when about ⅛₆ of an inch longer. The maximum lengths of male and female are, respectively, 1⅜₆ and 1⅜ inches. Hinckley states that females first lay in the spring following the year of their birth. No one knows how long these small amphibians live.

Habits.—The call of the spring peeper is a series of shrill whistles in a high pitch approximately two octaves above middle C. A single whistle lasts less than a second and is followed by ten to thirty similar notes in about as many seconds. There is some variation in pitch from frog to frog and an occasional trilled whistle is heard in every large chorus. The interval between calls emitted by an individual varies with conditions. Any chorus is sensitive to the least disturbance, and often the approach of a human being will bring instant silence. As fright wears off, the renewed notes of the boldest frog are quickly answered until the chorus has resumed its former intensity and the separate calls can no longer be made out; a din audible half a mile or more is the result. At a little distance a moderately strong chorus reminds one of jangling sleigh-bells. The spring peeper well illustrates two general rules: Frogs that commonly breed in temporary water have the loudest calls, and the smallest species have the shrillest voices.

The males call from vantage points just above the water, such as leaves, bunches of grass, or fallen rushes and sedges. Their greatly distended throats are reduced to about half the maximum size between whistles and completely collapse at the end of a call. First attempts to catch peepers are disappointing because silenced individuals are exceedingly hard to find; it is best to search at night in small, relatively open breeding sites where the concentration of specimens is great and the cover low. Hunting in a large swamp for widely scattered peepers is all but hopeless for the inexperienced.

After breeding, the peeper is silent until late summer and autumn when it is again heard but not from the spring breeding sites. This fall activity, most noticeable in October, may be correlated with the ripening of sperm; Rugh's detailed investigation of the male's reproductive processes shows that the sperm are developed in the autumn and stored in the testes during hibernation.

The winter is spent in deep retreats under fallen leaves and other cover, or even in springs. Hibernation on land is presumably the more usual. Frost found shed skins in the stomachs of Pennsylvania specimens collected on April 5; this frog apparently molts soon after emergence and eats its slough.

Food.—The tadpoles subsist almost entirely on diatoms and algae. After transformation and throughout adult life small insects and spiders are eaten.

Enemies.—On two occasions Hinckley actually witnessed the capture of a mature tadpole by a large spider. The arachnid dived, seized its victim, and dragged it out of the water. No doubt innumerable other aquatic invertebrates, not to mention some vertebrates, devour these tender morsels.

Habitat.—Like other frogs that often breed in temporary water, the spring peeper is faced with disaster if summer heat dries up its breeding site. The tadpoles that are able to metamorphose in time leave the water as they acquire the adult form, and hide near-by in grass and other vegetation. Soon they spread over the land, seeking moist, shady places such as the dead leaves and low vegetation of damp forests. Eventually some of them wander into orchards and other relatively dry, open areas where they may ascend into bushes or even low trees. The discovery of a peeper in midsummer is unusual.

Captivity.—Any shaded, well-planted terrarium makes a suitable home for an adult. House flies, small worms, aphids, and the like are readily taken. The tadpole is even more easily raised and will eat lettuce and the yolk of hard-boiled eggs if its natural food is not available.

Occurrence.—*Hyla crucifer* is widely distributed over the eastern United States and adjacent Canada from the Atlantic Coast to a little beyond the Mississippi River. The population inhabiting the coastal plain of southern Georgia and northern Florida has recently been set off as a subspecies, *Hyla crucifer bartramiana.*

Considering the apparently general distribution of the spring peeper in the Chicago area, the list of counties with definite records is surprisingly short: Lake and Cook counties, Illinois; Lake, La Porte, and Porter counties, Indiana; Berrien County, Michigan.

References.—The Frog Book. By Mary C. Dickerson. Doubleday, Doran & Company, New York, 1931. A good general account, somewhat out-of-date.

North American Anura; Life-histories of the Anura of Ithaca, New York. By A. H. Wright. Carnegie Institution of Washington, Publication No. 197, 1914. A detailed account of reproduction.

TREE FROG
Hyla versicolor versicolor
Plate 5

Recognition.—The skin of this arboreal species is moist and moderately rough, the toes webbed and their tips expanded into disks that facilitate clinging to smooth surfaces. The back may be uniform in color or blotched, but it is never striped. The white spot under the eye and the yellow and brown vermiculations evident on groin and outstretched leg are not obscured by the remarkable color changes of the individual.

The Sexes.—In breeding specimens, the male's thumb bears a pad on its inner side, the skin of chin and throat (covering the vocal sac) is loose and dark, and in the floor of the mouth there is a pair of slit-like openings leading to the vocal sac; the female lacks these modifications. In five mated pairs examined by Wright, every male was shorter than its mate, but Wright does not state how the pairs were selected. There is, however, a noticeable sexual difference in size, substantiated by these maximum head and body lengths: female $2\frac{3}{8}$, male 2 inches.

Reproduction.—Secluded woodland pools are perhaps the most typical breeding sites, but marshes, ponds, flooded ditches, backwaters of streams, and borders of lakes sometimes serve the same purpose. These tree frogs require quiet, shallow, plant-grown water that is relatively permanent and at least partly surrounded by high vegetation. Night is the time of greatest activity, although on rainy and heavily overcast days breeding choruses may be heard. The loudly calling males gather at the water a few days in advance of the females.

No one has determined just how the males recognize the females, but Wright carefully observed the behavior of mated pairs in the field and the laboratory. The male mounts his mate, gripping her in the armpits with his fore limbs. While the pair floats free or partly supported by stems or leaves, the male fertilizes the eggs beneath the surface in lots numbering from four to forty. Immediately after a lot has been fertilized, the female raises her rear end so that the eggs spread out on the water, the transparent mucus surrounding them swelling to form a mass that usually becomes attached to stems or leaves. In a

few seconds the process is repeated once or twice before a
two- or three-minute period of rest intervenes. The eggs
of one mating, from one to two thousand, thus come to
lie in numerous masses several inches apart, each mass
containing from four to forty eggs. An hour more or less
is spent in actual deposition, but the pair may linger in
embrace for several hours.

The transparent mucus that holds the eggs of one mass
together is of loose consistency, and each egg is enclosed
by two transparent envelopes or capsules; the outer, much
the larger, measures about ¼ of an inch in diameter
and seems to merge into the mucus. The eggs, yellow or
cream at one pole, brown at the other, are $\frac{1}{32}$ of an inch
in diameter.

According to Bragg, the embryo becomes active long
before hatching and often makes violent movements.
From ten to sixty minutes before emergence, it lies with
the side of its head pressed against the wall of the capsule
and is rotated by cilia which, together with the secretion
of the frontal gland, weaken the capsule until its wall
suddenly gives way, allowing the embryo to twitch itself
free.

The gathering at a breeding site is a gradual process
and two weeks may elapse between the arrival of the
advance males and the first actual deposition of eggs.
Just how long individuals remain has not yet been determined. In the latitude of Chicago, the height of breeding
fervor falls between the middle of May and the middle of
June but laying may take place before and after these
dates. An air temperature of at least 72° F. is required
for maximum activity, although breeding may occur
when the mercury stands ten degrees lower; rain and high
humidity are also important factors. The eggs hatch in
four or five days, depending on the water temperature.

Growth and Age.—The hatchling, about ¼ of an inch
long, is such a good swimmer that it seldom uses the
relatively small adhesive organs. The external gills

develop a day or two after hatching and entirely disappear within a week. The larva or tadpole, which reaches a maximum length of 2 inches, metamorphoses in from forty-five to sixty-five days at a length ranging from ½ to ¾ of an inch. The newly transformed frogs are green above without markings. Wright estimates that late yearlings are about an inch long, whereas two-year-olds measure approximately 1⅜ inches and are sexually mature; this same rate of growth continues through the third year. His calculations do not take into consideration the difference in size between the sexes and are therefore open to criticism.

Two tree frogs, taken as adults, survived almost seven years of captivity and must have lived at least nine.

Habits.—The normal call of the tree frog is a melodious trill that lasts about two seconds and is audible at a surprising distance. A feeble bleat is uttered at times. Breeding males call incessantly; after mating they are heard now and then on damp or rainy nights when the mercury stands above 60° F. Because of its fondness for humidity, this frog has long been considered a forecaster of bad weather. The moist, slightly sticky skin and toe disks enable it to perform astonishing acrobatics such as saving itself from a fall by catching to a branch with one leg or landing safely on a vertical pane of glass. The long legs often propel it such distances through space that it appears to fly. As it leaps, the yellow "flash colors" of the groin and legs come suddenly to view and presumably serve to confuse an enemy. The winter is spent in cavities of tree trunks and roots or in similar deep retreats.

Individuals assume various shades of brown, gray, or green (Plate 5), changing from one to another in an hour or two. (Some specimens cannot turn green because certain pigment cells of the skin known as lipophores are too feebly developed.) This ability has led many workers to assume that the colors always harmonize with those of the surroundings. Such an assumption is unjustified, since amphibian color changes, largely controlled by hormones, are strongly influenced by temperature and humidity, low temperatures and excessive moisture producing dark hues. It is, therefore, somewhat coincidental when an ashy gray specimen is found on an ashy gray background. In general, colors are not only useful in rendering an animal inconspicuous, but may protect the internal organs from harmful rays and help regulate body temperature as well. In certain cases, the same color will not serve two purposes, the result being that, teleologically speaking, the species must take its choice between being conspicuous and thermally comfortable, or the reverse.

Certain flat-fishes quickly change their colors to match complex backgrounds so Parker kept tree frogs on various black-and-white-checkered backgrounds to see whether they have the same ability. No pattern modification whatsoever was discernible.

The larvae or tadpoles are shy and swim with great speed for short distances. They are not gregarious and frequent areas where bottom rubbish and aquatic vegetation afford ample concealment.

Food.—These herbivorous tadpoles subsist on minute algae and diatoms, which they secure with their horny beaks and rows of comb-like "teeth." Innumerable kinds of non-aquatic insects form the diet during the terrestrial or postmetamorphic life.

Economic Importance.—Insectivorous habits make this a useful as well as an attractive creature. As a weather prophet it is overrated.

Habitat.—Although partial to woodlands and bushy areas, this amphibian is also found in orchards and on vine-grown buildings, fences, and walls. It may occasionally turn up in such places as wells, cisterns, and piles of leaves, and among stones. In the summer and autumn it ranges far from any breeding site, but just how far nobody knows.

Captivity.—Captives thrive in almost any shaded terrarium and readily devour earthworms as well as insects. Meal worms are also eaten.

Occurrence.—*Hyla versicolor* is widely distributed over the eastern half of the United States and adjacent Canada. The numerous specimens on record from the Chicago area come from nine counties, including Racine County, Wisconsin, and Berrien County, Michigan.

A second subspecies, *Hyla versicolor chrysoscelis*, occupies the southwestern corner of the range.

References.—The Frog Book. By Mary C. Dickerson. Doubleday, Doran & Company, New York, 1931. A good general account, somewhat out-of-date.

North American Anura; Life-histories of the Anura of Ithaca, New York. By A. H. Wright. Carnegie Institution of Washington, Publication No. 197, 1914. A detailed account of reproduction.

WOOD FROG
Rana sylvatica
Figure 24

Recognition.—The wood frog is readily recognized by a black patch that lies behind the eye, covers the tympanum, and ends in a point above the base of the fore limb. No green is evident on the predominantly brown back and sides. The skin lacks conspicuous warts and the toes are pointed.

The Sexes.—Only the males have vocal sacs. Like those of the pickerel frog, they are lateral as well as "internal" and connected with the mouth by round openings. The females are lighter in color and somewhat larger. During the breeding season, the male's thumb bears a conspicuous pad on its inner side and the webs of the feet actually have convex rather than concave margins.

Reproduction.—Early in the spring, wood frogs leave their winter quarters and repair to the breeding sites. So quickly are emergence and migration accomplished that little is known about them. The breeding sites are usually woodland ponds and pools, but eggs occasionally appear in swamps and backwaters of streams. The body of water chosen may be either large or small, temporary or permanent, open or shaded, but it is always quiet.

The males apparently reach the water first and sprawl on its surface; the females enter it but do not float. No

Fig. 24. Wood frog, seen from the side.

good observations of the selection of mates have been made under natural conditions, but Noble and Farris experimented in the laboratory and concluded that males indiscriminately seize any available frog and retain their hold only if it is plump and resists compression. Silence is a secondary factor; a male when seized always makes a warning sound, a receptive female invariably remains silent.

Mating immediately follows arrival at the breeding sites and takes place in both daylight and darkness but most actively by night. The male grips his mate behind the arms, pressing his thumbs into her chest. Actual expulsion of the eggs requires only five or ten minutes, the speed of this act probably being facilitated by storage of sperm in a reservoir of the Wolffian duct. The strong gregarious tendencies of this species often result in the crowding of one or two scores of clusters in as many cubic feet at various depths. Attachment of each cluster to a stem, twig, or similar object is the rule, and sites near the edge of shallow water are most frequently chosen.

The egg cluster is roughly spherical, from two to six (usually from three to five) inches in diameter, and contains from 1,000 to 3,000 eggs, which are white at one pole, black or deep brown at the other, and $\frac{1}{16}$ to $\frac{3}{32}$ of an inch in this same dimension. Each egg is enclosed in two transparent capsules, the diameter of one being approximately $\frac{3}{16}$ of an inch, that of the other a little less than twice as great. Wood frog egg clusters sometimes harbor algae, which give them a greenish hue and no doubt aid development. This subject is treated in the discussion of the spotted salamander (see p. 37).

This frog is an "explosive" breeder; it appears suddenly, lays promptly, and disappears into the woods, leaving its spawn in bunches to puzzle the casual observer. At one place in any one year the vast majority of eggs may be laid within a week, although stragglers will appear in the breeding sites through a much more extended period. In the latitude of Chicago when, during late March or early April, the temperature of air and water reach 41° F., the frogs show slight breeding activity; when the water has become six or seven degrees warmer and the mercury has risen above 52° F., breeding reaches maximum intensity.

Wood frog eggs develop normally between 35° F. and 75° F. As might be expected, they have greater tolerance for cold and less for heat than eggs of any of the other four northeastern species of *Rana* studied by Moore. Their rate of development is also the most rapid. Pollister and Moore studied this rate under controlled conditions and found that, at 65.5° F., hatching occurs about 100 hours after actual fertilization. Nevertheless, the low tem-

peratures of natural conditions sometimes keep the eggs
in their capsules for two or three weeks; the clusters laid
early when it is still cold may hatch little if any sooner
than those deposited later in the season when warmer
weather prevails.

Growth and Age.—The careful investigations of Pollister and Moore show that the newly hatched larva is
only $\frac{9}{32}$ of an inch long, its external gills are still poorly
developed, and it is barely able to swim. Sixty-four hours
later (at 64.5° F.) the larval mouth has formed, the gills
are about to be covered by the opercular fold, a length of
$\frac{7}{16}$ of an inch has been attained, and the larva swims
actively and spontaneously; in short, it is now a minute
but perfect tadpole.

At Ithaca, New York, according to Wright, the tadpoles have a maximum length of $1\frac{7}{8}$ inches and transform
when from forty-four to eighty-five days old and only $\frac{1}{2}$
to $\frac{3}{4}$ of an inch long. The elaborate laboratory experiments of Lynn and Edelmann proved that development
under crowded conditions not only prolongs the larval
period but causes the tadpoles to metamorphose at a
smaller size.

It is hard to believe that few measurements of sexed
wood frogs are in print, but such is the case. Wright gives
these snout-to-vent dimensions of adults: males $1\frac{3}{8}$ to
$2\frac{3}{8}$, females $1\frac{3}{8}$ to $3\frac{1}{4}$ inches. He apparently had only
one female more than $2\frac{11}{16}$ inches long, so the degree of
sexual dimorphism in size is not great.

Habits.—The wood frog is silent except during the
breeding season when the males, calling in chorus, remind
one of the clucking (not the quacking) of domestic ducks.
The individual frog usually emits in rapid succession from
two to six short, sharp clacking sounds, which have but
little carrying power. Occasionally, a male will call when
submerged. The female is able to call weakly and even
emit a "yeow" when pinched, but she seldom utters these
sounds. Hinckley noticed that captive young frogs in the

excitement of catching flies "give a musical 'chip' not unlike the call note of the song-sparrow." She also heard a breeding chorus in full swing when the mercury stood at 30° F. Although this occurred after a rapid fall in temperature, it shows how resistant to cold this amphibian is. Specimens ready to breed are sometimes seen under ice.

Except during the breeding season, this species is solitary and shy. It is an astonishingly good jumper and, when pursued, turns in the air and lands facing the pursuer. Its brown colors match the hues of the woodland floor, and the black patch over the tympanum "disrupts" the uniformity of the brown and renders the frog even more inconspicuous. The individual often changes its shade of brown in a few minutes, but whether in doing so it ever more perfectly matches the background has not been determined.

Authorities generally state that the winter is passed in logs or stumps, or under stones and heavy leaf cover of the forest floor, whereas Schmidt has seen Wisconsin populations gather during late autumn in roadside ditches and believes that they hibernate there under water.

The remarks on molting of green frogs apply to the wood frog as well, since Frost concluded that the process in one of these species is about the same as in the other.

An individual from Long Island, New York, demonstrated its ability to learn by avoiding a disagreeable hairy caterpillar after making only seven "mistakes."

Food.—The diet has been as well investigated as has that of the green frog, and the tadpoles have approximately the same feeding habits. The newly transformed wood frog's food includes 13 per cent of aquatic forms, whereas that of the adult, as might be expected, is 98 per cent non-aquatic. This amphibian is chiefly insectivorous but also eats small millipeds, snails, and various other invertebrates of moderate size. In feeding behavior it is more alert than many other frogs and may even walk or creep for some distance after its prey before making the capture.

Enemies.—Fortunately for the wood frog, few amphibian-loving snakes inhabit our northeastern forests. The early spring nuptial madness of this frog has method, since, at that chilly time of the year, few reptiles are active and even if they were they would never be common at the type of woodland pool in which the wood frog holds its rendezvous. In spite of this, an occasional specimen falls victim to a snake; a ribbon snake being carried by Conant in a collecting bag disgorged a wood frog and promptly swallowed it again. Hinckley saw leeches insinuate themselves into egg masses and devour many or all of the eggs.

Habitat.—This species is well named, for it nearly always inhabits woods. Occasional individuals are encountered in open areas adjacent to woods or even in moist grassy sites along streams flowing through farmlands. Damp woodlands perhaps attract the larger populations, but dry, shady uplands are also frequented.

It is astonishing that no other frog of the northeastern quarter of this country competes with this species in its forest habitat niche. The other kinds that live in woodlands are either arboreal or too small to offer effective competition; the terrestrial ones are, moreover, confined to moist areas and at best only partly occupy the wood frog's niche.

Captivity.—This amphibian is an attractive addition to any vivarium imitating woodland conditions. It readily becomes tame.

Occurrence.—Wood frogs are found from South Carolina and Arkansas northward through all of northern North America (except the western United States and the southwestern corner of Canada) south of the line of permanently frozen subsoil beyond which no amphibians live. No one yet knows just how many forms exist, but two or three subspecies of a single species are usually recognized. The foregoing account is based on the relatively homogeneous population of the area approximately delimited by the Mississippi River and the Atlantic Coast (including Canada from Georgian Bay southward). Of recent years, the local wood frogs have been called *Rana sylvatica cantabrigensis*, but I have left off the subspecific name pending further taxonomic studies.

There are records for the following counties of the Chicago area: Racine County, Wisconsin; Cook and Lake counties, Illinois; La Porte and Porter counties, Indiana; Berrien County, Michigan. Apparently the species occurs locally wherever suitable woodlands exist.

References.—The Frog Book. By Mary C. Dickerson. Doubleday, Doran & Company, New York, 1931. A good general account, somewhat out-of-date.

North American Anura; Life-histories of the Anura of Ithaca, New York. By A. H. Wright. Carnegie Institution of Washington, Publication No. 197, 1914. A detailed account of reproduction.

The Method of Sex Recognition in the Wood-frog, *Rana sylvatica* Le Conte. By G. K. Noble and E. J. Farris. American Museum Novitates, No. 363, 1929.

BULLFROG

Rana catesbeiana

Figures 25–28

Recognition.—Fully webbed hind feet with pointed toes, a green back without large warts, and lack of paired ridges of skin arising behind the eye and extending along either side of the back are characteristics that, in combination, set the bullfrog off from other local species. The size of full-grown individuals (more than $4\frac{3}{4}$ inches from snout to vent) is in itself sufficient identification.

The Sexes.—An easy way to sex a bullfrog is to compare the diameter of the tympanum with the distance between the nostrils. In males, the tympanic diameter is almost twice as great as this distance (Fig. 25); in females,

only slightly greater. The yellow of the male's throat and,
in breeding individuals, the pad on the inner side of the
thumb, are not evident in the female, which, according
to Dickerson, is browner and more mottled than the male.
Two circular openings in the floor of the male's mouth

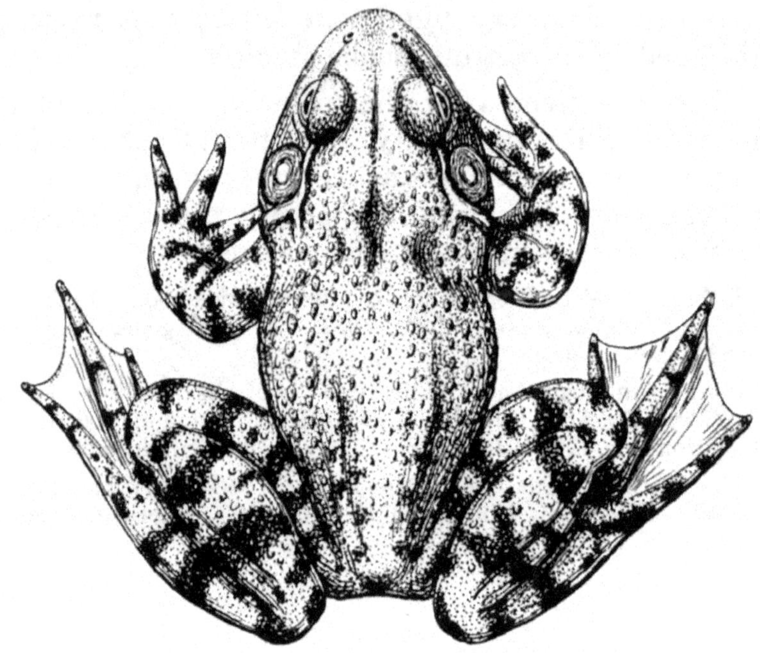

FIG. 25. Male bullfrog, seen from above.

(Fig. 26) lead to the single, median vocal sac, which is
"internal"; that is, the skin of chin and throat is never
modified in texture and color, so that, unlike most other
frogs, sex cannot be determined at a glance without
opening the mouth of the specimen. Females are said
to attain a little the greater size, but few data have been
accumulated to establish this character.

Reproduction.—This species ordinarily breeds in the
vegetation- and rubbish-choked shallows of pond or lake.
The males become evident first and begin to call two or
three weeks after emergence from hibernation. They soon

take up separate stations a short distance from shore in well-protected sites, as, for example, on a fallen tree in dense brush. There they sit half-submerged, calling nightly and, to some extent, through rainy and cloudy days. The rest of their time is spent hiding under heavy cover and banks near shore where the females are also

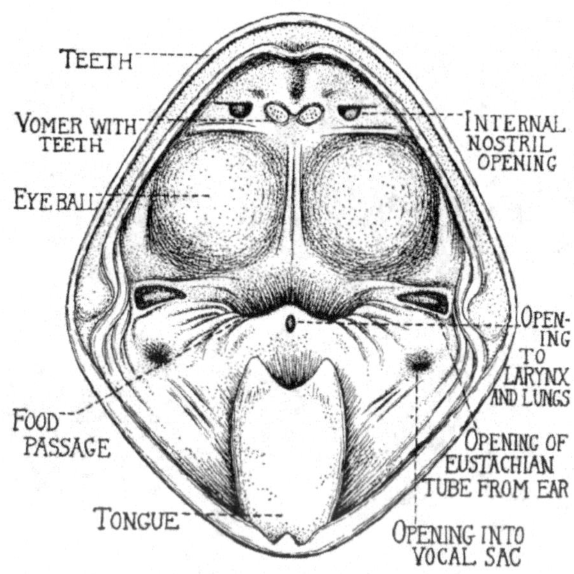

FIG. 26. Looking into open mouth of bullfrog. After Dickerson.

concealed. The latter, when ready to lay, go out to the calling males. Aggregation is seldom evident, although Wright found ten breeding males "within a space of 8 feet."

Details of laying have never been observed under natural conditions, but Aronson, after many unsuccessful attempts, induced a pair to mate in his laboratory by giving them pituitary injections. The process was essentially like that of the green frog; the minor differences possibly were individual rather than specific and will not be enumerated here. Figure 27 shows the position assumed by the laying pair.

The egg cluster or mass spreads out at the surface where it covers from two to five square feet (Fig. 28). It is attached in many places to the plant stems and brush in the midst of which mating took place, and it often acquires a stringy appearance as the water-level changes. Wright gives 10,000 to 20,000 as the number

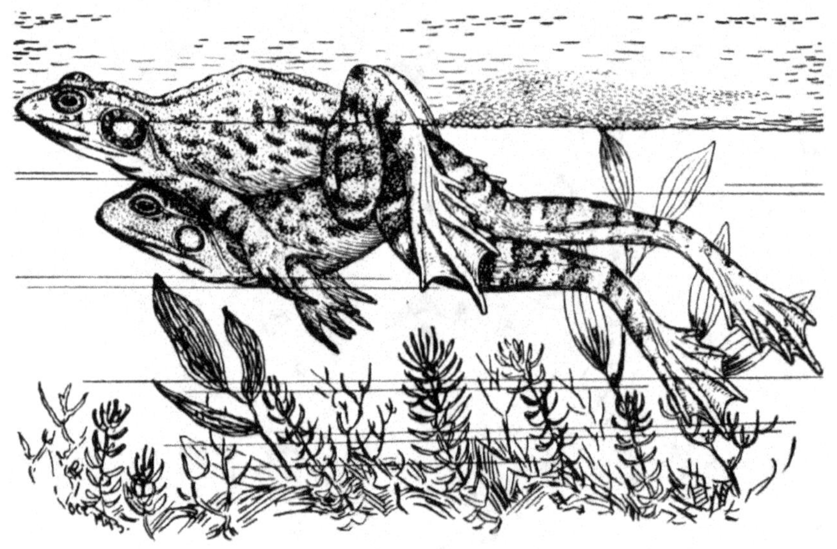

FIG. 27. Laying position of bullfrogs. After Aronson.

of eggs in a single complement, presumably meaning those in one cluster. The eggs, black at one pole, cream at the other, measure about $\frac{1}{16}$ of an inch in diameter; each is enclosed in a single envelope from $\frac{1}{4}$ to $\frac{7}{16}$ of an inch in this same dimension. These envelopes merge into the mucus surrounding the eggs and are seen with difficulty.

Considerable information has accumulated, showing that, in the southern half of New York, the eggs are laid during the last two or three weeks of June or the first three of July. There, in any one year, the season lasts two or three weeks; in Albany County, New York, these frogs bred approximately during the last fifteen days of June in 1940, whereas in the previous year they did so through the first three weeks of July. This late breeder does not lay until the air has reached a temperature of 72° F. and prefers one of 83° F.; the water near the bottom must be up to 66° F. but is more often above 70° F. By careful laboratory experiments Moore determined that

FIG. 28. Bullfrog egg cluster in situ. After Wright.

the eggs develop normally between 59° and 90° F. and hatch in 134 hours at 68°; New York and Louisiana specimens have the same temperature tolerance and rate of development.

In his comparative study of five northeastern species of the genus *Rana*, Moore shows that the bullfrog's flat, floating egg mass is correlated with late breeding when the water is warm and all danger of freezing has passed. The relatively small amount of oxygen dissolved in such water is compensated by the proximity of each egg to the air itself. This interesting subject is treated more fully in the discussion of the pickerel frog (see p. 130).

Growth and Age.—The bullfrog, like many other thoroughly aquatic species, has a long larval life. One might say facetiously that there is no need for hurry because the eggs are laid in permanent water. Late breeding and large size may also be contributing factors. The mature tadpole varies greatly in length, usually being between 4 and 6 inches long, occasionally measuring 6.6 inches. At Ithaca, New York, where conditions probably approximate those of our area, the legs seldom develop during the summer after that of hatching, and transformation occurs during the last three weeks of July and most of August when the tadpoles are two years old; in rare cases it is delayed so that a third winter must be spent in the larval state. For the great majority of specimens the length at transformation ranges from $1\frac{3}{4}$ to $2\frac{3}{8}$ inches.

Raney and Ingram tagged bullfrogs in Albany County, New York, and found considerable variation in rate of growth. Data based on several cases indicate that, under good conditions, a female will reach a head-and-body length of $3\frac{1}{2}$ inches at the age of one, $4\frac{3}{8}$ at the age of two years, at which time it should be sexually mature. Two or even three more years would be required to approximate the maximum size of $5\frac{1}{2}$ to 6 inches. Females may measure 7 inches but such giants are very exceptional. Males grow almost as rapidly; information on comparative growth rate of the sexes is meager.

A bullfrog lived fifteen years and eight months in the London Zoological Gardens and five others have survived seven or more years of captivity. Two of these, a pair from Long Island, New York, lived eight years after beginning their confinement at a size that could not have been attained in less than four years after hatching. Since this species was long confused with allied ones of the southeastern states, confirmatory records are needed.

Habits.—It is not surprising that a giant like the bullfrog has a call in keeping with its size. The sonorous sound can best be imitated by shouting a prolonged "rum" into an empty barrel as deeply and loudly as possible. The frog repeats the sound four or five times at intervals of a second and then remains quiet for several minutes. A pond inhabited by many individuals will resound with their chorus. Lone adults often call; this species is relatively solitary and has little propensity for forming choruses. The booming of a group is audible, so it has been stated, more than five miles. Seldom is a bullfrog heard after the breeding season. Dickerson writes that the female, although lacking a vocal sac, can call like the male but with less force.

This remarkably vociferous amphibian emits two other sounds: a "yelping snurp," given as it dives when frightened, and an agonized scream so disturbingly human that it makes a collector's conscience hurt. This sustained scream issues from the wide-open mouth of a frog suffering sharp pain or shock. We might consider the "snurp" a warning to other frogs, the scream an alarm that may make certain enemies such as skunks and raccoons release their prey. Observations substantiating this conjecture would be welcome. A snake, being deaf, would scarcely be deterred.

This species is aquatic, wary, and, as might be expected, a good jumper, swimmer, and diver. It does not understand the art of hiding as well as smaller species do; a bullfrog often buries its head and body in the mud but leaves its long legs in full view. The large tadpoles are protectively colored and escape danger by rapid swimming as well as by stirring up a shielding cloud of mud as they scuttle for cover.

The seasonal activity is relatively limited, especially in the adults, which Wright did not find abroad at Ithaca, New York, until the middle of May, when the air temperature had climbed at least to 68° F., that of the water near the bottom to 57° F. The smaller individuals make their appearance a few weeks earlier, but just when is hard to determine because of their size and secretive habits.   Frog and tadpole hibernate alike in muck under several feet of water.   However, the larvae have been seen swimming about under ice in the middle of winter.

In 1921 McAtee related how a bullfrog with only one front foot returned in two days to its home site after being caught and released at a point a quarter of a mile away.   Since then other workers have studied this homing ability and found that individuals will sometimes return after having been transported distances up to 675 feet, traveling by night or during and after rain.   The usual time required is two days, and the return may be overland or even across an intervening area of alluring habitat. Raney and Ingram studied the summer movements and pronounced them variable and without rhyme or reason, some frogs remaining in one place, others moving hundreds or even thousands of feet.   The champion traveler was retaken on July 28 about 4,000 feet from the point at which it had been released nineteen days earlier.

Food and Feeding Habits.—The diet of this voracious eater has been carefully investigated by five workers, who together have tabulated the contents of about 200 stomachs.   In addition, there are various more or less casual observations.   The combined results show that the larvae eat diatoms and algae, the very young frogs insects and other small invertebrates (at least half of which are non-aquatic), and the larger frogs almost any animal that can be overpowered, their victims including innumerable invertebrates and such vertebrates as fish, frogs, salamanders, young turtles, snakes, moles, mice, and birds. Frogs, other small vertebrates, and crayfishes seem to be the chief items devoured by large specimens, the prey sometimes weighing a third as much as the predator. One individual was found dead, in its mouth a 7-inch bullhead catfish firmly anchored by the pectoral spines.

Patterson's study of the bullfrog's hunger reactions explains how this amphibian is able to retain large objects and eat greedily whenever food is plentiful. The hunger contractions are astonishingly powerful and persist without slackening for hours or even days on end. As the stomach is dilated by food, it continues to contract with full strength until stretched to utmost capacity; thus it is made to serve as a reservoir while the process of digestion goes on unabated.

Enemies.—There is surprisingly little concrete information on the non-human enemies of this our most prolific amphibian, although an enormous toll must have been taken even before the white man developed an appetite for frogs' legs. It is, of course, known in a general way that numerous aquatic invertebrates eat the tadpoles, while vertebrates such as fish, snakes, turtles, mammals, and birds devour tadpole as well as frog.

Economic Importance.—Bullfrogs are of considerable commercial value as food and have long been protected by law. In Louisiana alone, the catch during 1928 was 715,540 pounds valued at $107,331, figures that must include the southern species, *Rana grylio.* Biological supply houses annually sell tens of thousands for dissection by students of zoology. Capture is generally made at night after the victim has been blinded by a strong light. Although such large frogs are easily collected with gun or gig, it is better to net or seize them with the hand, so that, being uninjured, they do not have to be marketed immediately. The traditional method of using a piece of red flannel on a fishhook as a lure is slow and more romantic than practical. Raising frogs on "farms" has never been successful in this country, enticing advertisements of "breeders" notwithstanding.

The destruction of countless numbers of small frogs and toads by large bullfrogs presents the conservationist with a complex problem. Young bullfrogs themselves destroy noxious insects, so perhaps the good done by these industrious juveniles offsets the damage done by their parents in eating the valuable insectivorous toads and frogs.

Habitat.—The most typical haunts are small lakes and permanent ponds with vegetation- and rubbish-choked shallows adjacent to a bank shielded by willows and other low trees.   Any permanent aquatic situation combining quiet, shallow water with abundant cover in the form of pickerel-weed, arrowhead, water-lilies, and brush or rubbish may be frequented.   The young require less cover than the adults.   At every good site the newly transformed individuals are encountered in season as countless numbers of them leap across floating débris or the broad leaves and matted stems of the water plants in lakes and ponds.

Captivity.—There is little difficulty in keeping a bullfrog if it is provided with shade and enough water for submersion.   But do not forget that sooner or later it will attempt to swallow all other small animals confined with it, young bullfrogs not excepted.

Occurrence.—The original range probably included nearly all of this country east of the Rocky Mountains and much of adjacent Canada.   Introduction into many areas for commercial purposes has spread the species widely through the western states to the Pacific region and even to foreign countries such as Japan, where it forms the basis of an extensive industry.   The distribution in the Chicago area is general, with records for Racine County, Wisconsin, Berrien County, Michigan, and four Indiana as well as four Illinois counties.

References.—The Frog Book. By Mary C. Dickerson. Doubleday, Doran & Company, New York, 1931.   A good general account, somewhat out-of-date.

North American Anura; Life-histories of the Anura of Ithaca, New York.   By A. H. Wright.   Carnegie Institution of Washington, Publication No. 197, 1914.   A detailed account of reproduction.

The Amphibians of Kansas.   By Hobart M. Smith.   The American Midland Naturalist, vol. 15, pp. 377–528, 1934.   A good general account.

GREEN FROG

Rana clamitans

Figures 29 and 30

Recognition.—Webbed feet with pointed toes, a predominantly green back without bold, crowded spots (small, obscure, widely separated ones may be present) and paired ridges of skin arising behind the eye and extending along either side of the back, are characteristics that combine to identify this species. The bullfrog and

FIG. 29. Male green frog, with vocal sacs inflated; seen from above.

the green frog are much alike but the former lacks the paired ridges of skin.

The Sexes.—The differences between the sexes (Fig. 29) are essentially the same as in the bullfrog, except that the green frog has two additional ones: Only the male has a greenish yellow spot or ring in the center of its tympanum, and the head of this sex is relatively wider. The sexual dimorphism in size of body probably is more marked than in the bullfrog, a character that, as explained under "Growth and Age" below, has not been carefully investigated (see p. 124).

Reproduction.—Breeding takes place in quiet, shallow, plant-grown water of the normal habitat, the males calling most actively at night from sites near shore or bank or from matted vegetation farther out.

Oddly enough, the mating of this ubiquitous frog was not described in detail until recently, when Aronson induced pairs to lay in the laboratory. A male ready to breed will apparently clasp any other green frog that happens to be near; if the one seized is plump (with ripe eggs) and gives no warning croak, the male retains or improves his hold, his arms encircling the female just behind her arms and his hands pressing against the sides of her chest. Thus his selection of a mate seems to depend on relative bulk plus vocal response. Since Aronson did not intensively investigate the involved problem of sex recognition in this species, he reached tentative conclusions only.

After a male has successfully attached himself to a receptive female, the latter lowers the head, often enough to submerge it, bows the back downward so that her cloaca is raised just out of the water, and extends her hind limbs, spreading them well apart. The male then shifts himself far forward, moving his hind limbs so that their shanks rest on his laterally projecting thighs (Fig. 30, left). Now, as the female's abdomen contracts, the male moves his feet still farther forward, bringing them almost together and placing his heels anterior to the two cloacas. About the same time, the female expels a batch of thirty to fifty eggs that spread out between the male's feet, come near to or actually touch his cloaca, and (presumably) are suffused with seminal fluid emitted by him (Fig. 30, center). Next, he pushes the eggs away so that they spread out at the surface a short distance behind the pair (Fig. 30, right). New abdominal contractions initiate

a second cycle of these characteristic movements, which
continue rhythmically until the female is spent, from ten
to twenty-five minutes later.

Under natural conditions, the pancake-shaped cluster
of eggs becomes attached to stems or twigs and ordinarily
is less than a foot in diameter. In the north, the number

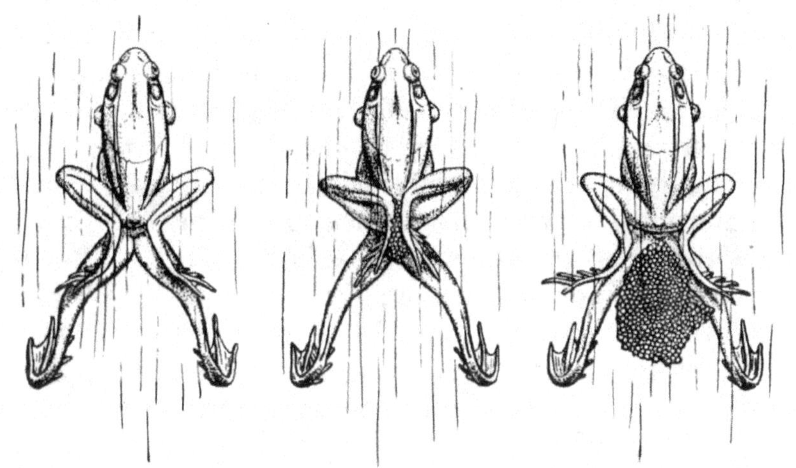

Fig. 30. Laying stages of green frog. Left: Just before first
batch of eggs appears. Center: Reception of eggs by male. Right:
Cluster of eggs forming between legs of female. After Aronson.

of eggs per cluster varies from 3,500 to 5,000; green frogs
from the southern states are smaller and may lay as few
as 1,000 eggs. The individual egg, white at one pole,
black at the other, and about $\frac{1}{16}$ of an inch in diameter,
is enclosed in two transparent capsules or envelopes, the
inner one spherical or nearly so, the other spherical and
so closely joined to the surrounding mucus that it is seen
only with difficulty. The diameter of one capsule is
approximately $\frac{1}{8}$ of an inch, that of the other almost or
fully twice as great.

The laying season of the green frog is late and extensive. At Ithaca, New York, eggs may be laid from late
May to early August, but in any one year the season lasts
only three or four weeks, its height usually coming in the

last weeks of June or the first one of July. Deposition
does not occur until the air has reached a temperature of
65° F. and one at least ten degrees higher is preferred.
The surface of the water must be as warm as that of the
air or warmer, a condition that frequently prevails in
shallows. The eggs hatch in three days when the mercury
stands above 80° F., in four or five when it is a little
below this point.

Growth and Age.—In New York, Wright found that
tadpoles reach a maximum length of $3\frac{5}{16}$ inches and nearly
always transform when 370 to 400 days old; they may
occasionally spend a second winter as larvae. Newly
metamorphosed green frogs measure from $1\frac{1}{8}$ to $1\frac{1}{2}$
inches in the north, somewhat less in the south. The rate
of growth has not been accurately determined. Wright's
calculations of one that adds $\frac{3}{8}$ of an inch to the length
every year for three or four years may be taken as approximately correct for the smaller southern frogs, which would
be about $2\frac{1}{4}$ inches long at the end of their third year and
presumably sexually mature. Few accurate measure-
ments of adults are available, but in the northern states
and Canada large males are usually from 3 to $3\frac{1}{2}$ inches
long, large females from $3\frac{1}{4}$ to 4, the sexual difference
being marked.

One green frog lived ten and two others seven years in
the London Zoological Gardens. These must have been
at least one and probably were three or four years old when
their captivity began.

Habits.—The green frog is not a persistent singer. As
the male sits half-submerged he emits from three to six
deep notes, each reminding one of the plucking of the
string of a bass viol. Sometimes a single "ctung" is
sounded, and there is considerable variation in the sound,
due no doubt to the singer's position in relation to the
water's surface. An individual frightened while sitting
on the bank of pond or stream will emit a short, high-
pitched cry as it leaps into the air in its dive to safety.

This cry has given rise to the name "screaming frog." Dickerson maintains that only the young scream, whereas, under the same conditions, the adults make a nasal sound more like the regular call.

This species has solitary habits. Although thoroughly aquatic, green frogs often leave the water to sit at its edge during day or night. They are good divers, swimmers, and jumpers. The tadpoles' behavior resembles that of larval bullfrogs.

In April, when the temperature of the air reaches 64° F., green frogs of the north first appear. Even in this part of their range they retire late in the autumn and are active during mild winter weather, especially about springs. They hibernate in the mud or débris of stream or pond bottom or under submerged stones and similar objects. The tadpoles usually burrow down several inches into the mud. Laboratory experiments have shown that at low temperatures these amphibians will move away from light, at room temperature toward it. Such results are well correlated with normal behavior in nature.

Some individuals of this species seem to wander at random within the region they inhabit, whereas others have a favorite spot in which they stay and to which they will return if taken away. This homing ability was studied by the Breders and Redmond, who tagged green frogs and moved them from place to place. One of their subjects might, for example, actually cross a suitable stream or pass by an inviting pool in returning to its home site, which, to the human judgment, had no special attributes as a frog home. Since green frogs can run a familiar maze that they have not seen for a month, presumably they would recognize their own pools after an absence of several weeks.

Differences of opinion have been expressed over the process and frequency of molting. Dickerson states that the skin is shed three or four times a year and devoured if it comes off out of water. Frost, on the other hand, maintains that a molt occurs several times a month and that the skin is not eaten. His records show that the act consumes from one to three days.

Food and Feeding Habits.—The diet of this species has not been as carefully investigated as has that of the bullfrog, but two workers have dissected large series of stomachs. The tadpoles contained diatoms and algae and a very small proportion of minute animal forms. The young frogs as well as the adults had eaten insects, crustaceans, and other small invertebrates, among them spiders, snails, and earthworms. Some 90 per cent of the forms consumed by frogs of all ages were non-aquatic, a surprising fact in view of marked aquatic tendencies. Green frogs resemble the bullfrog in voraciousness, and without doubt any vertebrate small enough to be over-powered will be swallowed by either kind. Small amphibians as well as reptiles are well known to fall victim to green frogs, even though the stomachs examined contained almost no vertebrates.

Frost, who fed captive green frogs and regularly examined their feces, found that undigested parts of insects were usually passed one or two days after acceptance; he concluded that the stomach would be emptied once in two or three days. This is not surprising in view of the strength of frog digestion (see under BULLFROG).

Enemies.—Water snakes devour large numbers of green frogs, and man also rates high as an enemy. The remarks made concerning the bullfrog apply here as well.

Economic Importance.—In many parts of its range, the green frog is eaten locally and even appears in markets. Small size alone keeps it from competing with its giant cousin, the bullfrog.

Habitat.—The bullfrog and the green frog are similar in habitat preference except that the latter requires much less cover and is therefore found in almost every permanent, plant-grown aquatic situation. Ponds, lake borders, swamps, river backwaters, and streams meandering through meadows or open woodlands are the favorite haunts. Altitudes of 4,200 and 2,230 feet are attained in North Carolina and New Hampshire, respectively.

Captivity.—As a readily available tadpole that will not metamorphose in too short a time, the larval green frog is an interesting inmate of any aquarium. Although it breathes with gills (which are concealed) it has such a low oxygen requirement that the aquarium does not have to be balanced with plants. These tadpoles are good scavengers that will devour scum and small particles of animal matter. A few individuals in a large, well-planted aquarium do not have to be fed, but in close quarters tadpoles can be given lettuce, yolk of hard-boiled eggs, and meat in small quantities; over-feeding should be avoided, as any excess food will merely decay and will pollute the water.

Occurrence.—Widely distributed over approximately the eastern half of the United States and adjacent Canada. The species has been introduced into Washington; apparently its tadpoles were transported inadvertently with those of the bullfrog. The distribution in the Chicago area is general, with records for the three Wisconsin, the single Michigan, five Illinois, and two Indiana counties. Thus it is definitely known to occur in more than half of the local counties.

References.—The Frog Book. By Mary C. Dickerson. Doubleday, Doran & Company, New York, 1931. A good general account, somewhat out-of-date.

North American Anura; Life-histories of the Anura of Ithaca, New York. By A. H. Wright. Carnegie Institution of Washington, Publication No. 197, 1914. A detailed account of reproduction.

PICKEREL FROG

Rana palustris

Figure 31

Recognition.—The back is conspicuously spotted, the spots being more or less angular in outline and, for the most part, arranged in two rows between the paired ridges of skin that arise behind the eyes and extend along either side of the back. The concealed surface of the thighs, together with the adjacent area of the belly, is bright orange-yellow. The toes are pointed.

The Sexes.—The male is larger and somewhat darker and its feet have a little fuller web. Two circular openings

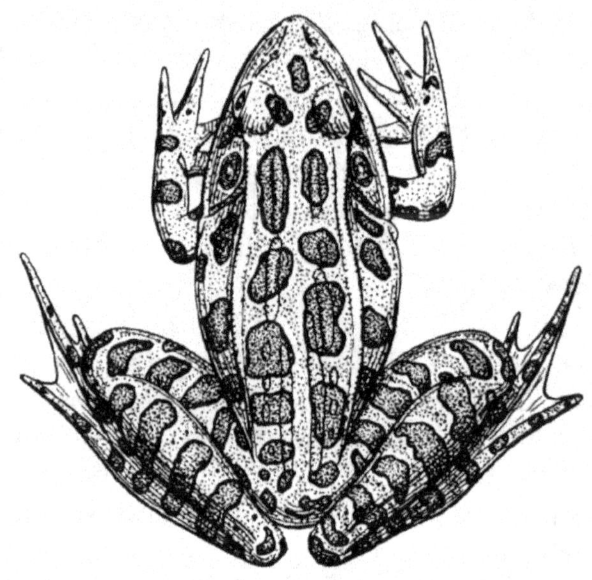

FIG. 31. Pickerel frog, seen from above.

in the floor of its mouth lead to the paired, lateral vocal sacs, which are "internal"; that is, the skin over them is never modified in texture and color, so that the sex cannot be determined from the outside by a glance at the throat. The thumb of the breeding male bears a conspicuous pad on its inner side.

Reproduction.—Pickerel frogs breed in quiet, shallow, relatively cool and clear backwaters of streams, and in lake margins, marshes, bogs, and ponds. Muddy water is never chosen, and deep places are usually avoided. Large numbers congregate and mate with persistence by day and by night; a dozen or more pairs may be seen within a space only a few feet square, the arrival of an observer affecting their activity little. The laying females are restless and back around so much that they disturb one another. Although captive pairs may remain together for days before and after actual deposition, the eggs are extruded in a remarkably brief interval.

Wright describes the laying process of one unconfined pair as follows: The male had already mounted his mate and hugged her so that his hands pressed against her chest. She soon assumed a horizontal position with hind limbs flexed and paralleling those of her mate. As the eggs were being extruded, the male repeatedly extended his legs as if helping to get the eggs out. A cluster, laid in three minutes, was accompanied by 10 or 12 emissions of the male. This action went on beneath the surface.

The females lay from 1,500 to 2,000 eggs in globular masses or clusters surrounded by firm, transparent mucus. The diameter of a single cluster at first may be only one or two inches, but in time it increases to three or four. The clusters are submerged and attached to twigs, stems, or similar objects. The egg itself is brown at one pole, yellow at the other, and enclosed in two capsules. The diameters of egg and capsules are, respectively, about $\frac{1}{16}$, $\frac{1}{9}$, and $\frac{1}{4}$ of an inch.

Wright kept records of breeding activity for many years at Ithaca, New York, and determined that there the pickerel frog rarely lays before the last week in April and usually deposits most of its eggs during this and the following week. Depositions may occur over a period of three weeks in any one year, but this period is doubled by records kept for several seasons. In Connecticut Babbitt found mated pairs on October 16. The average air temperature at which laying occurs is 67° F., the lowest 50° F. Ovulation nearly always takes place in water with a temperature between 50° F. and 65° F.; careful laboratory experiments by Moore determined that development is normal between 46° F. and 86° F. The eggs hatch in about two weeks.

Moore experimented further to show a correlation between form of egg mass and time of breeding. Since oxygen does not reach the eggs of a submerged, globular cluster as readily as it reaches those of a flattened, floating one, it is an advantage for the former type to be laid early while the water is still cool enough to have a high content of dissolved oxygen. This worker also emphasized certain other correlations: The embryo's need of oxygen is not as great at low as at high temperatures, and a poor supply of this gas may be compensated by hatching at an early stage before the requirement has reached a high level.

In his comparative study of five northeastern species of the genus *Rana*, Moore relates the early breeding of the pickerel frog to its globular egg mass. He further shows that, among the three species producing such a mass, this one breeds latest, a contingency that it makes up for by hatching at a relatively early stage of development.

Growth and Age.—The tadpole reaches a length of 3 inches at maturity, and transformation occurs from seventy to eighty days after hatching. Newly metamorphosed individuals vary in length from ¾ to 1¼ inches. The adult males and females, respectively, measure from snout to vent 1⅞ to 2½ and 2 to 3⅛ inches. Sexual maturity is attained during the second spring after hatching.

Habits.—The call, low in pitch and with little volume, sounds like a "gentle, musical snore" and lasts but half a second. It is often thought to be the subdued note of a leopard frog. Both of these species actually croak under water. The pickerel frog seldom calls after the breeding season, and its female is silent.

This frog, which is active in the day as well as in the night, spends much time out of the water but usually dives to avoid danger. Once in this element, it hides in the soft mud of the bottom, among vegetation, or under over-hanging banks. Catching one in rank grass is no simple matter because its yellow and green colors are highly protective and its ability to make long, swift leaps leaves one in a state of bewilderment.

The habit of living in springs and spring-fed bodies of water is linked with the extensive period of activity enjoyed by the pickerel frog. Even in the latitude of Chicago, populations inhabiting the relatively warm water of springs and streams issuing from ravines are more or less active all winter. Wright found at Ithaca, New York, that large numbers migrate to ravines to hibernate in deep pools.

Food.—The tadpoles subsist chiefly on diatoms and algae, the transformed individuals on a great variety of insects and, among other invertebrates, crustaceans, snails, and spiders. Munz gives evidence that the diet of recently metamorphosed frogs consists of 21 per cent aquatic animals, that of the adults of only 4 per cent. A progressive independence of water is thus evident.

Enemies.—Collectors soon learn to isolate their catch, because the poisonous secretion of the skin quickly kills other amphibians confined with pickerel frogs. Babbitt saw a ribbon snake that had made the "mistake" of seizing a young specimen quickly release its grip, rub the sides of its head on the ground, and show other signs of distress. Garter and water snakes are also said to respect the poisonous nature of the pickerel frog, but I know of no real investigation of this subject. Bullfrogs and green frogs, on the other hand, relish small specimens and show no signs of discomfort after devouring them; newts frequently eat the eggs. It would be interesting to know whether such frog-loving mammals as skunks and raccoons are repelled by the poisonous skin; dogs are alleged to be.

Economic Importance.—Various obnoxious insects and other harmful invertebrates are eaten by this voracious amphibian, which can survive in areas where other frogs have been all but exterminated by snakes. Pickerel frogs are eaten locally and even appear in markets.

Habitat.—All types of aquatic situations combining cool, clear water with high grass or other low vegetation are frequented by the pickerel frog. Clear, spring-fed streams flowing through wet meadows with an abundance of rank grass form the most typical habitat. Where the ground is damp the frogs frequently wander beyond the bank of pond or stream, but their presence is a sure sign that water is not far off. Altitudes of 4,200 and 2,100 feet are reached in North Carolina and New Hampshire, respectively.

Captivity.—A young one-legged specimen kept by Murphy thrived on pieces of earthworms (presented to it in tweezers), live house flies, and crickets. In spite of having only one hind limb, it leaped with precision distances of twelve or fourteen inches to catch the crickets. The food was grasped in the jaws rather than picked up with the tongue. This adaptable creature also swam with direction.

Occurrence.—The range embraces the eastern United States as far west as Minnesota and the eastern extremity of Kansas, with the exception of the southeastern coastal region; in the adjacent part of Canada, it is known as far north as Hudson Bay.

The pickerel frog is apparently lacking in the Illinois part of the Chicago area, but it has been recorded from Porter County, Indiana, and Walworth and Racine counties, Wisconsin. The explanation of this avoidance of the middle of our area probably lies in the scarcity there of the requisite spring-fed type of aquatic situation; the clear-water bogs of Porter County seem to approximate this habitat niche well enough.

References.—North American Anura; Life-histories of the Anura of Ithaca, New York. By A. H. Wright. Carnegie Institution of

Washington, Publication No. 197, 1914. A detailed account of reproduction.

The Amphibians of Kansas. By Hobart M. Smith. The American Midland Naturalist, vol. 15, pp. 377–528, 1934. A good general account.

LEOPARD FROG
Rana pipiens pipiens
Figures 32 and 33

Recognition.—The leopard and pickerel frogs are alike, but when alive may be distinguished by the color of the concealed surface of the thighs and the adjacent part of the belly. This area is white in the leopard frog, bright orange-yellow in the other kind. In addition, the spots on the back of the leopard frog are round or oblong rather than angular, irregularly distributed rather than arranged in two rows.

The Sexes.—During the breeding season, the male is somewhat darker than the female and has a fuller web. The vocal sacs, found only in this sex, are paired, one lying just above the base of either fore limb (Fig. 32). The skin over them is more or less modified, and a round opening connects each with the mouth. This frog is unusual in having a pad on the inner side of the male's thumb throughout the year, not only during the mating season. The females are but slightly longer than the males; the sexual difference between the averages of snout-to-vent measurements of Rugh's large series of Vermont adults amounted to barely $\frac{1}{8}$ of an inch. Nevertheless, in all series examined by him the largest individuals were female.

Reproduction.—This handsome frog breeds in shallow, quiet water of almost any plant-grown aquatic situation. Favorite sites are lake margins, ponds, swamps, bogs, and backwater or marginal pools of watercourses. Under some conditions, migrations down ravines occur, but ordinarily the frogs lay where they live. Breeding takes place by day and by night but most actively at night. Mating frogs frequently croak under water.

As in the case of the wood frog, it is necessary to draw on laboratory investigations for details of reproduction. Rugh has outlined with great thoroughness the internal

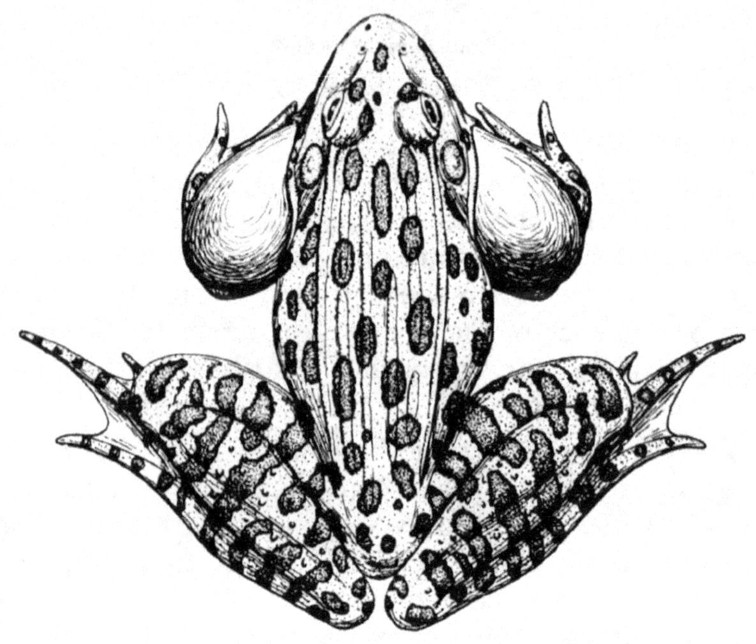

FIG. 32. Male leopard frog with vocal sacs inflated; seen from above.

processes of both sexes, but his accounts scarcely come within the scope of this work. Nevertheless, it is impossible to resist giving a few of Rugh's data that explain how the eggs get their mucous coatings. After an egg has been released by the ovary, ciliary currents carry it across the body cavity to the oviduct, a much convoluted tube fully eight inches long. Having gained entrance, the egg is passed through this tube in two hours (at 72° F.) by spirally arranged cilia, which rotate it once every fourteen seconds. During the passage, mucus is deposited in layers by special glands. A buckshot inserted into the body cavity of an ovulating female will come out coated like an egg. The cilia are lacking in the body cavities of males.

The studies of Noble and Aronson give a picture of mating and laying induced by special technique and observed under carefully controlled conditions. According to them the breeding male seizes any available frog but retains his grip only if the one seized is plump and remains silent; a male invariably gives a warning croak and is of course thin compared with a female ready to lay and presumably unable to croak because of the internal pressure exerted by the mass of eggs.

Having found a receptive female, the male encircles her body just behind the arms with his fore limbs so that his thumbs press against her chest. The female next makes, for a varied length of time, a characteristic shuffling movement with the hind limbs, propelling the pair slowly backwards. As laying time approaches, each frog assumes a special posture, the female taking the initiative. She extends the thighs laterally and bends the legs inward at the knees so that the hind limbs enclose a diamond-shaped area; in shallow water, the feet rest on the bottom. The male moves slightly forward, rotating his flexed legs somewhat downward and inward. Actual laying is started by a sharp contraction of the female's abdominal walls and a responsive spreading of the male's legs accompanied by an arching of his back that brings his cloaca forward past hers. The female now raises her cloaca by bending her back downward as the male presses his legs against her abdomen to complete what Noble and Aronson call an "ejaculatory pump." After each pump, the female ejects a cluster of eggs numbering from ten to twenty-three, and the male emits sperm. The eggs gather in the area enclosed by the female's legs. Laying requires from two to eight minutes and may take place at the surface or several feet below it, but the pair always clings to a stem or some similar object for support.

Wright found as many as forty clusters crowded together in a small space and noticed that this species not infrequently lays in shallows that soon dry up. The egg mass is a somewhat flattened sphere with one diameter from 3 to 6, the other from 2 to 3 inches long. It contains from 3,500 to 5,000 eggs $\frac{1}{16}$ of an inch in diameter and black at one pole, white at the other. Two transparent capsules enclose each egg, one $\frac{3}{16}$, the other $\frac{1}{8}$ of an inch in diameter.

At Ithaca, New York, this species begins to lay in early April when air and water temperatures approach 50° F.; the crest of laying comes as soon as these temperatures rise above 54° F. No records are available for the Chicago area; eggs may be laid in March in southern Michigan. Development is normal between 42° F. and 82° F.

Growth and Age.—The early development of no other frog of the Americas has received so much attention as has that of the leopard frog. In spite of this, there is but one completely satisfactory description, and this, unfortunately for the present work, is based on material from Bloomington, Indiana, that may represent the southern leopard frog usually known as *Rana sphenocephala*. The author of the account, Dorothy Miller, was the only one of five workers to state clearly the origin of the eggs used. Rugh has specifically shown that the rate of development of eggs from Vermont specimens differs noticeably from that of eggs laid by Florida frogs.

Dickerson's account of development, six stages of which are shown in Figure 33, is based on eggs from Providence, Rhode Island, laid on April 9. Hatching took place in nine days, and the escaping embryos measured $\frac{5}{16}$ of an inch, had well-developed gills, and could swim. They were feeding on the sixteenth day after deposition. Dickerson failed to record temperatures, but it is a safe guess that the growth took place at room temperature. Comparative estimates based on the charts

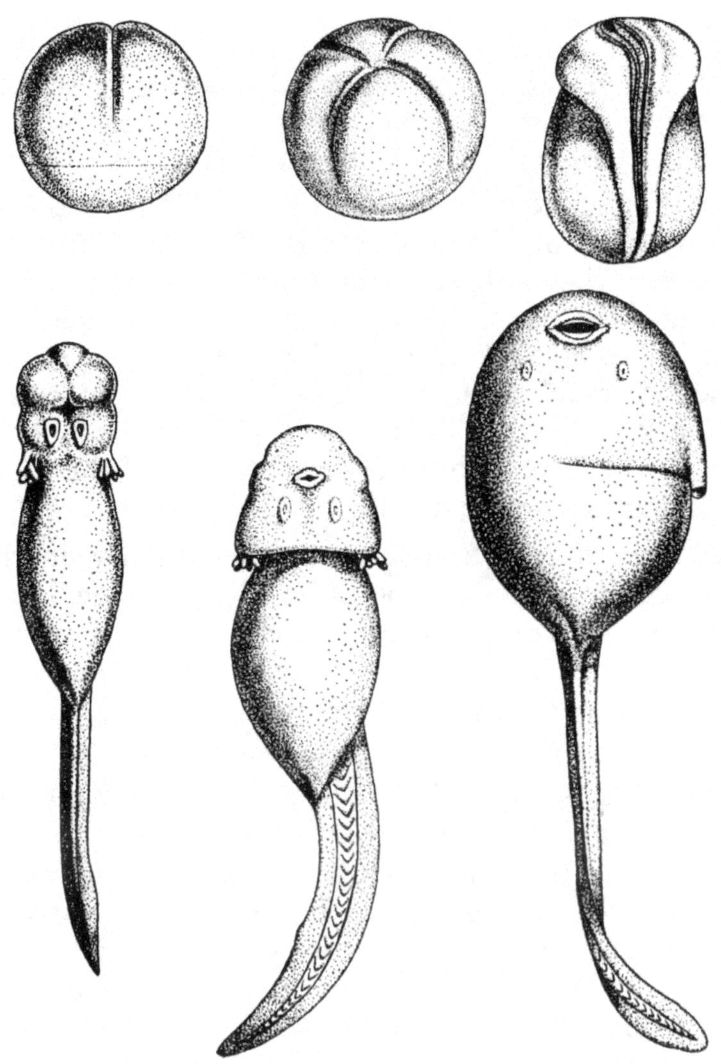

FIG. 33. Development of leopard frog, showing commencement of cleavage of egg on day of laying (two drawings), and successive stages on fourth, ninth, eleventh, and sixteenth days. On the eleventh day, a fold of skin is forming a cavity over the disappearing gills, which will be replaced by the pair that function throughout tadpole life. After Dickerson. Greatly enlarged.

of Miller and Shumway, both with careful temperature records, convince me that development to this point should require not more than twelve days.

At Ithaca, New York, according to Wright, the tadpoles reach a maximum length of $3\frac{5}{16}$ inches and metamorphose when an inch long, from 60 to 80 days after hatching, the peak of transformation usually coinciding with the third week of July. The females measure $2\frac{7}{8}$ inches at sexual maturity and attain a maximum length of 4 inches. The adult males are slightly smaller. Sexual maturity is apparently reached at the age of three years (including the larval period).

A leopard frog from an unknown locality survived six years and nine months of captivity in the London Zoological Gardens; probably it was at least nine years old at death. Another lived there five years and eleven months. Its origin was not recorded.

Habits.—Noble and Aronson state that the male leopard frog emits a "sex call and a warning croak," whereas the female, lacking the resonating vocal sacs, gives only a weak warning croak. Cries of pain something like those of a young chicken are made by an individual when overpowered by an enemy such as a snake. The sex call, a quavering sound that lasts about three seconds and may be written "ir–a–a–a——a–a–h," is often repeated several times by an excited male. Scores of these frogs calling together produce a chorus so subdued that it readily goes unnoticed. The musical warning croak is represented by Noble and Aronson as "ir–a–a–a–h—— ir–a–a–h——ir–a–a–h" and suggests talking or singing. A frog held in the hand or touched on back or sides will "talk." Dickerson mentions "low purring tones" induced by pouring water on the back of a contented male. Most vocalization is confined to the breeding season; summer showers and warm spells in the autumn sometimes cause males to set up a weak chorus.

Catching a leopard frog in high grass is not easy because it is apt to give several surprisingly long leaps in succession, not all of them in the same direction. It also has the habit of emptying the bladder on an annoyer. The ability to swim is well developed.

Dickerson watched a captive shed its skin after the manner of the American toad, and Frost's tables show that this act is accomplished several times a month.

Investigation of intelligence from two angles has given leopard frogs a comparatively high rating. An individual from Long Island, New York, learned to avoid disagreeable, hairy caterpillars after making but four "mistakes," and another frog (from an unspecified locality) was able to run a maze almost without error after only twenty trials.

Food.—Two workers have examined large series of leopard frog stomachs from Pennsylvania and northern Ohio and determined that insects and spiders form the principal diet, the number of the former consumed being roughly twice as great as that of the latter. A small proportion of crustaceans, still fewer mollusks, and a scattering of other invertebrates are included. Nearly all of the prey is non-aquatic. It should be remembered that the food of any animal having migratory habits and living in a variety of habitats must differ from time to time and place to place. Drake secured his 209 Ohio specimens between August 8 and 22 in a non-aquatic habitat. The tadpoles live on algae and diatoms, even the newly transformed consuming 83 per cent non-aquatic prey. Oddly enough, very few spiders fall victim to these juveniles.

Enemies.—Newts eat the eggs; fish and various insect larvae devour the tadpoles. Reptiles of different kinds, especially garter and water snakes, are fond of both larvae and adults. Man and many other mammals must be included among the leopard frog's enemies.

Economic Importance.—This amphibian is a friend of farmers because it destroys vast numbers of noxious insects, including potato bugs and grasshoppers. Sixteen of twenty-five individuals caught at the same time on golf links of Kingston, Ontario, held at least one potato bug, whereas twenty-one of the same twenty-five contained one or more grasshoppers.

Bass and pickerel fishermen use countless thousands of juveniles as bait. The demand is so great that the frogs can be bought by the dozen at all fishing stations and have been given special names, one of which is "policemen." The individuals that escape the anglers and grow up are in danger of being collected for their legs, as this is one of the species relished by man and commonly seen in the markets of Chicago and other large cities. Biological supply houses regularly stock adults to be sold to schools and colleges for laboratory use; students of zoology dissect the frogs while professors use them for experimentation. In this country, laboratory workers in various branches of zoological research have usually meant *Rana pipiens* when they spoke of "the frog," assuming that its universal use made further designation unnecessary. This habit was unfortunate, since now we know that "the frog" might actually be any one of several forms of the leopard frog.

Habitat.—It seems best to describe together the hibernation, migratory habits, and habitat preference. Winter is spent in bottom mud or under some object such as a log or stone submerged in the water of an aquatic situation. In the latitude of Chicago, no winter activity occurs except where the water temperature is modified by springs. Actual tests have shown that a leopard frog can survive being chilled to 30° F. but dies before its temperature reaches 28° F. Not until the breeding season has passed do the frogs scatter over swamps or migrate to damp meadows and other low, open, grassy areas, some even reaching dry fields and places far from water. In the autumn, they return to water. Most of them have retired by the first of November at Ithaca, New York, where

Wright kept careful records. Thousands of newly transformed individuals are sometimes seen on the move in summer, presumably migrating from the rapidly drying site in which they developed.

This ability to live in a dry environment is especially interesting because frogs in general, and especially those of the genus *Rana,* are unable to conserve moisture, the inner tissues supplying the skin with water as fast as it is lost through evaporation. Thus the body behaves like a wet bulb thermometer and has a lower temperature on a dry, sunny day than on a cool, rainy one. Experiments by Hall and Root proved that, at 68° F. in a relative humidity of 50 per cent, the leopard frog's body temperature is depressed 8° F. below that of the environment.

Captivity.—This is one of the easiest frogs to keep because it requires little or no water and will thrive in almost any shaded vivarium, readily becoming tame. Specimens can be bought at all seasons from any biological supply house.

Occurrence.—Leopard frogs are found from southern Canada southward over nearly all of North America. No one knows how many forms exist, but incomplete investigations indicate that the population inhabiting this country is divisible into three or four forms that may include two distinct species. To be on the safe side, I have based my account on the population living east of the Mississippi River and north of the latitude of the southern boundary of Pennsylvania, including adjacent parts of Canada.

The local distribution is general, specimens from all but four of the nineteen counties in the Chicago area being on record. Little collecting has been done in these counties: Kane and Kendall in Illinois, Jasper and Starke in Indiana.

References.—The Frog Book. By Mary C. Dickerson. Doubleday, Doran & Company, New York, 1931. A good general account, somewhat out-of-date.

North American Anura; Life-histories of the Anura of Ithaca, New York. By A. H. Wright. Carnegie Institution of Washington, Publication No. 197, 1914. A detailed account of reproduction.

The Sexual Behavior of Anura. Part 1. The Normal Mating Pattern of *Rana pipiens*. By G. K. Noble and L. R. Aronson. Bulletin of the American Museum of Natural History, vol. 80, pp. 127–142, 1942.

REPTILES

Lizards are rare in the Chicago region, only the six-lined race-runner occurring in numbers sufficient to make capture at any given time a certainty. The only poisonous lizards live in Mexico and the dry southwestern part of the United States, so the three local species should not be feared. One of them, the glass-snake, is often mistaken for a snake because all signs of legs are lacking.

The lizards comprise the Suborder Sauria (formerly Lacertilia) of the Class Reptilia.

GLASS-SNAKE
Ophisaurus ventralis
Figure 34

Recognition.—This legless, snake-like lizard can be recognized at once by the ear openings and the ability to close the eyes. The two other local lizards have well-developed limbs.

Reproduction.—The six known clutches of eggs, all laid in captivity, contained from four to seventeen eggs, an average of twelve apiece. Four of the six clutches were deposited between July 2 and 24, one in early June, and one presumably in late May. Only four eggs hatched, their period of incubation ranging from fifty-six to sixty-one days. The eggs have a white, flexible shell, with the two diameters varying in length from ⅜ to ½ and ¾ to ⅞ of an inch. They swell noticeably before hatching.

Laboratory experiments by Noble and Mason showed that females brood (Fig. 34), but, in contrast to the blue-tailed skink, fail to defend their eggs. When these are moved to a new location, the parent will search for them.

Growth and Age.—The hatchlings from the four eggs mentioned above were 4½ to 5 inches long. A good rate of growth is indicated by a young individual (in Chicago Natural History Museum) from Georgia that measures 9½ inches (in spite of a missing tail tip) and was killed in April, presumably having doubled its length in a few growing months. Ditmars records one that measured 37½ inches, and Holbrook states that he saw specimens more than 40 inches long. Most adults are about 2 feet in length.

Habits.—The few casual remarks about the disposition of this innocuous reptile describe it as shy, but sometimes exhibiting enough pugnacity to bite when handled. The movements in grass and other low vegetation are graceful. Although it may bask in mild sun of spring and autumn, during the hottest weather it comes out early, late, or after rain. Being a hardy lizard, the extent of its seasonal activity is great. The skin, often shed in a single piece, is not turned inside out like that of a snake. One captive shed several times during the spring and summer. Late in November a hibernating individual was found coiled eighteen inches below the surface at the foot of a hedge tree; during midwinter another was unearthed near a

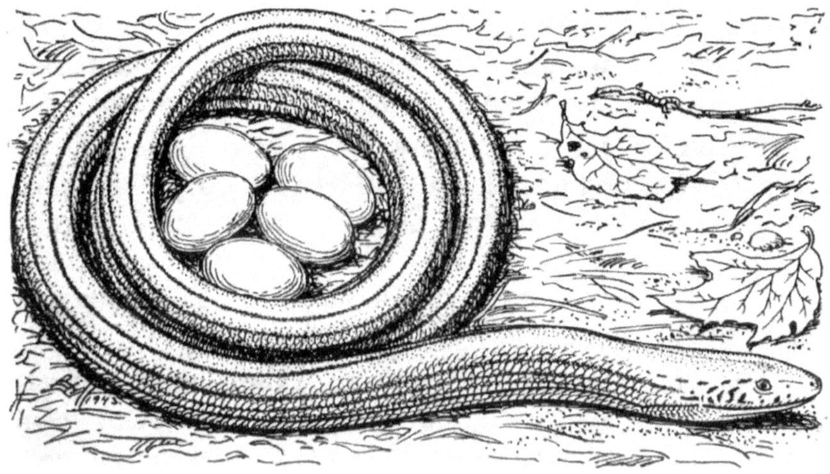

FIG. 34. Glass-snake brooding her eggs. After Noble and Mason.

stump from the depth of a foot. The first was in Kansas, the second in Mississippi.

The most interesting attribute is an ability to break at a point that is apparently near the middle of the body. This is possible because the tail is twice as long as the head and body, and the glass-snake, when it breaks in two or more pieces, is doing no more than many other lizards that leave a wriggling tail in the jaws of a predator. The belief that parts of a shattered tail become joined to the body once more is erroneous; a new but shorter tail grows out of the stump of the original one.

Food and Feeding Habits.—Although the glass-snake feeds largely on insects, the diet includes other invertebrates such as spiders and snails. Grasshoppers are a favorite food since all of the four stomachs that have been examined contained remains of these insects and, in one case, nothing else. Even vertebrates such as small snakes and other lizards are said to fall victim to the bigger adults. The tongue is slowly and repeatedly protruded while the animal drinks.

Enemies.—A young individual was once taken from the stomach of a blue racer.

Economic Importance.—The habit of feeding on insects makes this reptile welcome in agricultural regions.

Habitat.—Grassy or bushy places with loose soil, or piles of brush and dead leaves are frequented. This lizard has been reported from both dry and wet areas. It spends much of the time in cavities under roots, flat stones, and the like, or burrowing through loose soil and decaying vegetation.

Captivity.—In confinement, the glass-snake thrives and will learn to take grasshoppers, crickets, and meal worms from the hand; earthworms and even chopped beef may be substituted. A cannibalistic tendency has been noticed in captives.

If the specimens are not handled with great care, part of the tail will be lost.

Occurrence.—The range embraces the southeastern United States and eastern Mexico to the state of Vera Cruz. In the east, it reaches Virginia, whereas in the Mississippi region it occurs as far north as southern Wisconsin. Locally, the glass-snake is rare, excessively so in the northern part of the Chicago area, where it has been taken at Evanston. There are records for Cook, Kankakee, and Grundy counties in Illinois; Lake, Porter, and Starke counties in Indiana.

Reference.—Experiments on the Brooding Habits of the Lizards *Eumeces* and *Ophisaurus*. By G. K. Noble and E. R. Mason. American Museum Novitates, No. 619, 1933.

SIX-LINED RACE-RUNNER
Cnemidophorus sexlineatus
Figure 35

Recognition.—Three conspicuous, narrow, light stripes extend down either side of the back of this four-legged lizard. The minute scales of back and sides contrast sharply in size with the large ones lying in eight rows along the belly.

The Sexes.—The male of this species can be recognized at once by its wider vent and the two swellings made by the pair of hemipenes concealed just behind this orifice. The femoral pores (extending in a row along the lower surface of each thigh) are larger in this sex and, at least during the breeding season, the male's belly, in contrast to that of the female, is tinged with brilliant blue. Judging by a series of thirteen males and twelve females from Mason County, Illinois, all apparently mature, the females are slightly longer from snout to vent, the average difference being somewhat less than $\frac{1}{16}$ of an inch. The male and female ranges in this series are, respectively, 2 to $2\frac{3}{4}$ and $2\frac{1}{16}$ to $2\frac{7}{8}$ inches. The tails are left out of consideration because they vary greatly in length and are often incomplete or regenerated.

Reproduction.—The sexually excited male begins to court by rubbing his pelvic region from side to side on the ground, often running about in a figure eight as he rubs. He then chases other individuals, biting and poking at their necks. After successfully straddling a female (Fig. 35, above), he repeatedly rubs his pelvic region across her back, continuing to bite and poke her neck. Finally, a twist puts his tail beneath hers, and, as the cloacas meet, he seizes her side just in front of her hind leg and arches his body over her back (Fig. 35, below). As his jaws take a firm grip on her flank, one hemipenis is inserted. Copulation lasts from five to fifteen minutes and is accompanied by convulsive forward thrusts of the male's pelvis.

Noble and Bradley, who worked out the mating behavior of this race-runner in the laboratory, concluded that the brilliant belly of the male does not stimulate the female but is used by one male in challenging another to

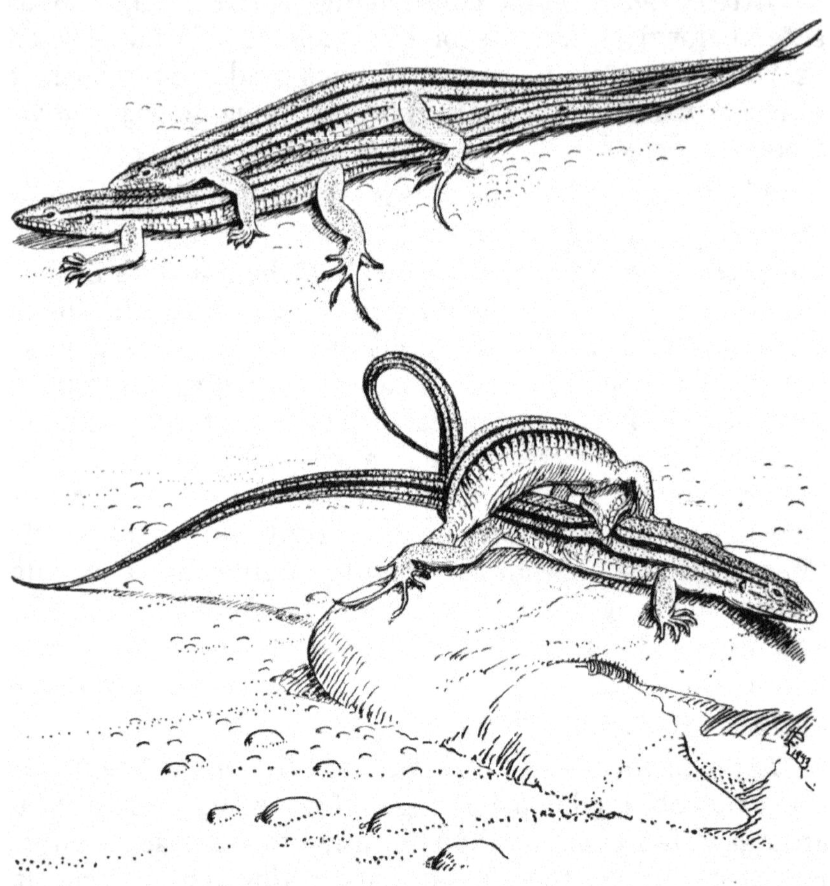

FIG. 35. Six-lined race-runner courting (above) and copulating (below). After Noble and Bradley.

battle. These workers tried in vain to determine which sense organs are essential to courtship.

Five dissections and counts of three clutches indicate that from one to six eggs are laid at a time, the average falling between three and four. The following data show how extensive is the laying season: In Mason County, central Illinois, I secured on May 30 four adult females, two of which held advanced eggs; in the same region, on June 28, eight more were collected, at least two of them gravid and four apparently spent. (There is an actual record of a June 5 deposition in Oklahoma.) By August 9, the Mason County population included numerous recently hatched individuals measuring from $1\frac{3}{16}$ to $1\frac{1}{4}$ inches from snout to vent. The eggs have a flexible white shell; although variable in size, they usually measure about $\frac{3}{8}$ by $\frac{3}{4}$ of an inch. The nests, made in the ground, are said to lie from four to twelve inches beneath the surface.

Growth and Age.—No one has ever studied a series of hatchlings, but Burt's smallest individual (among hundreds) measured $1\frac{1}{16}$ inches from snout to vent and may be considered a hatchling. Our Mason County lot includes juveniles that on May 30 were $1\frac{1}{2}$ to $1\frac{5}{8}$ inches long. These probably are about to enter their second year after growing approximately $\frac{1}{2}$ of an inch. Two gravid females secured in the same county on May 30 and June 28 are only $2\frac{1}{8}$ inches long or about $\frac{1}{2}$ of an inch longer than the advanced yearlings. If the rate of growth to maturity is uniform, this species mates during its second spring and certainly not later than its third.

The maximum length is $3\frac{1}{4}$ inches exclusive of the tail, which, according to Burt, occupies from 55 to 72 per cent of the total length. His minimum figure is probably based on a regenerated tail, since this appendage is rarely if ever so short unless it has sustained damage.

Habits.—The chief characteristic of this lizard is the astonishing speed of its dashes for safety; at such times it appears as a streak across the ground and indeed is called "streak-field" in Georgia. If these dashes do not end at its burrow, the lizard will halt in cover as suddenly as it began and thus seem to disappear. At such times the pursuer must exercise great care, since the race-runner, taking advantage of the cover, will try to sneak slowly and quietly away until again closely approached.

The speed of the wild dashes has not been accurately determined, although it is claimed that a rate of eighteen miles per hour may be attained. There is a strong tendency to live in colonies, one group occupying an area perhaps a few acres in extent.

All observers agree in describing this race-runner as diurnal, but there is disagreement as to which part of the day it remains abroad. No doubt the intensity of a southern midsummer sun reduces its hours of activity, since lizards cannot survive exposure to high temperatures. Barden experimented with a series kept under controlled conditions of light and heat, concluding that the activity depends in part on environmental factors and in part on the inherent physiological constitution of the species.

Food.—The thirty-eight stomach contents analyzed show that the diet includes a great variety of invertebrates, among them adult and larval butterflies and moths, grasshoppers and their allies, beetles, bugs, ants, flies, spiders, and land snails. The presence of mayfly nymphs and mosquito larvae corroborates the discovery of a specimen foraging along the edge of a pond. An individual was once seen to catch a butterfly on the wing.

Enemies.—The blacksnake has been known to eat six-lined race-runners in Georgia.

Economic Importance.—The habit of feeding on insects makes this lizard a friend of the farmer.

Habitat.—The most successful colonies occur in dry, open areas with sandy soil and low vegetation, but the species actually frequents almost every type of country. Throughout Kansas, for example, Burt found it in a greater variety of habitats than any other lizard. In the Great Smoky Mountains National Park it does not attain an altitude greater than 2,000 feet. It is strictly confined to sandy places in the Chicago area.

Captivity.—Captives feed voraciously on insects, and to this diet may be added raw egg and chopped meat.

Occurrence.—The range covers the southeastern quarter of the United States with northward extensions through Maryland along the Atlantic seaboard, and, farther west, up the Mississippi Valley into southern Wisconsin. The colonies inhabiting sandy regions of the southern part of the Chicago area (Porter and Lake counties, Indiana; Kankakee and Grundy counties, Illinois) mark the northernmost occurrence in the territory lying between the Mississippi River and the Appalachian Mountains.

Reference.—A Study of the Teiid Lizards of the Genus *Cnemidophorus*, with Special Reference to Their Phylogenetic Relationships. By Charles E. Burt. Bulletin of the United States National Museum, No. 154, 1931. A general account.

BLUE-TAILED SKINK

Eumeces fasciatus

Figure 36

Recognition.—This lizard has four limbs; the scales of the belly are large and about the same size as those of the back. A five-striped pattern is usually discernible, although the juvenile's brilliant colors fade with growth.

The Sexes.—Old males become uniform brown, whereas females always retain some of the juvenile pattern; the head of the mature male is wider and, at least during the breeding season, redder than that of the adult female. The largest individual among 140 Ohio specimens examined by Conant was a male 7½ inches in total length. Taylor's table also suggests that males exceed females in length, but he does not state how he selected the lizards measured.

Reproduction.—The sexually excited male, after a few preliminaries, approaches a female and turns his head sharply at an angle so that he can readily seize her neck just behind the ear opening. After securing a firm grip, he throws the two limbs of one side over her back and works his tail under hers so that the two cloacas come together. As soon as she has quieted down, he inserts one hemipenis by pushing his pelvic region forward as he pulls back on her neck. Copulation is accompanied by rhythmical forward and backward movements of the male and lasts from four to eight minutes. Noble and Bradley studied the mating behavior of captive skinks, but no one has made observations on specimens living under natural conditions. Reynolds recently made a laboratory study of the male's reproductive cycle.

The nests are usually just beneath the hard shell of logs with well-rotted cores but may be in other situations —rotten stumps, under a rock or the loose bark of a log, in dirt accumulated among the roots of a windfall. Cagle, working in southern Illinois, found that he could make a good guess as to which logs held nests, and noticed that the females selected those that were exposed to the sun during part of the day. Some logs held several nests apiece, and three were found in an area eight inches square. The female evidently hollows out a cavity in which to lay her white, soft-shelled eggs. At first these measure in inches from $\frac{5}{16}$ to $\frac{7}{16}$ by $\frac{1}{2}$ to $\frac{9}{16}$ and vary considerably in shape, some being almost spherical, others much longer in one diameter than in the other. All swell noticeably before hatching. The number per clutch ranges in twenty-nine cases from two to fourteen and averages seven; twenty-six Illinois clutches examined by Cagle contained from six to fifteen and averaged nine. Thus, those from one site in Illinois have a higher average and smaller range than the twenty-nine others from widely scattered localities.

The first sign of hatching is a jerky movement in the egg made by the young as it struggles to slit the shell with the egg-tooth; either the tip of the snout or the whole head is thrust out first. Final emergence usually takes place from forty-five minutes to a few hours after rupture of the shell. The hatching of an entire clutch commonly

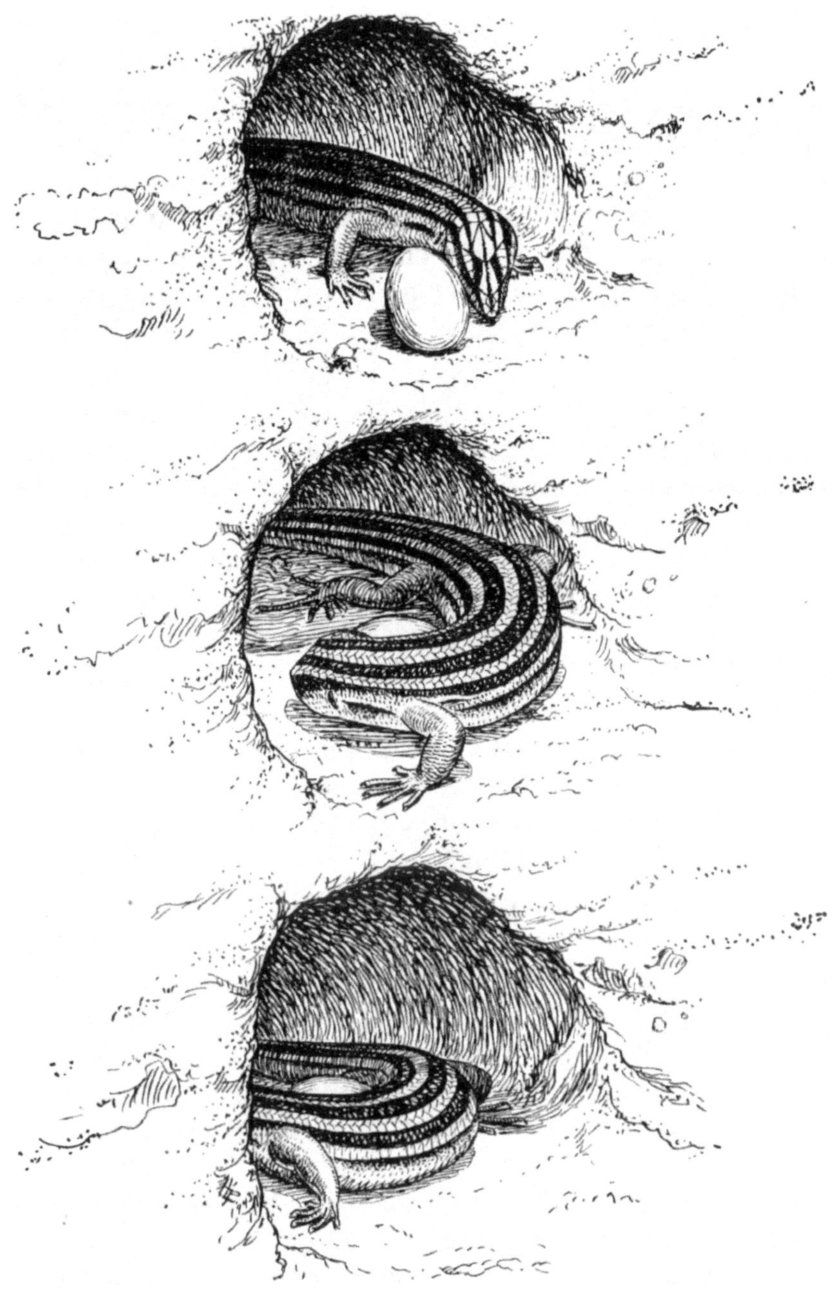

FIG. 36. Female blue-tailed skink retrieving its egg. After Cagle.

requires twenty-four hours. In one case, the egg laid last hatched last; presumably only one attempt has ever been made to correlate order of laying with that of hatching. The hatchling is very active and, if startled, will even rush forth from its shell. Within a few hours the skin has been shed, an appetite developed, and the ground color has changed from dull green to iridescent black.

The earliest date of laying is May 23, the latest July 23; since nearly all of the clutches involved were laid in captivity, it would be gratifying to have additional records based on field observations. Cagle describes the hatching during nine consecutive days (July 14 to 24) of twenty-six clutches from his site in southern Illinois, so it would seem that the laying season in any one region is not extensive. Dates of other hatchings are well distributed through July with two in August, but most of these likewise are captivity records that need support. There are no data on the duration of incubation under natural conditions, but eight clutches laid in the laboratory required from twenty-four to about fifty-five, or an average of thirty-six days.

The brooding habits have attracted much attention and can only be summarized here. The female forms a semicircle about her eggs, curves the body between them, or lies over them, always being in contact with some. She leaves the nest at intervals to feed and bask, her increased temperature after sunning apparently aiding incubation. Upon returning to the nest, she turns some of the eggs, using either tongue or snout. Foreign bodies resembling eggs, and eggs of distantly related lizards are rejected, but not those of close allies. The tongue is used in identification. Intruders such as mice or other reptiles of moderate size are attacked, and Cagle found that the hand of a collector is often bitten. Exposed eggs are reburied, scattered ones brought together. Dirt is moved with the fore limbs, snout, and tail; an egg is covered by burrowing under, and pushing dirt over it. The eggs are either seized in the mouth and carried, pushed with the snout, or rolled while caught in a curve of the body (Fig. 36). Reassembling a lot of scattered eggs requires hours of patient effort.

Growth and Age.—The brilliant livery of the young gradually loses its contrasting colors until, in the adult, all brilliance is gone, the gorgeous, azure-tailed lizard having become more or less uniform olive brown. Hatchlings are about one inch in length from snout to vent. Noble and Bradley saw a male only $2\frac{3}{8}$ inches long (exclusive of the tail) copulate, and the few breeding females that have been measured were about the same size ($2\frac{3}{16}$ to $2\frac{1}{2}$ inches). Lack of uniformity in method of mensuration and failure to sex specimens make it difficult to state the dimensions these lizards usually reach. Conant found that the tails of his Ohio series averaged 1.42 times the length from snout to vent. Nothing is known about the rate of growth under natural conditions or the age attained.

Habits.—This diurnal skink shows a distinct preference for bright, sunny days, when its alertness and agility are astounding. Alarmed individuals disappear in a crevice or scamper for the nearest object under which to hide. If captured, they generally bite, but only the old males are strong enough to inflict more than a painless pinch. Conant noticed certain individuals that habitually lived on the same sawdust piles and used the same retreats, even to the point of running across an intruder's feet to reach them. The basking habit is well developed. A young blue-tailed skink was found in Ohio on January 22 under a log, where it was apparently hibernating.

When seized, the tail breaks off easily, an event that doubtless confounds an enemy and often allows the skink to make its escape while the predator is struggling with the violently wriggling appendage. A new tail soon grows out of the stump of the old one.

Males sometimes attack one another with great vigor, the ensuing battles being real tests of strength and endurance, in which bluffing, so commonly evident in the aggressive behavior of many other lizards, plays no part. The male's wide head and powerful jaws are correlated with this genuine fighting.

Food and Feeding Habits.—Examination of twenty-five alimentary tracts containing food shows that relatively large, active insects such as grasshoppers and their allies and beetles form the bulk of the diet. Various other insects as well as spiders, isopods, and snails are also taken. The remains of a tail in one and *Eumeces* scales in another are evidence of cannibalistic tendencies. It seems likely that the former had eaten its own missing appendage, as a recently hatched captive once did. Another confined individual killed and ate a smaller lizard of a different family.

Economic Importance.—The habit of feeding on insects makes this a useful animal.

Habitat.—The blue-tailed skink typically frequents dry to damp but not actually swampy or boggy woods. It is usually found on stumps and logs, the bark of which has become loosened by decay. Piles of brush, dead leaves, or sawdust, and cavities under large flat stones are also inhabited. Decayed driftwood and logs form a specialized haunt on the shores of the Great Lakes. Although individuals may occasionally take refuge in trees, these lizards normally remain near the ground.

Occurrence.—The range covers the approximate eastern half of the United States exclusive of northern New England, most of Minnesota, and possibly all of Florida. There are many locality records for southern Ontario, but the few for New York lie in its southeastern tip. This is a rare reptile in the Chicago area, the few records being for Berrien County, Michigan; Lake County, Indiana; Cook County, Illinois; and Walworth County, Wisconsin.

References.—A Taxonomic Study of the Cosmopolitan Scincoid Lizards of the Genus *Eumeces.* By Edward H. Taylor. University of Kansas Science Bulletin, vol. 23, 1935. A general account.

Experiments on the Brooding Habits of the Lizards *Eumeces* and *Ophisaurus.* By G. K. Noble and E. R. Mason. American Museum Novitates, No. 619, 1933.

Snakes fascinate as well as frighten people, and reptile houses of zoos draw large crowds because there most visitors experience the greatest thrill—or chill. Strange as it may seem, man comes by his horror of snakes through learning, not inheritance. Progressive educators like to experiment with this fear to see how readily such a deep-rooted and general obsession can be eliminated. In many places, great progress has been made, and the younger generation is not alarmed by snakes. Numerous adults of the Chicago suburbs are made miserable by proximity to harmless garter snakes, but relatively few of our boys and girls are so easily disturbed. Only one of the eighteen local kinds is poisonous, and that one, the massasauga, sounds a warning with its rattle when annoyed.

Nothing about a snake is more remarkable than its feeding habits. One might expect a limbless animal to eat small, weak creatures, but such is not the case; snakes overpower and devour large animals without tearing them apart or even chewing them. The needle-like teeth are curved and slanted rearward to ensure a firm hold; certain bones of the skull move independently and are readily spread apart to allow large objects to pass; the skin stretches like rubber. Digestion is moderately rapid, and surplus nourishment is stored as fat. A well-fed snake easily survives a year without food and yet, during seasons of plenty, eats voraciously.

The method of reproduction is far from uniform. For example, seven of the local kinds lay eggs, eleven bear living young. In some species, the female guards the eggs, but neither hatchlings nor new-born young are cared for by the parents. Infant snakes in general are able to live at least a year without food. They resemble their parents in form but tend to have brighter colors; a more or less complete loss of pattern occurs during early life in the blue racer and the pilot black snake.

The rate of growth has been determined in few of the local species, but probably sexual maturity is attained in $2\frac{1}{2}$ or $3\frac{1}{2}$ years, full size in another three. Garter snakes have unusually large broods and one female was still fertile at the estimated age of twenty years. Such a snake might well give birth to 450 young in a lifetime.

The snakes comprise the Suborder Serpentes (formerly Ophidia) of the Class Reptilia.

My *Snakes Alive* (1937) is a general account, with emphasis on habits. *What Snake Is That?*, written by Roger Conant and William Bridges and published in 1939, is the simplest reliable guide to our snakes east of the Rocky Mountains. A more detailed and technical account, by Karl P. Schmidt and D. Dwight Davis, covers the entire country. The title is *Field Book of Snakes*, the date of publication 1941.

The simple form of a snake makes identification difficult; the novice must either determine the relationships of various scales after first learning their names, or compare details of color patterns. When few species are involved, differences in pattern suffice, so I have based the key largely on these. It must be remembered that stripes extend along, bands across the body. The latter are better called "crossbands." Dryness of the skin tends to obscure the pattern; old common water snakes often appear to be uniform in color until the skin is wet.

Determination of the number of rows of scales extending along the body often helps, and this scale count is given for nearly all the species. Such a count should be made as indicated in Figure 37, about halfway between head and base of tail. A narrow ridge running from the front to the rear edge of a scale is called a "keel," and the scales of all eighteen local species except the milk snake, the blue racer, and the green snake are keeled. The pilot black snake has keels only on the hind half of the body. Small snakes should be examined with a hand lens for this character, which is best seen along the mid-line of the back. A row of large scales or "ventral plates" (Fig. 37) extends down the belly from throat to vent and continues under the tail as a single or double row of "subcaudal

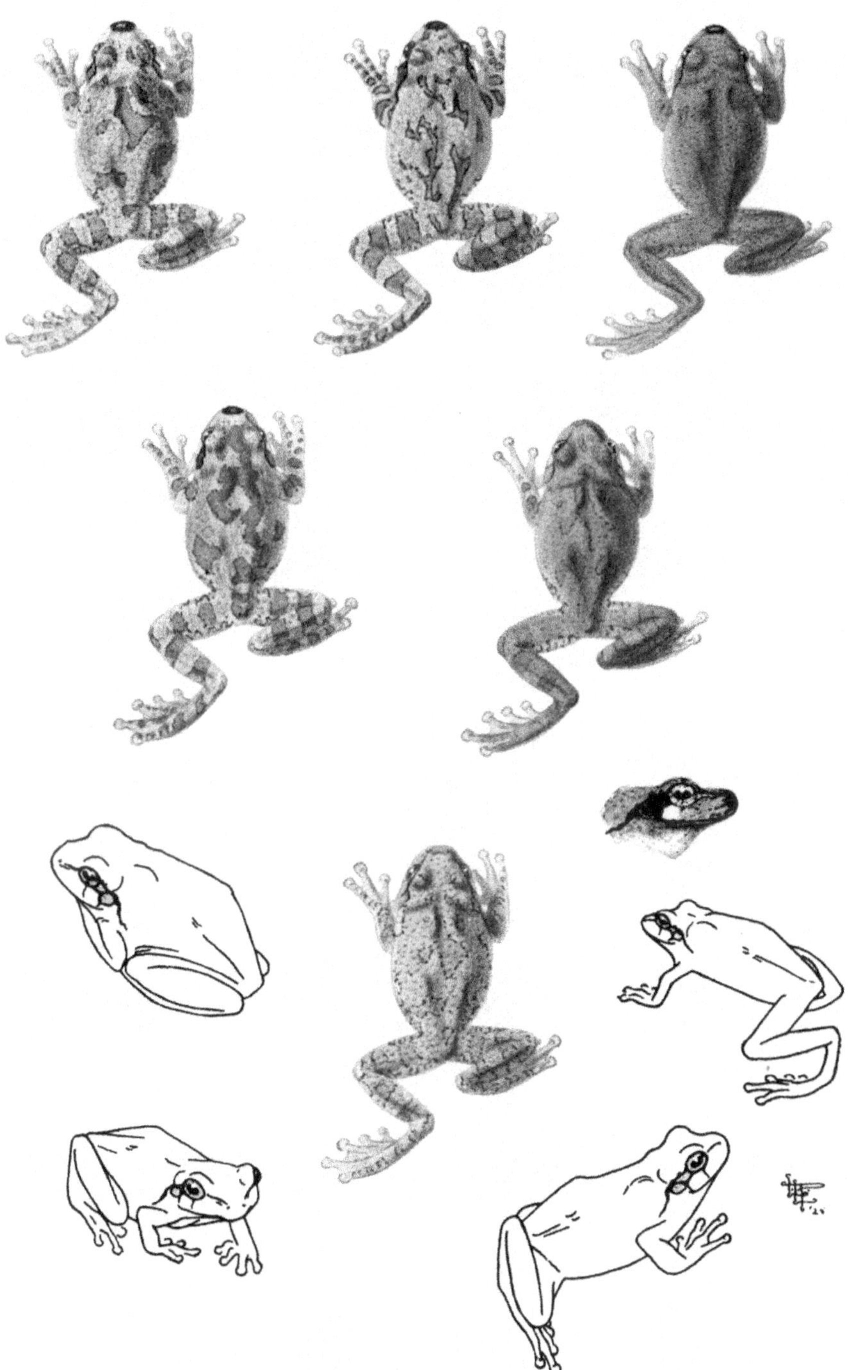

COLOR CHANGE OF THE TREE FROG (*Hyla versicolor versicolor*)
Painted from a single individual

plates." Double or paired subcaudal plates are counted by pairs to correspond to the ventral plate count.

Since many workers find a long key confusing, I have made a short one that does not always carry the user to

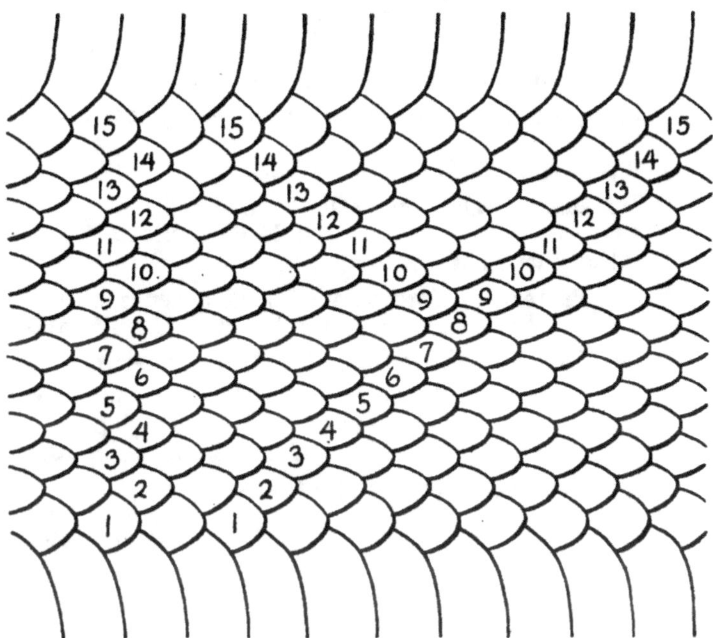

FIG. 37. Flattened-out section of snake's skin, with fifteen lengthwise rows of scales. The numbers show how these rows may be counted across the section or, before skinning, around the body of the snake. The ten scales or "ventral plates" seen at the upper and lower sides of the drawing have been bisected.

a final decision. This can be reached only after comparing the description at the beginning of each species involved.

The coloration of DeKay's snake is so variable that a specimen sometimes falls into the wrong category of the key. This species never exceeds sixteen inches in total length and has heavily keeled scales in seventeen rows, a combination of characters that will help to identify puzzling individuals.

No rattle on tip of tail.

  Back without three light stripes.

    Back and belly without markings; belly not red.

              Green Snake, p. 169, or Adult Blue Racer, p. 171

    Back or belly with markings, or belly red.

      Back with conspicuous blotches, spots, or crossbands.

        Four rows of black spots along back, spots of outer
rows larger than those of inner.

                  Kirtland's Water Snake, p. 189

        Back without four rows of black spots.

          Tip of snout a three-sided, sharp-edged scale.

                    Hog-nosed Snake, p. 165

          Tip of snout a flat, smooth scale.

            A sharp angle along either side of belly; arboreal.

                  Juvenile Pilot Black Snake, p. 174

            Belly without sharp angles.

              Pattern on fore part of back obscure in con-
trast to that on hind part....Bull Snake, p. 179

            Pattern on fore part of body not obscure.

              Crossbands of neck break up to form on
body three rows of alternating spots.

                  Common Water Snake, p. 194

              Pattern of neck like that on body.

                         Fox Snake, p. 177

                          Milk Snake, p. 184

                   Juvenile Blue Racer, p. 171

      Back without conspicuous blotches, spots, or cross-
bands.

        Belly without dark stripes; usually less than a foot
long; found in dry places.

          Red-bellied Snake, p. 201, or DeKay's Snake, p. 200

        Usually at least one dark stripe on belly; seldom
thirty inches long; aquatic.

                  Graham's Water Snake, p. 188

                        Queen Snake, p. 192

        Belly white, back with remnants of a blotched
pattern; more than thirty inches long; arboreal.

                  Adult Pilot Black Snake, p. 174

  Back with three light stripes.

    Ribbon Snake, p. 211, or Garter Snake, pp. 204, 208, 213

A rattle on tip of tail; back blotched, belly largely black.

                      Massasauga, p. 220

HOG-NOSED SNAKE
Heterodon contortrix contortrix
Plate 6

Recognition.—This chunky, conspicuously blotched and spotted snake can be definitely identified by the hard, three-sided plate forming the upturned tip of the snout. The lower and much the larger face of this plate presents a slanting, flat surface bordered by a sharp, curved edge. The scales are keeled and usually in twenty-five rows at the middle of the body.

The Sexes.—The average number of ventral plates in females exceeds the average number in males by a few plates, whereas the reverse is true for subcaudals. The figures given by Conant for Ohio follow (numbers in parentheses are averages): ventral plates in males 122 to 134 (129); in females 122 to 141 (134); subcaudal plates in males 47 to 57 (50); in females 40 to 52 (46). The largest specimen on record is a Minnesota female that measured 43 inches and weighed about two pounds and ten ounces. Disregarding a 41-inch individual of unknown sex, the next to the largest specimen, 39 inches long, is also a female. The longest recorded male measured only $33\frac{7}{8}$ inches, so females probably exceed males in size. Until a large series has been measured, 28 inches may be taken as the average adult length.

Reproduction.—Dissections of eight females and records of ten clutches show that from four to sixty-one, an average of twenty-five eggs, are laid at a time. Omitting the highest and the four lowest of the eighteen records leaves the extremes as twelve to forty-two, figures representing the usual range in size of clutches.

There may be a brooding habit since a female was once found coiled about her clutch.

The eggs have a white, flexible shell and measure about $\frac{3}{4}$ by $1\frac{1}{4}$ inches. They are deposited four or five inches below the surface of sandy fields or other dry, open areas. The only female that has been seen laying was a captive that deposited eggs at intervals of ten to sixty minutes, requiring about one minute for expulsion of an egg. The surprisingly few records indicate that, in the north, eggs are laid during the last half of June and hatch in late August or early September. Cagle reports for extreme southern Illinois a fifty-day incubation period for a confined female and, in addition, a late September hatching of eggs incubated under natural conditions. The young escape by slitting the shell with the egg-tooth; the skin is first shed three or four days after hatching.

Growth and Age.—Ten captive-hatched young of a southern Illinois brood had an average initial length of 8⅛ inches, but individuals only 5½ inches long are on record. One hog-nosed snake survived six years of captivity.

Habits.—The alarming antics of a threatened hog-nosed snake are among the wonders of reptile behavior. An attitude of uncompromising hostility more ominous than that of many really dangerous snakes is at once assumed. The head and neck are expanded and flattened so that new colors appear as if by magic; air is expelled from the inflated body in short, violent hisses as the head is thrust forward in quick jabs. Close inspection shows that, during these jabs, the jaws are barely if at all opened, and only rarely will an individual actually bite. This mock ferocity persists for a varying length of time and is followed by a still more interesting if less disturbing set of reactions.

Allowing the body to resume its normal shape, the snake coils and, at first slowly, then more and more rapidly, twists and writhes about in a curious manner. The wide-open mouth, with trailing tongue and lips oozing blood, is rubbed in the dirt, and convulsive movements run through the body until a climax has passed and the snake relaxes, slowly coming to rest with the belly up. The apparently lifeless form can now be freely handled without showing signs of consciousness but, if placed on the belly, it immediately rolls over on the back! When left alone for a short time, the "dead" snake cautiously raises the head, looks around, and, if the coast is clear, crawls off to safety.

The sharp-edged, upturned snout is used in burrowing, but there have been no good field observations to determine the reasons why this reptile burrows. These reasons suggest themselves: to construct a nest; to reach a resting place or hibernation site; to secure concealed toads. Toads being nocturnal, the diurnal hog-nosed snake might have difficulty in finding them if it could not burrow into loose soil or force its way under logs, roots, flat stones, and other objects beneath which toads like to hide.

Food and Feeding Habits.—Toads form the main diet. A pair of lance-shaped teeth, a loose skin, and a thick body enable this snake to devour these tough, warty amphibians, which have a skin so poisonous that few other animals molest them. When attacked, the toad inflates its already rigid and bulky body until the snake is forced to use its long teeth to puncture and thus deflate its balloon-shaped victim. Although these teeth lie flat at the back of the upper jaw, this bone can be elevated in front, bringing the teeth into play.

Other kinds of frogs and even salamanders are not infrequently eaten. Occasionally mammals and birds have been found in stomachs. More than one investigator has reported insects as an element of the diet, but, due to the fact that insect remains are often left over from digested amphibians, one is at a loss to say how often insects are taken. Very young hog-nosed snakes may resort to a diet of insects more than do the older ones. A small captive that ate crickets supports this supposition.

Enemies.—How does the elaborate bluffing and death-feigning of the hog-nosed snake affect its relationships with such snake-eating mammals as raccoons and skunks? Although it is reasonable to believe that a feigning snake would be quickly devoured, conclusions should be based only on concrete evidence. In the case of man, the threatening attitude has merely brought about relentless persecution, through the conviction that where there is so much smoke there must be some fire. Many people believe that even the breath of the hog-nosed snake is poisonous.

Economic Importance.—Since toads are beneficial, an animal that destroys them cannot be considered useful; but as an entirely innocuous and extremely interesting element of our fauna, this reptile deserves to be spared.

Habitat.—Beaches, open woods, and dry, sandy fields are the preferred habitats, but hog-nosed snakes are sometimes encountered in various other types of country.

Captivity.—A gentle nature, a beautiful pattern, and even the reputation of being a dire menace to life and health enhance the value of this novel reptile to any collection of animals. Unfortunately, its defensive behavior and even the death-feigning habit are given up after a short time in captivity.

Occurrence.—This snake ranges over the eastern half of the United States except southern Florida (where a subspecies occurs) and parts of the extreme north. It is also found in southern Ontario. The distribution in the Chicago area appears to be general, with records for Walworth County, Wisconsin; Lake, Cook, Will, and Kankakee counties, Illinois; Lake and Porter counties, Indiana; and Berrien County, Michigan.

Reference.—The Reptiles of Ohio. By Roger N. Conant. University Press, Notre Dame, Indiana, 1938. A good general account.

GREEN SNAKE
Opheodrys vernalis blanchardi
Plate 6

Recognition.—This slender snake is easily recognized by its uniformly green back and whitish, yellow-tinged belly. The scales are smooth and in fifteen rows.

The Sexes.—Judging by counts of twenty-five males and twenty-nine females from the Chicago area, the sexes can be recognized by the number of ventral plates. The ranges and averages (in parentheses) in fifty-four local specimens follow: males 123 to 135 (132); females 136 to 154 (143). There is a considerable overlapping in the ranges of subcaudal plates as shown by forty-nine local specimens. In twenty-three males the range is 78 to 95, the average 87; for twenty-six females these figures are 65 to 86, and 76. In the local population, females are larger than males, the average length of nineteen adult females being 17¾ inches, that of twenty adult males only 15⅛. The longest female measures 20⅞ inches, the longest male 19½.

Reproduction.—Six eggs of the green snake were discovered under a tie of a deserted railroad in northern Cook County on July 10. They were white and from ¾ to ¹⁵⁄₁₆ of an inch long (Plate 6).

Although the reproduction of the eastern subspecies, *Opheodrys vernalis vernalis,* has been studied in considerable detail by Blanchard and others, that of the western form remains virtually unknown. According to Blanchard, in northern Michigan the eggs of the eastern form are laid in August or late July and hatch between August 4 and September 5, the variable incubation period lasting from four to twenty-three days.

Habits.—This inoffensive and docile snake often climbs about in bushes and grass.

A hibernating colony of 8 plains garter snakes, 101 red-bellied snakes, and 148 green snakes was taken from an ant hill in southern Manitoba, a region in which the eastern and western green snakes intergrade. The ant hill, a flat mound about thirty-six inches in diameter and six high, was located among hazel and hawthorn scrub at the edge of a small opening surrounded by oak and aspen woods. Not far away were willow swamps and muskegs. The snakes were distributed from near the surface to depths of 57 inches, the deepest ones being partly submerged in water. All but two were dug out on October 6 and 10. The smallest of the 112 green snakes measured was only 4⅝ inches long, obviously a young of the year.

Food.—No information on the feeding habits under natural conditions is available. The eastern form is chiefly insectivorous, but other invertebrates and even salamanders form a small part of the diet.

Habitat.—Grobman's intensive study of the green snake revealed two interesting facts: First, the western subspecies is a grassland reptile that, from Ohio to Nebraska, ranges only as far south as the southern limit of Pleistocene glaciation; second, intergradation between eastern and western forms occurs along a line connecting the present eastward extensions of the prairies. This line runs from central Ohio northwestward to extreme southern Manitoba, skirting the southern end of Lake Michigan.

Occurrence.—The green snake ranges from New Mexico and Utah northeastward through the Middle Atlantic and New England states, including adjacent parts of Canada as far west as Manitoba. The line of intergradation between eastern and western subspecies is given above.

The population of the Chicago area is composite, though predominantly made up of the western form plus intergrades nearer to this than to the eastern one. Specimens from the southeastern corner of Wisconsin are actually *Opheodrys vernalis vernalis* (the eastern subspecies), those from Indiana, *Opheodrys vernalis blanchardi.*

HOG-NOSED SNAKE (*Heterodon contortrix contortrix*)

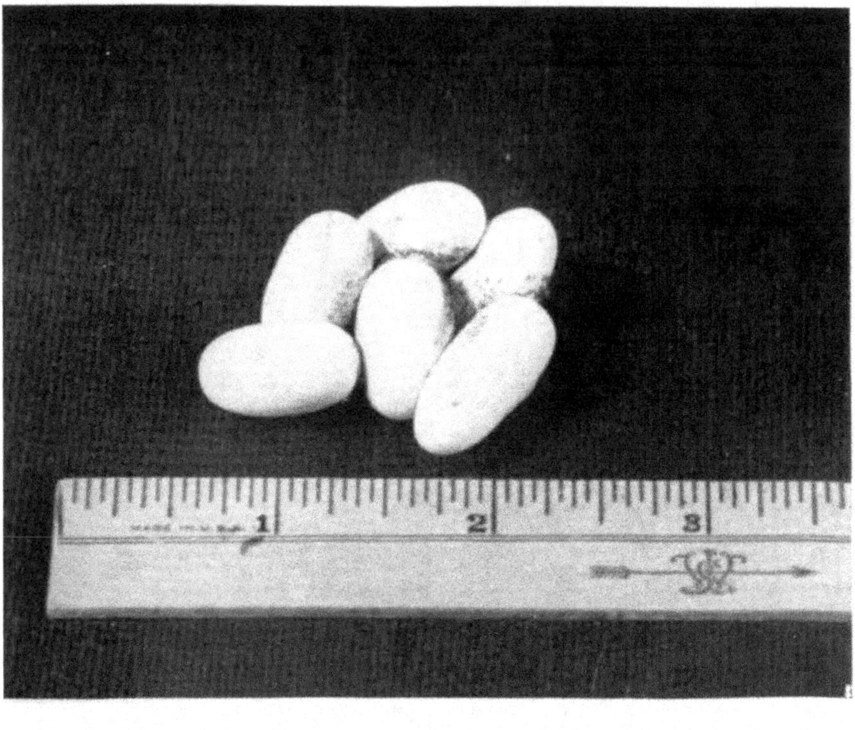

EGGS OF THE GREEN SNAKE (*Opheodrys vernalis blanchardi*)

The local Illinois population seems to be closer to the latter than to the former, hence the use of the name *blanchardi*. There are records for Kenosha and Racine counties in Wisconsin; Lake, Cook, and Du Page counties in Illinois; Lake and La Porte counties in Indiana.

Reference.—A Contribution to the Knowledge of Variation in *Opheodrys vernalis* (Harlan), with the Description of a New Subspecies. By Arnold B. Grobman. Miscellaneous Publications, Museum of Zoology, University of Michigan, No. 50, 1941.

BLUE RACER
Coluber constrictor flaviventris
Plate 7

Recognition.—The adult blue racer is recognized at a glance by its blue- or olive-gray back and much lighter belly, which may be blue, greenish-gray, or yellow. Juveniles, in strong contrast to the patternless adults, are spotted and blotched. A row of large, dark cross-blotches along the back is flanked on either side by two or three rows of irregular, alternating spots that tend to, run together, and each ventral plate has from one to three spots (Plate 7). The scales are smooth and in seventeen rows on the forward, in fifteen on the hind part of the body.

The Sexes.—The average number of ventral plates in females slightly exceeds the average number in males, but the reverse relationship holds for subcaudals. Fourteen males and twenty females from Nebraska have, respectively, the following counts (averages in parentheses): ventrals 171 to 181 (177); 174 to 188 (180); subcaudals 83 to 92 (88); 74 to 87 (81).

Reproduction.—On May 12, Conant found a pair of blue racers mating in northern Ohio. The details of courtship have never been recorded, but courtship of the blacksnake, the eastern subspecies of *Coluber constrictor*, has been described in part by Noble. When sexually excited, the male blacksnakes dash wildly about before paying court to individual females. In captivity, these dashes excite all specimens confined together. A male, after picking out a mate, moves his chin lightly along her back while undulations run forward along his sides and he extends his tongue now and then. Later, he throws the part of his body near his vent over the corresponding part of the female, the two tails sometimes becoming loosely entwined. Snakes courting under natural conditions had cloacal temperatures at or near 87° F.

On June 26, a female from Ohio laid twenty-five white eggs. They did not stick together and the lesser and greater diameters averaged $\frac{7}{8}$ and $1\frac{3}{8}$ inches. All failed to hatch. Only four other clutches have been recorded, three of them with ten, thirteen, and nineteen eggs. The laying dates cover June and include the first two days of July. Some eggs ploughed up in Coles County, Illinois, about September 22 hatched soon after.

Growth and Age.—The smallest specimen in the Chicago Natural History Museum measures $12\frac{1}{2}$ inches and is from Cumberland County, Illinois. Since it was collected in August, it could not have been more than a few weeks old. Thirteen adults from Nebraska had an average length of $40\frac{3}{4}$ inches. Two individuals 71 inches long have been recorded but neither was sexed. The remarkable juvenile pattern already described begins to fade when the young snake has grown three or four inches and disappears when it is between 30 and 40 inches long. The belly spots are last to go; I have even seen traces of them on a 42-inch male. It is obvious that the original pattern fades rapidly during the first year, but the age at which it completely disappears is unknown.

Habits.—Graceful, agile movements and a nervous temperament are characteristics of the blue racer. Stories of attacks on man are probably based on the erratic behavior of males interrupted during courtship. If cornered, an adult will vigorously defend itself at any time, but rapid flight is the normal reaction to the approach of man. An aroused individual vibrates the tip of the tail. This reptile is a good tree-climber, often reaching points from twenty to thirty feet above the ground.

A remarkable hibernation site was discovered in the Indiana Dunes a few years ago by Karl P. Schmidt of the Chicago Natural History Museum. Scores of blue racers aggregate in October on and around an old, oak-covered dune, but their exact winter retreats have not been detected. Before retiring for good, they bask during the warmest hours of the day when the shade temperature reaches 67° F. or thereabouts. Conant found three Ohio specimens hibernating together in a hole about three feet deep. Winter quarters are sometimes shared with other kinds of snakes, a surprising fact in view of the blue racer's snake-eating proclivity.

Food and Feeding Habits.—Small mammals, reptiles (snakes and lizards), frogs and toads, birds, and birds' eggs make up a large part of the diet. The items are named in their approximate order of preference. Insects are also frequently found in the blue racer's stomach, but it is likely that many of them had been eaten by other animals that in turn fell prey to the snakes. For example, Ortenburger dissected twenty-two stomachs and found that only one of them held anything but insects. This, by far the most extensive investigation ever undertaken, makes the blue racer appear to be almost entirely insectivorous. Further studies are needed.

In spite of its scientific name, this reptile is not a typical constrictor; it overpowers its victims by throwing loops of the body over them rather than by tightly coiling around them. A blue racer that overcame a copperhead apparently did so by chewing its head and neck. The poisonous snake was swallowed in about an hour's time.

Habitat.—The blue racer prefers dry, open situations with abundance of low cover such as thickets, hedge rows, and old, overgrown stone walls. Less often it occurs in woods and damp meadows or fallow fields.

Captivity.—Marked nervousness and a tendency to bite make this snake anything but a quiet, gentle pet. Constant, careful handling will induce many individuals to become perfectly tame.

Occurrence.—This racer is found in the southern part of the Chicago area from Berrien County, Michigan, to Grundy County, Illinois, with records for the five intervening counties. There is also a preserved specimen from an unknown point in Cook County. Whether the blue racer did not occur in the area just north of Chicago, or has been exterminated there by man, will probably remain a mystery. It ranges from the Rocky Mountains eastward to central Ohio, where it intergrades with the blacksnake. Farther south, intergradation takes place in the valleys of the Mississippi and Ohio rivers. The blue racer is absent from the region west and south of Lake Superior but it is well known in the southern half of Wisconsin, including Walworth County.

Reference.—The Whip Snakes and Racers, Genera *Masticophis* and *Coluber*. By A. I. Ortenburger. University of Michigan, Ann Arbor, Michigan, 1928. A good general account.

PILOT BLACK SNAKE
Elaphe obsoleta obsoleta
Plate 8

Recognition.—In this, the most arboreal snake of the Chicago area, the upturned ends of the ventral plates produce a pair of edges that greatly facilitate climbing and make the belly flat or even concave. A row of about thirty large, dark blotches extends down the middle of the back from head to vent, most of the blotches being longer than wide and hexagonal in shape. The pattern, though

ADULT BLUE RACER (*Coluber constrictor flaviventris*)

JUVENILE BLUE RACER (*Coluber constrictor flaviventris*)

distinct in juveniles, is always more or less obscured by dark pigment in adults. The scales are in twenty-five or twenty-seven rows at the middle of the body and their keels are noticeable only to the rear of this point.

The Sexes.—The average number of ventral plates in females exceeds the average number in males by a few plates, and the reverse relationship holds for subcaudals. Counts of seven specimens of each sex from Nebraska follow (averages in parentheses): ventral plates in males 223 to 234 (227); in females 226 to 241 (232); subcaudal plates in males 79 to 84 (81); in females 71 to 84 (78).

Reproduction.—A pair of six-foot captives from eastern Kansas copulated in late May and the female laid fourteen fertile eggs on July 30. Nine eggs deposited on July 11 by another female living under the same conditions hatched on August 22. The largest and smallest eggs of the first clutch measured in inches $2\frac{1}{4}$ by $\frac{15}{16}$ and $1\frac{3}{4}$ by $\frac{15}{16}$. Boyer and Heinze report the deposition of a clutch in Jefferson County, Missouri, on the night of May 22. The longest of the sixteen almost spherical eggs measured only $1\frac{1}{4}$ inches, so they may have been premature.

Growth and Age.—Recently hatched specimens are from $11\frac{7}{8}$ to $15\frac{3}{4}$ inches long. The average length of six adults from southeastern Nebraska is 52 inches, or just $5\frac{1}{2}$ inches less than the average length of as many (three of each sex) from eastern Kansas. Among forty collected at Darlington, Oklahoma, in a year, only one exceeded six feet in length. The longest specimens on record are two 75-inch individuals, one from Ontario, the other, a female, from Indiana. Longer ones doubtless exist.

Habits.—This largely arboreal snake spends much of its time in bushes, trees, and brush piles, often reaching points from twenty to thirty feet above the ground. Cagle records the discovery of a specimen in an abandoned woodpecker's hole in a barkless tree twenty inches in diameter. The single entrance to the hole was at a height of thirty-five feet, so the snake must have climbed the outside of the tree. The shape of the belly that facilitates climbing has already been described. The movements, except those of alarmed individuals, are slow, and the habit of "freezing" to avoid detection is sometimes practiced. The temperament is variable; some pilot black snakes bite viciously and vibrate the end of the tail when annoyed, others remain quiet and docile even after being picked up.

Gloyd reports the discovery in eastern Kansas of eight individuals preparing to hibernate in crevices of rocks lining a tightly closed well. They were less than twelve feet below the surface in company with two blue racers and a small bull snake.

Food.—The diet consists of mammals, birds, and birds' eggs. Five stomachs contained, respectively, two fledgling downy woodpeckers, a sparrow, a small chicken, three birds' eggs (unbroken), a white-footed mouse. A baby rabbit was once seen in the coils of a three-foot individual, a second is known to have killed and swallowed three young robins, and a third, found dead, had devoured a large, decomposing chipmunk.

Economic Importance.—Such a large snake is capable of devouring a great many useful birds as well as harmful rodents, so its economic status must vary from place to place; for example, in seven months thirty-three specimens were killed along a fence protecting an Oklahoma quail hatchery, and one that gained entrance ate a full-grown quail measuring $10\frac{1}{4}$ inches from the tip of the beak to the end of the toes. The snake, only $4\frac{1}{2}$ feet long, was trapped because the bulge made by the bird rendered escape through the inch-mesh poultry netting impossible.

Habitat.—As suggested by the arboreal habits, this snake frequents wooded areas. In southern Illinois, Cagle found it generally distributed but abundant in forests of river bluffs and canyons. A liking for farm buildings has been noted.

Occurrence.—Snakes living in an extensive area stretching from eastern Nebraska and eastern Kansas to the Atlantic Coast are now commonly identified as *Elaphe obsoleta obsoleta,* but it is by no means certain that they belong to the same subspecies or even species. I have therefore restricted the foregoing account to the population found farther west than Ohio and Lake Huron.

In the Chicago area, the pilot black snake has been taken in Cook County, Illinois, and in Lake and La Porte counties, Indiana. It is excessively rare in the local Illinois counties, and anything but common in those of northern Indiana.

Fox Snake

Elaphe vulpina vulpina

Plate 1

Recognition.—The fox snake is described with the milk snake because the two species look so much alike.

The Sexes.—The average number of ventral plates in females exceeds the average number in males, whereas the reverse relationship holds for subcaudals. The following figures are given by Conant for a large series (approximately 100 specimens) from all parts of the range (averages in parentheses): ventral plates in males 190 to 210 (200); in females 198 to 216 (207); subcaudal plates in males 52 to 68 (63); in females 51 to 59 (55). The male fox snake exceeds the female in size, a most unusual condition clearly shown by Conant's extensive series. The longest male measured by him was 60⅝ inches long, the longest female only 53⅛; his ten longest males and females averaged, respectively, 53¼ and 47¼ inches.

Reproduction.—Two fox snakes were once seen near Chicago in a curious position, one having swallowed the other's head and neck. Since their bodies were undulating synchronously, and the one did not continue to engulf the other, their behavior must have been of a sexual nature; probably the male had bitten the female in courting her and carried his normal biting technique a little too far.

With the exception of a clutch of unknown size dug out of a manure pile in Bureau County, Illinois, the only three clutches on record were laid by captive females and had seven, seven, and thirteen eggs in them. The largest was deposited in Iowa on July 24; the hatchlings appeared fifty-four days later and were $9\frac{1}{2}$ to 11 inches long. The white eggs measure about $\frac{7}{8}$ by $1\frac{5}{8}$ inches, and those that happen to come in contact at laying adhere together. The shell is flexible. Such are the surprisingly meager data on the reproduction of this familiar reptile.

Habits.—Nearly everything that has been written on the habits of fox snakes concerns the eastern subspecies, *Elaphe vulpina gloydi,* so it is time that observations on the behavior of the western form were recorded. The habit of vibrating the tail when alarmed is common to both subspecies and in Ontario has given rise to the name "hardwood rattler" because in dry leaves the vibrating tail makes a noise similar to the rattling of a rattlesnake.

Food.—Presumably this subspecies, like the eastern one, lives on a diet of small mammals supplemented by birds, birds' eggs, salamanders, and even earthworms. Our knowledge of the feeding habits of *Elaphe vulpina gloydi* is slight enough, and the diet of the two forms may differ more than one might suppose. Earthworms were found in a specimen of *gloydi* only two feet long, so perhaps young individuals eat more invertebrates than do the adults.

Habitat.—Dunes bordering Lake Michigan, woods, stream valleys, prairies, and farm lands are frequented by this snake. It is sometimes found in fields under shocked grain.

Occurrence.—The distribution in the Chicago area is general with records for twelve of the nineteen counties, including Starke County in Indiana, Grundy County in Illinois, and Racine County in Wisconsin. The city of Racine is, in fact, the type locality. The range extends from the northern peninsula of Michigan, Wisconsin, and northeastern Indiana westward to eastern Nebraska and the southeastern tip of South Dakota. There are records for Lincoln and Charles counties in eastern Missouri.

BULL SNAKE
Pituophis sayi sayi
Plate 8 and Figures 38–40

Recognition.—There is a marked difference between the patterns of the front and hind thirds of this large snake, the transition from one to the other being gradual. The dark spots of the forward third are obscured by their close proximity, by being connected, especially on the sides, or by the presence of numerous dark scales between them. In contrast to this, the well-separated spots of the last third are seldom connected or obscured by intervening dark scales. The fact that the bull snake is found only in the southern part of the Chicago area will often help in its identification. The scales are in twenty-nine to thirty-five rows at the middle of the body and heavily keeled.

The Sexes.—The average number of ventral plates in females is slightly higher than it is in males, but the overlap in range is so great and the difference in average so slight that ventral counts do not help in determination of sex. The subcaudal counts, higher in males, also differ too little to be useful. In many snakes, the female is decidedly larger than the male, but such is not the case in the bull snake. Measurements given by Stull do not present conclusive evidence but suggest that, if a difference exists, it is slightly in favor of the male.

Reproduction.—The few data on the laying habits show that the eggs are deposited the second week in July and hatch during the last two weeks of September. The six recorded clutches contained from ten to eighteen eggs apiece, averaging thirteen. The only lot of eggs found in situ was "partially imbedded in soft earth under a stone" lying in a field. The eggs adhere to one another if they come in contact at laying. Sixteen eggs deposited by a Kansas female averaged about 2 by 1½ inches in greater and lesser diameters. There is much variation in the size and shape of eggs both from the same and from different clutches.

When fully developed, the embryo makes with its egg-tooth some slits in the white, flexible shell and pokes its snout out to begin a gradual emergence that requires several hours for completion.

Growth and Age.—Thirteen of a brood of sixteen from Kansas averaged 16⅜ inches in length when two days old and shed their skins for the first time about a week later. The largest adult on record measured 92 inches. Among the 192 bull snakes more than 30 inches long examined by Stull, the largest taped 83⅛ inches from tip to tip; the average length of Stull's twenty largest was 71⅛ inches. Most of the mature individuals encountered measure from 54 to 66 inches. Nothing is known about growth except that some captive hatchlings 15 to 15½ inches long attained a common length of 18 inches in two months.

Habits.—This is a terrestrial snake often seen abroad during the day. Many individuals are so docile when encountered that they merely attempt to crawl away and do not resist being picked up. Others defend themselves by vibrating the end of the tail, coiling, inflating the partly raised body, hissing loudly, and even striking. The forward jabs of head and neck are ineffectual, the vigorous hissing being the ominous part of this reptile's elaborate defensive bluff. The rapid expulsion of air against a flat structure in front of the windpipe produces the noise, which suggests an angry gander. All very young individuals are reported to be vicious and thus exhibit a greater uniformity of behavior than do the adults.

Food and Feeding Habits.—Although no one has ever examined a series of bull snake stomachs, numerous casual observers agree that the diet consists chiefly of small

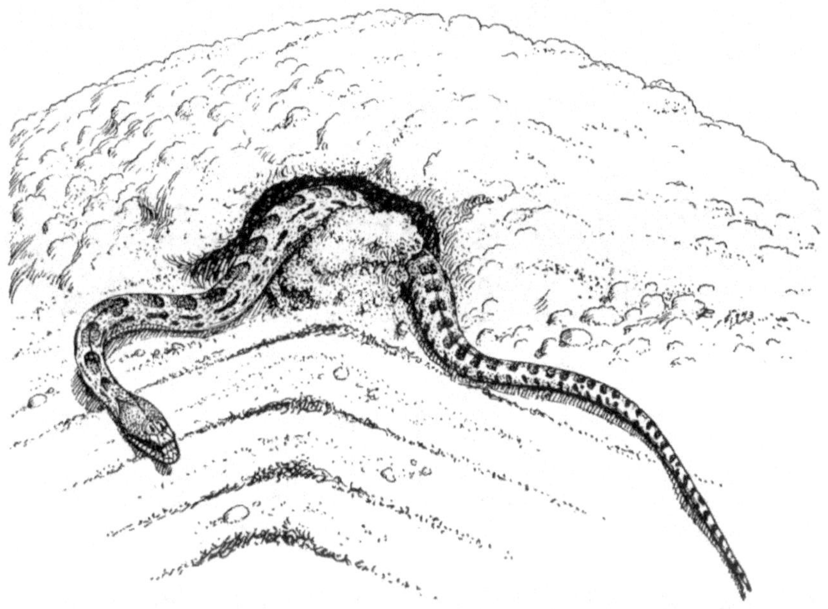

Fig. 38. Bull snake removing loose dirt from entrance to pocket gopher's burrow. After Hisaw and Gloyd.

mammals, such as rats, mice, gophers, ground squirrels, and rabbits. Birds and their eggs are also eaten. The feeding habits probably vary considerably from place to place; for instance, bull snakes are common in forests along the Illinois River in the region of Havana, where they frequently ascend the straight trunks of large trees to rob nesting boxes of the wood duck. Remarkable feats of climbing have been observed by Mr. Frank C. Bellrose (of the Illinois State Natural History Survey), who showed me the nesting boxes in question. A typical prairie snake thus demonstrates an astonishing ability to adapt its feeding behavior to special conditions.

Hisaw and Gloyd describe the method often used by bull snakes in entering the pocket gopher's burrow. Doing this may require a digging technique, because this mammal fills the numerous side entrances to its home with loose earth. The snake thrusts its head into this earth, catches a load of it in a coil of the body, pulls it out of the tunnel, and releases it near-by (Fig. 38). Repetition

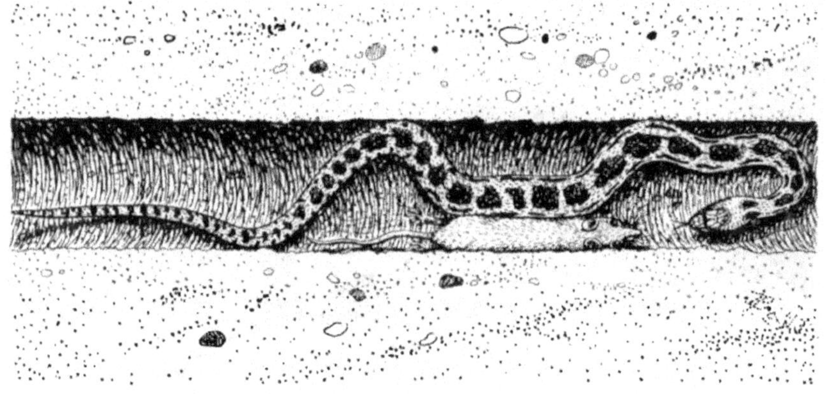

FIG. 39. Bull snake killing pocket gopher in its burrow. After Hisaw and Gloyd.

of this process enables the snake to reach the main tunnel. Once a gopher is found, it is quickly pinned against the wall of its burrow by a bend in the snake's body (Fig. 39). Although no capture was observed under natural conditions, numerous lateral tunnels obviously excavated by snakes were found, and captives repeatedly demonstrated their ability to trap small mammals in a similar manner, one even killing three half-grown rats at a time.

Enemies.—Strecker saw a bull snake that had been lifted into the air by a large hawk make its escape by striking at the hawk and struggling violently. No doubt a hawk finds little difficulty in overcoming small snakes of this species. Countless numbers are killed on roads by speeding automobiles. Large in size and relatively slow in movements, this reptile seems to be the chief highway victim of the great plains region.

Economic Importance.—Some feeding experiments performed in Kansas by Hisaw and Gloyd led them to conclude that a typical bull snake weighing 2½ pounds would normally consume in six months at least 6.7 pounds of food. The twelve pocket gophers estimated ordinarily to

FIG. 40. Range of bull snake.

inhabit an acre and a half of alfalfa also would weigh about 6.7 pounds. In other words, allowing for a six months' season of activity, a snake might account for the normal acre-and-a-half crop of pocket gophers, and, in doing so, prevent an annual loss of $3.75. Many farmers recognize this snake as a helper, and they release on their farms specimens that have been captured elsewhere.

Habitat.—The bull snake is typically a prairie inhabitant but it occurs in other types of country along the periphery of its range. An example of this is the population found in forests along the Illinois River and already mentioned. In northeastern Illinois, bull snakes are confined to open, sandy areas, but oddly enough they do not reach the Indiana Dunes.

Captivity.—A snake of such unusual dimensions makes a striking pet. The ordinary precautions against dampness, over-heating by sunlight that floods the entire cage, and chilling should be taken. Direct sunlight that can be avoided at will is beneficial. A specimen of *Pituophis sayi* lived four years and eight months in the National Zoological Park, Washington, D.C.

Occurrence.—The range extends from Lake Michigan and the region of the Indiana-Illinois boundary southwestward to extreme northeastern Mexico, westward through central Colorado, and northwestward to the southeastern corner of Alberta (Fig. 40). In the Chicago area, the bull snake has been found in sandy areas of Kankakee and Will counties, Illinois, and Jasper County, Indiana.

Another subspecies of *Pituophis sayi*, known as the Arizona bull snake, occurs west of the southern part of the range just outlined.

Reference.—Variations and Relationships in the Snakes of the Genus *Pituophis*. By O. G. Stull. Bulletin of the United States National Museum, No. 175, 1940. A general account.

MILK SNAKE

Lampropeltis triangulum triangulum

Plate 1

Recognition.—The milk and fox snakes, being readily confused, are described here together for the sake of clarity. Both have a black-and-white-checkered belly and a back with a median row of dark-bordered blotches flanked on either side by a single row of spots. The blotches are at least as wide as long and do not tend to be hexagonal in shape. The two species are most readily distinguished by counting the rows of scales between the blotches and the ventral plates. The fox snake has five or six such rows, the milk snake only three or four. At the middle of the body the scales of the milk snake are in twenty-one or twenty-three (rarely nineteen) rows and smooth, those of the fox snake in twenty-five or twenty-seven, and keeled.

The Sexes.—In Ohio, the ranges and averages of ventral and subcaudal plates show little sexual difference. The figures follow (averages in parentheses): ventral plates in males 195 to 208 (202); in females 197 to 210 (203); subcaudal plates in males 46 to 53 (49); in females 42 to 48 (46). Males appear to attain the greater length, the two largest specimens on record being of this sex. One, from Indiana, measures 44 inches (although the tail is incomplete); the other, from Ohio, 43½. The largest female known was collected in New York and is 39¾ inches long.

Reproduction.—Two lots of eggs, one of them possibly composite, have been found in situ. One was concealed under a bark slab in a pile of decaying sawdust, the other in a pile of manure. Records of six clutches and dissections of two gravid females show that from eight to sixteen, or an average of eleven eggs are laid at a time in July or late June. The few available data indicate an incubation period of about two months. The white eggs adhere in a clump if they come in contact with one another at laying, and measure approximately ⅝ by 1¼ inches. Ditmars states that the female broods its eggs.

Growth and Age.—Hatchlings vary considerably in length but usually are about 8 or 9 inches long. No large series has ever been examined to determine the average adult length, which a safe guess puts between 32 and 36 inches. One Connecticut female measuring only 30½ inches laid eggs. The third largest individual known is 42¾ inches long and comes from New York; it was not sexed. The maximum size by sexes has already been considered.

Habits.—At least during the day, the milk snake is secretive and hides under logs, boards, rubbish, or almost any other convenient object or material; presumably it prowls and feeds at night. Most individuals show some pugnacity when first encountered, vibrating the end of the tail and striking to the accompaniment of a short, sharp hiss. After being picked up, they often deceive the inexperienced by appearing to be docile but suddenly seizing the skin and chewing. Such biting without striking is unusual behavior for a snake. Two milk snakes were found on a tree in Connecticut, one three feet from the ground descending the vertical trunk, the other six feet higher in a crotch. This species is not ordinarily credited with arboreal tendencies.

In Pennsylvania, sixteen snakes (including seven species) and four salamanders (two species) were. dug out of a gravel bank where they had hibernated together 2½ feet below the surface. A milk snake 9½ inches long was among them.

Food and Feeding Habits.—Two attempts to determine the feeding habits of this snake have been made: In one case, the contents of twenty-nine stomachs from Pennsylvania were tabulated; in the other, the contents of nineteen from the mountains of Virginia and West Virginia. A shrew was found in one stomach, mice were found in twenty-nine, undetermined mammals in two, birds in three, birds' eggs in one, snakes or their eggs in seven, invertebrates in three, unidentifiable vertebrate remains in two. Several scattered records of one to four observations each confirm the strong preference for mice and snakes, give no further evidence of a bird diet, and add lizards to the list.

One 10-inch milk snake when captured disgorged a red-bellied snake of equal length; another was seen to constrict and swallow a copperhead about 18 inches long.

This struggle occurred in nature and the victor escaped without being measured. In spite of this incident, most of the snakes eaten are harmless kinds. Like certain other egg-eating snakes, this reptile crushes comparatively large eggs after swallowing them to a point not far from the head.

Economic Importance.—Many farmers believe that the milk snake enters barns and stables in search of cows to suck, whereas this reptile shows no interest in milk and is physically incapable of extracting it; any cow would be driven frantic by the numerous needle-sharp teeth of a snake, and no reptile is able to suck. Even if a 30-inch snake did drink milk, it could hold only a few tablespoonfuls since it displaces but a quarter of a pint of water, an amount equal to about a hundredth of the milk produced daily by a good cow. In other words, the milk that a cow might give in a day would be enough food to satisfy the most glutinous milk snake for a year. Of all our snakes this useful rodent-eater is the most maligned.

Habitat.—This common reptile has no well-defined habitat preference. It occupies a variety of situations such as woods, fields, meadows, farm lands and buildings, and even waste land of settled and suburban areas.

Captivity.—In spite of attractive colors and a sufficiently docile nature, the milk snake is not a perfect pet because many individuals feed indifferently or even refuse all food.

Occurrence.—There are records for eleven of the nineteen counties of our area, including at least one county in each of the four states. This is ample evidence of general local occurrence. *Lampropeltis triangulum triangulum* is distributed over nearly all the northeastern United States and much of southeastern Ontario. It follows the Appalachian Mountains into the southern states and reaches extreme southeastern Minnesota to the northwest. Several other subspecies of *Lampropeltis tri-*

angulum range through the middle-western and southern states southward to extreme northwestern South America.

Reference.—A Revision of the King Snakes: Genus *Lampropeltis*. By Frank N. Blanchard. Bulletin of the United States National Museum, No. 114, 1921. A good general account.

GRAHAM'S WATER SNAKE
Natrix grahamii

Recognition.—This species and the queen snake look much alike when viewed from above, but their bellies differ noticeably. The light belly of Graham's water snake is sometimes stripeless, but usually it has a single, dark median stripe that is stronger toward the rear. The scales are in nineteen rows at the middle of the body and heavily keeled.

The Sexes.—The females are thicker and attain a greater length than the males. This is illustrated by the series of three adult males and the eleven largest females, probably all of them also adult, in the Chicago Natural History Museum. The males are from 25¾ to 27½ inches long, whereas the females range in length from 23¾ to more than 34 inches (the two largest have incomplete tails), seven of them being longer than the largest male. The male's tail is proportionately longer. The two longest tails of the males measure 5¼ inches, a caudal length not equaled by any female less than 28¾ inches long. Strecker states that females are more often "dull or off-colored," a point I am unable either to confirm or refute.

Reproduction.—A pair of captive Missouri specimens copulated on May 10. Judging by the seven known broods, the number of young produced at a time varies from six to twenty-five and averages fourteen; birth may take place from late August to September 17. Such are the meager data on this important phase of the life history.

Growth and Age.—Beyer states that this snake has an egg-tooth, but I fail to find one on an advanced embryo in the Chicago Natural History Museum. An egg-tooth in a live-bearing snake is certainly a vestigial structure.

The average birth-length of the young of one reported brood was 7¼ inches, that of another 8½. The maximum length is about a yard; the 34-inch female in the Chicago Natural History Museum probably would be this long if it had a complete tail.

Habits.—Graham's water snake is aquatic and more secretive than the various crossbanded water snakes inhabiting the Mississippi region. Strecker found it active on cloudy days. When handled, it gives off an offensive odor but is docile and timid.

Food.—Strecker writes that the food consists of crustaceans, small fish, frogs, and salamanders, and gives evidence that crayfishes are most often eaten.

Habitat.—This snake frequents lagoons, streams, ponds, and rivers. It is prone to hide under driftwood and brush piles along the water's edge.

Occurrence.—From Cook County, Illinois, and the southeastern corner of Nebraska, *Natrix grahamii* ranges southward to the Gulf Coast of Louisiana and Texas. The only records from the Chicago area are based on the few specimens that have been taken in Cook County and a single one from Will County.

KIRTLAND'S WATER SNAKE

Natrix kirtlandii

Plate 8

Recognition.—Four rows of alternating, black spots along the back and sides of this locally rare snake give it a checkered pattern that is unmistakable. The spots of the outer rows are a little larger than those of the median ones. The belly is red, with a pair of conspicuous, black spots on each ventral plate. The scales are in nineteen rows at the middle of the body and heavily keeled; there are from 121 to 136 ventral plates.

The Sexes.—Males and females are alike in coloration, but the females are thicker and attain the greater length, the longest female and male on record being 21 and 17⅝ inches long. The tail of the male occupies about 25 per cent of the total length, that of the female only about 22 per cent. The proportionately longer tail of the male has more subcaudal plates, the range and average for 115 specimens being 57–69 and 62; the corresponding figures for 119 females are 44–61 and 54.

Reproduction.—Little is known about the breeding of this snake, which was long considered a rarity. The young are born in August or the first three weeks of September. Eight is the number in the average brood but there may be as many as thirteen or as few as four.

Growth and Age.—The young are almost without pattern and about 6 inches long when born; they shed the skin within thirty-six hours of birth. Nothing is known about the rate of growth under natural conditions, or the duration of life. There is a record of a female only 14⅜ inches long having produced a brood. An individual of this sex three inches longer is large, whereas a male but two inches longer may be considered a big specimen.

Habits.—This small, secretive reptile is the least aquatic of the local water snakes. Probably it prowls at night, since few individuals are encountered abroad during the day. Hiding places under logs, boards, and similar objects are preferred. There is some evidence that numbers hibernate together underground but no actual "dens" have been discovered.

Many snakes flatten the body when frightened but few do so to such a remarkable degree as does Kirtland's water snake; among them only Kirtland's water snake becomes rigidly immobile while flattened. If touched, or disturbed in some other way, a rigid individual sud-

QUEEN SNAKE (*Natrix septemvittata*)

PILOT BLACK SNAKE (*Elaphe obsoleta obsoleta*)

BULL SNAKE (*Pituophis sayi sayi*)

KIRTLAND'S WATER SNAKE (*Natrix kirtlandii*)

denly throws a fit of violent, erratic wriggling that makes capture difficult. Some specimens strike but seldom do they really bite, and all can be handled with safety.

Food.—No investigation of the feeding habits under natural conditions has been made, but three wild individuals disgorged earthworms and another a slug. Many captives have fed avidly on these same animals while refusing other small creatures usually relished by water snakes. Rarely has a captive accepted chopped fish.

Habitat.—This species typically inhabits moist situations of open prairies such as wet grasslands and meadows and the margins of lakes, streams, and swamps. Specimens are occasionally found near woodland pools.

Captivity.—In caring for about a hundred captives over a period of many years, Conant persuaded approximately half of them to eat earthworms or slugs, but he has never succeeded in keeping a wild-caught one alive through the winter. The cause of death is a mystery; perhaps it is improper nourishment. Confined specimens remain nervous and rarely grow accustomed to being handled.

Occurrence.—This reptile ranges from the eastern half of Illinois eastward to western Pennsylvania and seems to be a survival of the fauna that once inhabited the "prairie peninsula" that formerly extended at least as far as Pennsylvania but now terminates at the Illinois-Indiana boundary. The first specimen ever recorded in scientific literature, the "type," was taken at "West Northfield," Cook County, Illinois. There are several other records for this county as well as one for Du Page County, Illinois. The species has also been taken in the dune area of Porter County, Indiana.

References.—The Reptiles of Ohio. By Roger N. Conant. University Press, Notre Dame, Indiana, 1938. A brief general account.

Studies on Kirtland's Water Snake. By Roger N. Conant. The American Midland Naturalist, vol. 29, pp. 313–341, 1943. An excellent account.

QUEEN SNAKE

Natrix septemvittata

Plate 8

Recognition.—A light stripe extends along the lower part of the side of this dark brown snake. The pair of dark stripes usually evident on the belly may be obscured, especially toward the rear, by a general darkening of the ventral plates. There is no median light stripe on the back. The scales are in nineteen rows at the middle of the body and heavily keeled.

The Sexes.—Disregarding three large females with decidedly blunt tails, there are in the Chicago Natural History Museum twenty-two females and twelve males 19 or more inches long. The longest male and female measure, respectively, $24\frac{3}{4}$ and $30\frac{3}{4}$ inches, and eight of the females are longer than the longest male. The average lengths of these two series are 22 and $24\frac{1}{2}$ inches, adding to each a small fraction of an inch to make up for missing tail tips. The obvious sexual difference in size can be more accurately determined after we know at what lengths the sexes mature. The male's tail is proportionately longer; for example, in a pair $22\frac{1}{8}$ inches long, the male's appendage measures 6 inches, the female's only $5\frac{1}{4}$; in a pair with $6\frac{1}{2}$-inch tails, the male is but $24\frac{1}{2}$, the female $27\frac{1}{8}$ inches long. This difference is reflected in counts of the subcaudal plates. Conant gives these ranges for Ohio specimens: males 72 to 79 (average of 76); females 64 to 72 (average of 68).

Reproduction.—Counts of six broods and dissections of eight gravid females indicate that from six to fourteen, or an average of nine young are produced at a time. Two additional cases involving fewer than six young are apparently abnormal. Births may occur from the middle of August throughout September.

Growth and Age.—Most new-born young are between $7\frac{3}{4}$ and $8\frac{3}{4}$ inches long. An individual in the Chicago

Natural History Museum measuring only 21⅝ inches contains six well-developed embryos and is the smallest sexually mature female known. The largest queen snake on record is an Ohio female 33 inches long. An Illinois female in the Chicago Natural History Museum has a 25-inch head and body but its tail is incomplete. Since females of this size have tails about 7 inches long, it is safe to assume that this Illinois snake would have had a length of at least 32 inches.

Habits.—This aquatic reptile likes to sun itself on projecting logs and branches. At the least alarm it drops into the water, swims to the bottom, and hides under a bank or any suitable object. When first captured, it gives off a strong odor and usually struggles violently to escape.

Food.—No thorough study of the food of the queen snake has been made, but there is general agreement that it eats chiefly crayfishes. A toad was found in one stomach, and some of the specimens taken by Conant in Ohio disgorged small fish as well as crayfishes.

Economic Importance.—It is most unlikely that the fish consumed by such a small snake have much economic value, whereas its destruction of crayfishes is welcomed in areas where these crustaceans damage earth banks and dams. No doubt some of the fish eaten are carrion.

Habitat.—Slow-flowing or shallow, rocky streams are the preferred habitat, but ponds, canals, and edges of lakes and rivers are also frequented.

Captivity.—An individual lived in the London Zoological Gardens for five and one-half years.

Occurrence.—The queen snake ranges from the southeastern corner of Wisconsin southeastward to the Atlantic seaboard, reaching central Alabama in the south and Pennsylvania in the north. In the Chicago area, records for the following counties indicate a general distribution (with the possible exception of the Indiana Dunes): Racine and Walworth in Wisconsin; Cook, Du Page,

Grundy, Lake, and Will in Illinois; and Porter in Indiana.

Reference.—The Reptiles of Ohio. By Roger N. Conant. University Press, Notre Dame, Indiana, 1938. A brief general account.

COMMON WATER SNAKE
Natrix sipedon sipedon
Plate 9 and Figure 41

Recognition.—The dark crossbands on the neck of this heavily built snake break up along the back and sides to form three rows of alternating spots. The pattern becomes obscure with age but can be made out when the skin is wet. No conspicuous dark band connects the eyes across the top of the head and continues on from either eye to the angle of the jaws. The fact that this snake lives in or near water helps to identify it because the species with which it is most readily confused are not aquatic. The scales are in twenty-three (rarely twenty-five) rows at the middle of the body and heavily keeled.

The Sexes.—The females are thicker and attain the greater length. Grant gives the average lengths of twenty-one mature females and thirty mature males from central Indiana as 36⅜ and 28 inches, but does not state his criterion for maturity. The proportionate difference in tail length is also shown in this same series, the tails of thirty males and twenty-two females averaging, respectively, 35 and 29 per cent as long as the head and body. This difference is reflected in the number of subcaudal plates, the twenty-four females having from 61 to 70 (average 65), the males 73 to 83 (average 77). Presumably at least as many males as females are included. In scalation of body and head Grant detected minor differences that are not surprising in view of the larger size of the female.

Reproduction.—Common water snakes mate early in the spring, several males often gathering about a single female. The extent of the mating season is indicated by two copulating pairs, one seen in central Indiana on May 7, the other found in central Ohio on April 19. The details of courtship have not been fully described, but there is general agreement that it is much like that of garter snakes, the male rubbing his chin along the back of his mate and jerkily nodding his head from time to time. No doubt copulation is also similar to that of garter snakes.

Few species are more prolific. Counts of nineteen broods and dissections of seventeen gravid females show that from fifteen to forty-five, or an average of twenty-seven young are born at a time. A gigantic New Jersey female nearly five feet long held seventy-six embryos, but her case is very exceptional. A record of a specimen carrying only nine embryos has also been omitted from the calculations of average brood size. The female usually gives birth in September or late August, occasionally about the middle of August or early in October. There is even one record of a gravid individual found in northern Indiana on October 20.

Growth and Age.—The average length of a large series of new-born from northern Michigan is 8½ inches, or a fifth of an inch less than the average for an Ohio brood of nineteen. The young are much more distinctly banded than the adults.

By marking and recapturing specimens, Blanchard calculated that, in the annual five-months growing season of northern Michigan, juveniles show an increase in length of about 50 per cent. At this rate a length of nineteen inches would be reached at the age of two years, 28½ at the age of three. Breeding should begin not later than the following spring, since there is in the Chicago Natural History Museum a gravid female measuring but 29½ inches. This individual might well have been only 21 inches long when fecundated, a length that agrees with Grant's figure for mature females taken in the spring. Thus it is not improbable that maturity is attained at the age of 2½ years.

The largest specimen known measured 51 inches, unless we accept the gigantic New Jersey female with seventy-six embryos and a length "a little short of five feet" as the record.

Habits.—This is an aquatic snake that does not hesitate to wander hundreds of yards from water but never leaves its vicinity for an entirely terrestrial existence. It likes to bask on branches, logs, and brush piles over water and drop or slide in at the slightest sign of danger. An agile swimmer, it often crosses open water. Individuals marked and released by Blanchard sometimes wandered distances up to half a mile along a lake shore but, on the whole, their movements were not predictable. One even traveled $3\frac{1}{2}$ miles in six days. The temperament is often bad; a cornered individual will flatten its head and body, assume a defensive posture, and strike viciously at an approaching enemy. The sharp teeth can draw blood but inflict little damage. Most specimens become tame if handled constantly and may even give up the annoying habit of producing a strong, musky odor and defecating when picked up.

The common water snake is one of the first reptiles to appear in the spring and one of the last to disappear in the autumn. The males come out of hibernation before the females. In central Indiana, during the spring of 1933, the males emerged in early April and by the middle of the month the sexes were out in equal numbers; the young became evident early in May. Conant states that the Ohio period of activity extends from March to October, inclusive, a statement that allows for seasonal variation in weather. Exact hibernation sites have rarely been detected, although various observers have concluded that old animal burrows and natural cavities adjacent to the summer haunts are used. Noble and Clausen did find a young specimen hibernating with seventy-six DeKay's snakes and ten young garter snakes on Long Island, New York. The site was an old rat burrow only eleven inches deep in a small knoll on the edge of a swamp. The hardiness of this reptile is illustrated by one that crawled in late December from a snow bank in the Great Smoky Mountains National Park. Careful experiments have shown that temperatures below the freezing point cannot be tolerated, so a specimen abroad in winter would quickly succumb to severe cold.

Food and Feeding Habits.—The contents of one hundred stomachs from Pennsylvania, the Virginias, North Carolina, and Tennessee have been tabulated by the three workers who have made serious attempts to determine the feeding habits of this snake. Combining their results and using round numbers, I draw this conclusion: The hundred snakes examined had fed on fish sixty times, on amphibians (frogs, toads, and salamanders) forty, on invertebrates (almost entirely insects) fifteen, and on mammals five. Since these figures approximate the results of each of the three separate studies, it is safe to accept them as reasonably accurate and representative. Moreover, numerous but often casual reports are confirmatory and add the surprising datum that rare acts of cannibalism occur. It would be interesting to know the size of the snakes that held the insects; probably the young rather than the adults eat these invertebrates.

The ability of this snake to devour fish with spiny fins or pectoral spines is astonishing. A ten-ounce bullhead catfish $10\frac{1}{4}$ inches long was once taken from the stomach of a common water snake weighing, without the fish, only twenty-five ounces. If the pectoral spines of a catfish pierce the stomach and body walls, the spines drop off after the fish has been digested, the resulting wounds quickly healing. In these encounters, the catfish may lodge in the snake's throat and the two die together. A common water snake sometimes catches fish trapped in a side pool by swimming back and forth, mouth wide open and body writhing in a manner that keeps the fish on the move and increases the snake's chances of success.

Enemies.—Man is the chief enemy of this harmless reptile, which is universally called "water moccasin" and hopelessly confused with the true moccasin of the southern states. Sportsmen slaughter countless numbers because they believe that water snakes destroy many game fish. Bullfrogs devour the new-born.

Economic Importance.—Most of the fish eaten are slow-moving species not valued by sportsmen. The few trout taken are compensated by the destruction of species fond of trout eggs and fry, among them white suckers, star gazers, and catfish. The killing of water snakes in the vicinity of a fish hatchery is of course warranted.

Habitat.—Almost every aquatic situation is frequented. The greatest numbers occur where low but rank vegetation, overhanging banks, and abundant débris such as rotting logs, flat stones, and piles of brush provide safe retreats and abundant basking sites. Along many of the sandy and rocky shores of the Great Lakes, vegetation does not reach the water's edge and there water snakes live in deposits of driftwood. Mountain streams with heavily forested banks are not inhabited and even in flat country thickly wooded areas are avoided. An altitude of 4,800 feet is attained in the Great Smoky Mountains National Park.

Captivity.—It is a surprising fact that a captive will thrive without ever entering water, although it doubtless prefers to have a bathing pan in its cage. Dampness is eventually fatal, so part of the cage must be kept perfectly dry. Direct sun is an asset, but captives quickly die in a terrarium flooded with strong sunlight; a shaded retreat protected against over-heating must be constantly available. Room temperature is suitable. Zoo records list seven of these snakes, or another subspecies of *Natrix sipedon*, as having survived four or more years of captivity; one even lived nine years in the London Zoological Gardens.

Occurrence.—The range embraces almost all of the northeastern quarter of the United States with a westward extension in the central region to the northeastern corner of Colorado; also southern Canada from the upper St. Lawrence to the eastern tip of Lake Superior (Fig. 41).

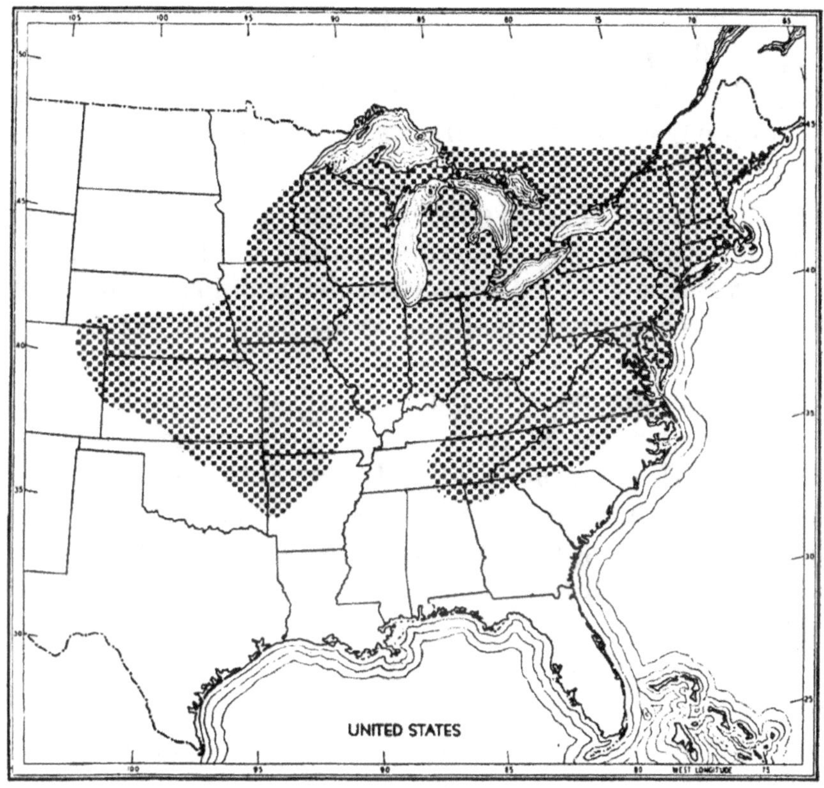

FIG. 41. Range of common water snake.

The distribution in the Chicago area is general, with records for more than half of the nineteen counties, including Walworth County in Wisconsin and Berrien county in Michigan.

References.—The Reptiles of Ohio. By Roger N. Conant. University Press, Notre Dame, Indiana, 1938. A good general account.

Natrix sipedon sipedon in Central Indiana, Its Individual and Sexual Variation. By Chapman Grant. The American Midland Naturalist, vol. 16, pp. 921–931, 1935.

DeKay's Snake
Storeria dekayi wrightorum
Plate 9

Recognition.—DeKay's snake is seldom more than 15 inches long. A light stripe bordered by black spots more or less fused into crossbands usually extends down the middle of the brown or gray back. The yellow, brown, or pink belly is without pattern but may have tiny black spots along its edges. The scales are in seventeen rows and heavily keeled.

The Sexes.—The average number of ventral plates in females exceeds the average number in males, whereas the reverse is true for subcaudals. Trapido's ranges and averages (in parentheses) for series from Illinois follow: ventral plates in forty-three males 121 to 131 (126); in thirty-nine females 127 to 140 (133); subcaudal plates in forty-three males 50 to 61 (55); in thirty-eight females 42 to 51 (47). Trapido also finds that in this state females are longer than males, twenty-nine apparently mature females averaging $11\frac{7}{8}$ inches in length, thirty-eight males only $10\frac{3}{4}$; the longest male and female measured $13\frac{5}{8}$ and $15\frac{3}{4}$ inches.

Reproduction.—A female about 13 inches long, collected in Cook County, Illinois, on July 2, was kept in the Chicago Natural History Museum until, on August 1, it gave birth to twenty-four young. Soon after birth, these young were from $3\frac{1}{4}$ to $3\frac{3}{4}$ inches long, only four of them measuring less than $3\frac{7}{16}$ inches. Judging by numerous data on the eastern subspecies, *Storeria dekayi dekayi*, this brood is exceptionally large.

Habits.—Almost no observations have been made on the habits of this small, secretive, and inoffensive reptile. Presumably its behavior is much like that of the eastern subspecies.

Food.—A captive from Jefferson County, Missouri, freely devoured earthworms and newly transformed toads.

Habitat.—This snake lives under all kinds of ground cover both in and out of forests. Trapido reports the discovery of specimens in the relatively dry part of an extensive swampy area of northwestern Tennessee. Small populations are found on vacant lots well within the limits of Chicago.

Occurrence.—DeKay's snake is of general occurrence in the Chicago area with records for Racine County, Wisconsin; Lake, Cook, Du Page, Will, and Kankakee counties, Illinois; Lake, Porter, and Starke counties, Indiana. The range of this subspecies extends from the Gulf of Mexico up the Mississippi Valley throughout Illinois and eastward over Indiana.

Reference.—The Snakes of the Genus *Storeria*. By Harold Trapido. The American Midland Naturalist, vol. 31, pp. 1–84, 1944.

Red-bellied Snake

Storeria occipitomaculata occipitomaculata

Recognition.—This, the smallest snake of the Chicago area, seldom exceeds a foot in length. The belly is bright red, and the gray or brown back may be faintly striped. The scales are in fifteen rows and heavily keeled.

The Sexes.—The average number of ventral plates in females exceeds the average number in males, whereas the reverse is true for subcaudals. Trapido gives the following ranges and averages (in parentheses) for specimens from an extensive area with Chicago at its approximate center: ventral plates in 126 males 112 to 132 (120); in 142 females 121 to 133 (125); subcaudal plates in 121 males 42 to 55 (49); in 135 females 37 to 51 (42). Trapido also finds that in this same area females are longer than males, 105 apparently mature females averaging 10⅛ inches in length, 95 males only 9⅜.

Reproduction.—Presumably this snake mates in the spring. That it does so in the autumn as well has been shown by the discovery of active sperm in female repro-

ductive tracts dissected in October. One Michigan specimen bore nine young in about three hours, the quickest
birth taking only four minutes. Detailed studies of
seventy-seven broods by Blanchard showed that, in northern Michigan, from one to thirteen, or an average of seven
young are born at a time, the range in two-thirds of the
cases being from four to nine. Births usually occur between
August 9 and 24, although some young arrive as early as
late July or as late as early September. Blanchard ascertained the sex ratio as 1:1 but collections of adults
showed a great preponderance of females taken from mid-
July through early August. This fact probably reflects
a temporary occupation by gravid individuals of places
near the surface where the greater amount of heat from
the sun benefits developing embryos.

Growth and Age.—In northern Michigan, the average
length at birth is but 3⅜ inches, the new-born being so
minute that they can coil on a dime with room to spare.
Maturity is attained at a length of about 8¾ inches, and
females only two years old bear their first broods. In this
same region the maximum length for males is 11⅝ inches,
for females 12⅞. In the northeastern states, where this
snake reaches somewhat greater dimensions, a female
length of 15¼ inches has been recorded.

Habits.—Although distinctive behavior is not readily
noticed in so small and secretive a creature, all observers
agree that the red-bellied snake is entirely harmless except
for the defensive act of exuding from the anal glands a
substance with a musky odor. Nocturnal habits have
been presumed rather than proved. In southern Ohio,
Conant detected a tendency to select the same hiding
places as other small secretive species.

Red-bellied snakes occasionally bask in the sun, especially on mild autumn days after search for a winter
retreat has set a population on the move. Two hibernating aggregates have been described: One, composed of
sixteen snakes (including seven species) and four sala-

manders (two species), was unearthed 2½ feet below the surface of a gravel bank in Pennsylvania; two of the sixteen were red-bellied snakes. The other aggregate, made up of eight plains garter snakes, 148 green snakes, and 101 red-bellied snakes, was found in southern Manitoba at a site described above (see GREEN SNAKE). Seventy-five of the red-bellied snakes ranged in length from 4½ to 12 inches.

Food.—Slugs have been found in six stomachs, so these invertebrates are the only known item of the natural diet.

Enemies.—No doubt this small reptile is frequently devoured by other kinds of snakes. In Ohio, Conant noticed that milk and red-bellied snakes often select similar habitats, and it is not hard to guess what attracts the former to the haunts of the latter. Conant also reports the discovery of seven red-bellied snakes in the stomach of a red-tailed hawk.

Habitat.—Although essentially a woodland species, this snake unhesitatingly invades various situations adjacent to woods. Among these are pastures, fallow fields, abandoned farms, and roadside ditches. It hides in and under all sorts of ground cover that retains a certain amount of dampness, thus showing a distinct love of moisture, even to the point of inhabiting bogs and wet meadows.

Captivity.—The preparation of a suitable terrarium for such a small reptile is a simple matter. Some specimens readily become tame and live on a diet of slugs and earthworms.

Occurrence.—This snake is widely distributed over the eastern half of the United States except Florida and adjacent territory where a recently described subspecies, *Storeria occipitomaculata obscura*, occurs. The center of abundance coincides with the forested regions of the northern states, extreme southern Canada, and the

Appalachian Mountains of the southeast. In the Chicago area, the range is limited to the forested morainal ridge (and vicinity) immediately west and northwest of the city. The only local records are for Cook, Du Page, and Lake counties, Illinois.

References.—Data on the Natural History of the Red-bellied Snake, *Storeria occipito-maculata* (Storer), in Northern Michigan. By Frank N. Blanchard. Copeia, pp. 151–162, 1937. A study of growth and reproduction.

The Snakes of the Genus *Storeria*. By Harold Trapido. The American Midland Naturalist, vol. 31, pp. 1–84, 1944.

BUTLER'S GARTER SNAKE
Thamnophis butleri
Figure 42

Recognition.—The presence of three light stripes, one down the middle of the back and one along either side, is a sure sign of a garter snake. In Butler's garter snake, the stripe on the side is relatively wide, involving, on the front of the body, the second, third, and fourth rows of scales. This snake is rare in the Chicago area and no specimens have been found south of the Wisconsin border.

The Sexes.—Male garter snakes are very unusual in having a higher average number of ventral as well as subcaudal plates. The overlap of range in ventrals is great, whereas in subcaudals it is slight and may not even exist in counts made on a series from one region. The following summaries based on forty-eight Wisconsin specimens illustrate the points in question, the numbers in parentheses being averages: ventral plates in males 135 to 150 (144); in females 136 to 151 (141); subcaudal plates in males 63 to 72 (67); in females 50 to 64 (58). Although no data on relative size of the sexes have been accumulated, it is a safe guess that females are larger than males, the two longest individuals on record being of the former sex; one, from Ohio, is 25 inches long, the other, from Ontario, 22¾.

Reproduction.—The courtship of this species differs from that of the common garter snake only in these minor details: The female elevates the tail more and the rhythmical waves that pass forward along the male's body have a higher frequency and a greater amplitude. Actual union may take place within a few minutes after commencement of the rhythmical waves, and, judging by two cases, may last from 40 to 135 minutes. Mating activity has been noted from March 23 to April 24, births from July 2 to September 18. Unfortunately, almost all observations on breeding have been made on specimens living in captivity, a condition that is well known to modify behavior. Conant found a free pair copulating in Ohio on April 4. Two workers have determined the period of gestation in five cases to be 90, 102, 104, 113, and 144 days. It is inadvisable to accept these data, not only because the parents were captive, but because so little is known about the relation between copulation and time of actual fertilization in snakes. Counts of thirteen broods and dissections of two gravid females give a range of four to nineteen, or an average of eleven young born at a time.

Growth and Age.—Tabulations of eight broods show that the new-born are usually $5\frac{1}{2}$ to $6\frac{1}{2}$ inches long, with 5 and $7\frac{1}{8}$ as the extremes. The largest female ever found (25 inches) bore fourteen young measuring from $6\frac{1}{2}$ to $7\frac{1}{8}$ inches, but, like her, these offspring are exceptional. The smallest known female parent had a length of only $16\frac{5}{8}$ inches. Next to nothing is recorded about the size of adult males.

Habits.—Butler's garter snake never defends itself by biting, but, if annoyed, emits a substance with a sweetish odor. When picked up, it wraps itself around the fingers, clinging with perceptible pressure, especially of the tail. It is graceful when crawling in grass or swimming; if frightened on bare ground, its undulatory movements become awkward and attain a speed out of all proportion to the rate of progress. Its hardiness is proved by early emergence and late hibernation, few other species being active so much of the year. In the spring, males are more abundant than females, whereas in midsummer the reverse condition prevails. Another characteristic is its occurrence in isolated colonies with such dense populations that scores of individuals are often seen in a single day. At least during the hot summer weather, it is most active from sunset to dusk.

Logier describes a colony of these snakes living in a temporarily dry swamp, and noticed during hot weather a tendency to congregate in shallow excavations and in pockets under sod. Aggregation of reptiles has been intensively studied by Noble and Clausen, who find that it benefits snakes by reducing the amount of water lost through evaporation. These investigators showed that the aggregation response of Butler's garter snake occurs at temperatures of 50° F. through 104° F. in relative humidity of 40 per cent. Lower temperatures make the snakes sluggish, higher ones produce restlessness. The maximum degree of heat that can be endured at a humidity of 35 per cent is about 118° F.

Food.—Leeches were found in one stomach, and some Ohio specimens, when collected, disgorged earthworms. Small fish are preferred by captives; earthworms and frogs are also accepted.

Habitat.—This reptile inhabits wet, open areas such as moist meadows, the grassy banks of streams, and the edges of marshes and drainage ditches. It does not require moisture at all times of the year, since it occasionally thrives in swamps that dry out during the summer months.

Occurrence.—Butler's garter snake has a continuous range from northwestern Pennsylvania and extreme southwestern New York through the southern tip of Ontario, southern Michigan, northern Ohio, and northern and central Indiana. An isolated population occurs in southeastern Wisconsin from Racine County (where it enters

COMMON WATER SNAKE (*Natrix sipedon sipedon*)

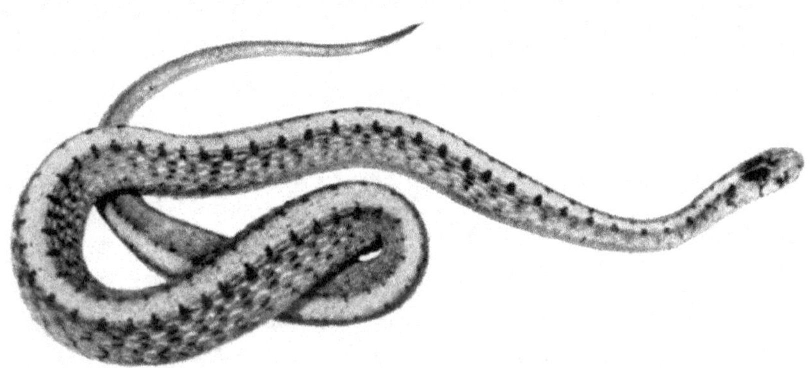

DEKAY'S SNAKE (*Storeria dekayi wrightorum*)

PLAINS GARTER SNAKE (*Thamnophis radix*)

the Chicago area) northward through Dodge County
(Fig. 42). Davis has investigated the problem presented
by this discontinuity and he concluded that the species
once had a continuous range around the southern end of

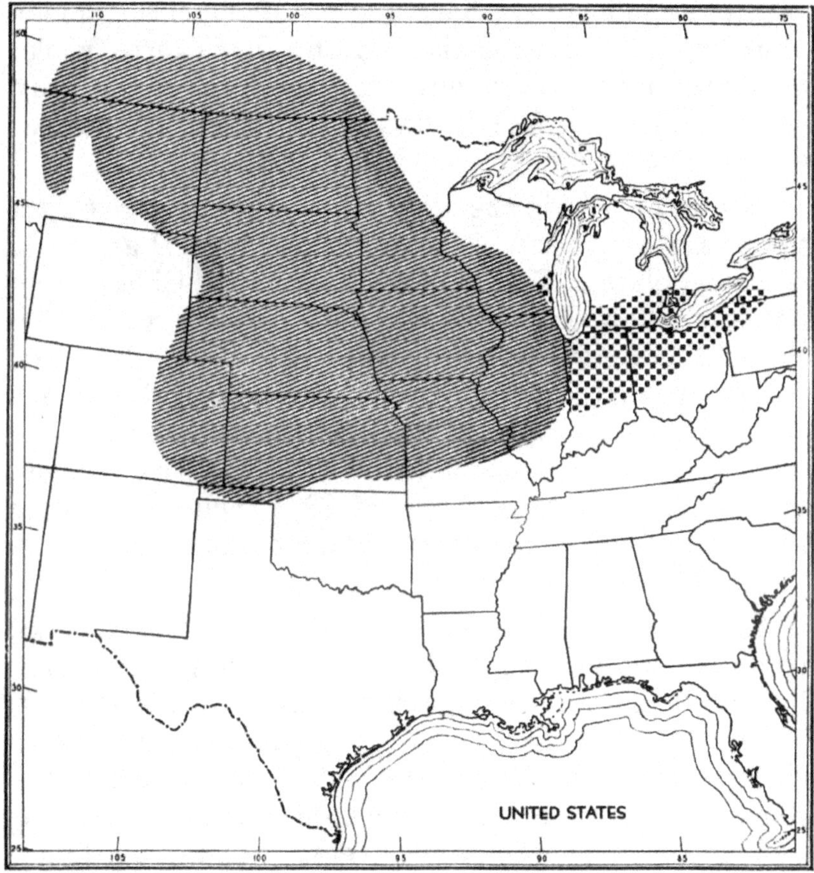

FIG. 42. Ranges of plains (lined area) and Butler's garter snakes.

Lake Michigan until an invasion from the south and west
by the larger and more aggressive plains garter snake cut
off the Wisconsin population.

    References.—The Reptiles of Ohio. By Roger N. Conant. University Press, Notre Dame, Indiana, 1938. A good general account.

    Occurrence of *Thamnophis butleri* Cope in Wisconsin. By D. Dwight Davis. Copeia, pp. 113–118, 1932.

Plains Garter Snake
Thamnophis radix
Plate 9 and Figures 42 and 43

Recognition.—The presence of three light stripes, one down the middle of the back and one along either side, is a sure sign of a garter snake.   In the plains garter snake, the stripe on the side involves, on the front of the body, only the third and fourth rows of scales, and the median stripe is usually orange.

The Sexes.—As in the other kinds of garter snakes, the males have a higher average number of ventral as well as subcaudal plates.   Counts of adults from the Chicago area show the following averages: ventral plates in eighty-five males 157; in seventy-two females 151; subcaudal plates in sixty-five males 74; in fifty-six females 65.   The females greatly exceed the males in size.   Hudson examined a large series from Nebraska and found that the seven largest males had an average length of $23\frac{1}{8}$ inches, the seven largest females $34\frac{1}{2}$; the maximum lengths by sexes were $27\frac{3}{4}$ and $37\frac{5}{8}$.

Reproduction.—The courtship of this species (Fig. 43) strongly resembles that of the common garter snake. Copulation has not been described.   According to Hudson, a mean of about seventy-five seconds elapsed between births in the case of a female that produced a brood of twenty-seven.   From six to forty babies are born at a time; twenty may be considered the average number until more data are available.   Mating has been noted in the Chicago area from April 19 to May 24, births during the first week of August.   Autumn mating has also been recorded, and Ruthven includes September in the birth season of western Iowa.   It is obvious that the reproductive habits of this common reptile call for further attention.

Growth and Age.—Twenty-nine of forty-two new-born from three local broods measure from $6\frac{3}{8}$ to $7\frac{1}{4}$ inches. Maturity is reached in males at an approximate length of 16 inches. The smallest individual among many gravid females in the Chicago Natural History Museum is 23 inches long. Additional information on size is given above.

Habits.—Plains garter snakes are so docile by nature that many of them do not even bite when picked up;

FIG. 43. Courtship of plains garter snake. After Davis.

most individuals do, however, discharge from the anal glands a substance with a strong, unpleasant odor. A common defensive habit is to flatten the body, presumably in an effort to frighten off the intruder. Diving to escape danger has been reported by some observers, whereas others have considered such behavior unusual. Basking has also been noted, and Ruthven states that excessive summer heat is escaped by early morning and late afternoon activity.

Small groups of hibernating individuals are found in postholes and under sidewalks of defunct real estate developments in the Chicago region. A large hibernating aggregate of 8 plains garter snakes, 101 red-bellied snakes, and 148 green snakes was discovered at a site in southern Manitoba (see the GREEN SNAKE). At this juncture, it is interesting to recall Lueth's careful experiments proving that the upper limit of temperature tolerance lies between 104° and 107.6° F., the lower at the freezing point.

Food.—A number of casual references indicate that the diet consists of frogs, tadpoles, earthworms, fish, and insects; even carrion may be taken occasionally. There is a hint that the juveniles have a distinct preference for earthworms. As far as I can discover, no one has ever tabulated stomach contents.

Enemies.—Hawks and bitterns frequently feed on plains garter snakes. Several of my pet raccoons have shown an unfailing interest in them and a marked willingness to eat them. No doubt wild raccoons devour many.

Habitat.—This snake is an inhabitant of plains and prairies, sometimes occurring in astonishing abundance. Although exhibiting a strong preference for marshes and the borders of lakes, ponds, and streams, it is by no means restricted to the immediate vicinity of water. No other snake is so abundant locally, and individuals often turn up in storm sewers near populous business districts of Chicago's outskirts. Many unduly alarmed persons telephone the Chicago Natural History Museum for advice about the striped snakes that infest their gardens.

Captivity.—Like most other garter snakes, this one thrives in captivity and makes an interesting pet.

Occurrence.—The range extends from Illinois and southwestern Wisconsin westward into eastern Colorado, and northwestward to extreme southern Canada and over much of Montana (Fig. 42). The species is common throughout the Chicago area except in the Indiana Dunes where it becomes rare and apparently fails to reach the southwestern extremity of Michigan. There are records for thirteen of the nineteen local counties.

Reference.—Variations and Genetic Relationships of the Garter-Snakes. By Alexander G. Ruthven. Bulletin of the United States National Museum, No. 61, 1908. A general account, somewhat out-of-date.

RIBBON SNAKE
Thamnophis sauritus proximus
Plate 10

Recognition.—The three light stripes of this snake, one down the middle of the back and one along either side, make it look like a garter snake, and actually it is nothing more than a slender kind of garter snake. The tail occupies more than 27 per cent of the total length, whereas, in the typical garter snakes, the tail is relatively shorter.

The Sexes.—Males have a higher average number of ventral plates than females, as shown by the following averages (in parentheses) and ranges for Chicago Natural History Museum specimens, most of which are from Texas: ventral plates in ten males 165 to 175 (170); in eleven females 160 to 174 (167).

Reproduction.—Judging by dissections of three gravid females and counts of two broods, this subspecies has from six to seventeen, or an average of twelve young at a time. One of the two broods was born on July 7, the other on August 24.

Growth and Age.—The average length of a brood of eight new-born from eastern Kansas is 9⅜ inches. There is little or no information on the size of this subspecies in the northeastern part of its range. The largest of the few local specimens in the Chicago Natural History Museum is a female from Porter County, Indiana, 31⅝ inches long; the longest male is from Lake County, Indiana, and measures 26⅞ inches, even though approximately an inch of its tail is missing. Our series from southern Texas and adjacent Mexico indicates that much greater dimensions are attained there, one male measuring no less than 44¾ inches from tip to tip. No doubt a length of more than four feet is reached by southwestern females.

Habits.—This innocuous and docile snake is quick in its astonishingly graceful movements. A good swimmer, it takes to water in times of danger, but, unlike the common water snake, does not dive and hide under objects lying on the bottom. It is also fond of climbing about low vegetation growing in and adjacent to water.

Food and Feeding Habits.—Two ribbon snakes with gaping jaws were once found swimming about a small pool. When the mouth of one came in contact with a fish, a capture was effected, so the pair appeared to have a method of fishing. One of these same snakes disgorged six perch, and the other had a distended belly. Gloyd saw specimens feeding on small frogs; a frog was taken from the stomach of a specimen in the Chicago Natural History Museum, a toad from another collected in Louisiana by Schmidt, and three cricket frogs were disgorged by a Missouri individual.

Habitat.—The few observers of these snakes under natural conditions have seen them on river banks and lake shores, in marshy ponds, and at the edges of swamps and marshes. A female almost ready to give birth was found under a stone in pasture land sparsely grown with sumac, coralberry, and mullen. This is evidence that the mothers leave the vicinity of water to bear their young.

Captivity.—Captives are hardy and thrive on a diet of salamanders, small frogs, tadpoles, and fish. They can be taught to eat strips of raw fish by first including a few strips with live tadpoles or other suitable prey and then reducing the proportion of living food until none is included.

Occurrence.—The ribbon snake, *Thamnophis sauritus*, is widely distributed over the eastern half of the United States and ranges south from Texas along the Gulf coastal plain. One subspecies occurs in the Florida region, another north of this southeastern one and as far west as the lower Mississippi Valley and the Indiana-Illinois boundary. Although the third subspecies, a prairie form, is here considered to be our local one, there is little concrete evidence of the subspecific identity of this form because of its rarity in the Chicago area. Specimens have been taken in Lake and Porter counties of Indiana, Racine County, Wisconsin, and at Sublette, a locality about halfway between the Chicago area and the Mississippi River. The apparent absence of ribbon snakes in the extreme northeastern corner of Illinois remains as much of a puzzle as does the relationship of the population living in and around the Chicago area.

Reference.—Variations and Genetic Relationships of the Garter-Snakes. By Alexander G. Ruthven. Bulletin of the United States National Museum, No. 61, 1908. A general account, somewhat out-of-date.

COMMON GARTER SNAKE
Thamnophis sirtalis sirtalis

Recognition.—The presence of three light stripes, one down the middle of the back and one along either side, is a sure sign of a garter snake. In the common garter snake, the stripe of the side involves, on the front of the body, the second and third rows of scales, and the median stripe is never orange.

The Sexes.—Males have a higher average number of ventral as well as subcaudal plates. The averages (in parentheses) and ranges of Ohio series illustrate this difference: ventral plates in males 145 to 160 (154); in females 142 to 158 (149); subcaudal plates in males 69 to 80 (74); in females 55 to 71 (63). Females are much larger than males, the largest known specimens of the former being 44, 43½, and 41 inches long, of the latter 30½ and 29¼.

Reproduction.—The sexually excited male begins to court by rubbing his chin along his mate's back, usually toward her head, until the two bodies lie together and his cloacal region is opposite hers. If more than one male is present, there may be some jockeying for advantage, but actual fighting is never evident. As soon as the proper position has been attained by a male, normally a matter of a few seconds, convulsive waves move rhythmically forward along its body at the rate of one every two seconds or even more frequently. Short periods of rest intervene between series of three to six waves. After five or ten (sometimes many more) minutes of courtship, copulation is accomplished by a maneuver too quick for the eye. Apparently the male pushes the female's cloacal region up with a wedge of his own and quickly inserts one of his hemipenes. Noble's experiments showed that the female takes an active part by certain movements as well as by opening the cloaca. When union has been consummated, the male's caudocephalic waves promptly cease; slow crawling of the female causes the bodies to lose their apposition and the male not infrequently is dragged about by his mate. The usual duration of attachment is from fifteen to twenty minutes. One male actually performed three fruitful matings in eighty minutes.

Additional experiments by Noble indicate that the male recognizes the female by the odor of her skin; that the rubbing of the chin along the female's back stimulates the male himself; that his knobbed anal ridges assist in the adjustment of the cloacas at the moment of insertion.

After years of experience with snakes kept in outdoor pits at the University of Michigan, the Blanchards became convinced that mating activities are not only seasonal but depend on weather conditions as well. Their snakes mated most readily from the first part of April through early May on sunny days with the mercury above 60° F. Courtship and occasional copulation also took place during Indian summer on bright, warm days following a cool spell. These fall copulations are frequently successful, the females becoming pregnant the following spring. Rahn has shown that sperm remain alive in the female for months and retain their ability to fertilize an ovum for at least one month. The Blanchards report several cases of broods born to females that had not mated during the previous spring. They believe, however, that fertility is carried over for one winter only. Frieda Cobb Blanchard's recent work strongly supports these conclusions: Sperm deposited by autumn matings do not actually fertilize the ova until spring; some broods are of mixed autumnal and vernal paternal parentage.

The duration of gestation has never been determined, but the Blanchards' records of twenty-seven successful pregnancies have shed some light on the problem of rate of development. Their conclusions, in highly abbreviated form, follow: During four years the mean period of development varied from 87 days in 1934 (the warmest year) to 116 in 1935 (the coolest). The difference of 29 days coincided with one of 7.2° F. in average temperature for the periods of development, or a difference of four days per degree. By "period of development" they mean the time between the start of preparation for fertilization by the ovum and the birth of the young. The beginning of this period was estimated, so the conclusions are open to question. It was impossible to determine just when fertilization took place.

In the northern part of this country, the majority of births occur during the first half of August, some as late as early September. The July records noted by Conant in Ohio seem to be exceptional. In Ontario, parturition dates fall between August 14 and October 9.

Dissections of twenty-one gravid females and counts of thirty-seven broods give a range from six to seventy-three, an average of twenty-six young born at a time; disregarding the five extremes on either end (17 per cent of the cases), the range is from twelve to forty-two. A female that attained the probable age of twenty years produced broods for the six successive years before her death. Thus it is patent that a common garter snake might give birth to as many as 450 young during her lifetime. It should be mentioned in this connection that Rahn presents some evidence that females living in Massachusetts may reproduce biennially rather than every year. This matter requires further investigation, since the Michigan snakes studied by the Blanchards lived under fairly natural conditions and reproduced annually. Rahn seems to be the first herpetologist to become convinced that the females of certain snake populations inhabiting the northern part of this country give birth only in alternate seasons.

Growth and Age.—Surprisingly enough, few broods of common garter snakes have been accurately measured. The thirty-one new-born of a Pennsylvania brood had an average length of $6\frac{1}{8}$ inches, minimum and maximum lengths of $5\frac{1}{2}$ and $6\frac{3}{4}$. The smallest gravid female on record measured but $19\frac{1}{8}$ inches. Males develop knobbed anal keels at a body length of about 19 inches; since these keels are a secondary sexual character, it is reasonable to assume that they appear at maturity. The Blanchards substantiate this conclusion by recording a male only $19\frac{3}{4}$ inches long that fathered a brood. The average dimensions of fully grown individuals of each sex have not been determined, although it is safe to guess that for males it lies between 22 and 25 inches, for females between 28 and 34. The maximum lengths have already been given.

Blanchard and Finster accumulated some information on growth rate under natural conditions by marking specimens and recovering them later. Unfortunately, only one really small snake was retaken, and it had increased but $2\frac{1}{8}$ inches in five growing months (August 16 to the following August 15). This can scarcely be considered normal growth since we know that a female kept by the Blanchards in outdoor pits reproduced at an age of three years; to do so it must have tripled its length in this time, a fact readily deduced from the size of hatchlings and the length of the smallest mature female.

More significant data were secured on a 17⅛-inch male. This snake, which might even have been sexually mature when first taken, added 5⅜ inches to its length in four growing months (August 18 to the following July 14) and, in doing so, supplied evidence that the annual increase of six inches may continue for a year after attainment of sexual maturity. A female of comparable size grew 1⅝ inches in forty-four days, a rate of increase almost as great as that of the male. In this case, allowance should be made for considerable error of measurement; securing accurate dimensions of a living snake is no simple matter. The larger specimens marked by Blanchard and Finster grew at relatively slow rates.

One female, already mentioned, lived fifteen years in outdoor pits and must have been at least five years old when secured by the Blanchards. There are few authentic records of snakes that reached such an age, and nearly all of those with a higher record are large constrictors (pythons and boas).

Habits.—The disposition of individual common garter snakes varies greatly, some being docile and refusing to bite, others flattening the body and striking repeatedly if annoyed. All give off a strong, unpleasant odor when handled. Although this is a terrestrial reptile, specimens will occasionally take to water or climb into bushes and thick vegetation. A tendency toward nocturnality has been noticed in hot summer weather, whereas basking in the mild sun of spring and autumn is a well-established habit. Periods of inactivity are spent beneath stones, logs, boards, rubbish, or in any other convenient hiding place.

The wanderings of this snake have been studied and found to be unpredictable; individuals may be recovered four or five miles from the point of release after an interval of one or two years, or they may remain in the same place for as great a length of time.

No other snake emerges from hibernation earlier in the spring or retires later in the fall. Conant collected specimens in Ohio every month of the year, but this perennial activity would hardly be expected in the Chicago area during a normal winter. Hibernation sites have rarely been discovered. Noble and Clausen found two on Long Island, New York. One of these, an abandoned rat burrow eleven inches deep in a small knoll on the edge of a swamp, held an immature common water snake, ten young common garter snakes, and seventy-six DeKay's snakes. The other site, near the first, was two feet deep and harbored several groups of the last two species. A third wintering aggregate, unearthed in Pennsylvania 2½ feet below the surface of a gravel bank, included seven kinds of snakes (sixteen individuals, four of which were common garter snakes) and four salamanders of two species.

Food and Feeding Habits.—Approximately 100 stomachs containing food have been dissected. Frogs (including toads), salamanders, and earthworms are the three main items of the diet and no doubt comprise some 90 per cent of the total. The relative amounts of these undoubtedly vary with the time and the place, and, in the case of earthworms, with the age of the snake, since juveniles depend more on them than do adults. The minor items accounting for 10 per cent include insects and various other invertebrates, birds, mammals, snakes, and even carrion. The numerous records of insects and the like have to be discounted because it is impossible to say how many of them were first eaten by frog or toad. The total absence of fish from the lists of stomach contents is puzzling since common garter snakes are well known to devour fish greedily; in some habitats these aquatic vertebrates are certainly eaten.

Wilde's extremely careful experiments have shown that the common garter snake finds and identifies its food through chemical stimulation of Jacobson's organs, a pair of blind sacs opening on the roof of the mouth. The origin, structure, and nerve supply of these sacs prove that they are essentially organs of smell. The delicate tips of the tongue convey to these organs "scent" from a trail or microscopic particles from the prey itself. Previous investigations had indicated that the nose was depended on more than Jacobson's organs, but Wilde's work is convincing.

Enemies.—Two of these snakes were found in the stomach of a red-tailed hawk collected in Ohio. No doubt other large birds and various mammals such as raccoons and skunks frequently dine on garter snakes. Countless numbers are killed on roads by automobiles; farmers, villagers, and suburbanites also take a heavy toll. Any snake so prone to frequent farm lots, city outskirts, and almost any part of small town or village is bound to suffer. During the warm days of spring and autumn when garter snakes are breeding or migrating, a score or more of crushed individuals may be seen on every mile of major highway. It is easy to calculate that in Illinois alone millions are killed annually during such periods of activity.

Economic Importance.—The garter snake should not be regarded as useful, since it destroys beneficial animals such as toads and earthworms. Just how much harm it does in this indirect way can scarcely be measured and must vary enormously with each locality.

Habitat.—All relatively open aquatic situations are frequented by large populations. Smaller numbers are found in woods and dry areas. Few snakes occur in such a wide variety of habitats.

Captivity.—The Blanchards raised successive generations in outdoor pits with natural earth bottoms measuring five by six feet. Cement rims five feet high projected eighteen inches above the outside ground level and boards covered half of each pit. A low, poorly drained area would not be a suitable location for such pits. Chopped fish was chiefly used for food.

Snedigar worked out a method of conditioning garter snakes to supplement a diet of fish, frogs, and earthworms with raw hamburger. He first included many squirming earthworms with the meat and then gradually decreased their number until the snakes were devouring the hamburger alone. Liver is a good substitute for beef. A ring of garter snakes eating chopped meat off a plate is a rare and amusing sight for anyone accustomed to their usual feeding behavior.

Occurrence.—The four subspecies of *Thamnophis sirtalis* range from coast to coast in the United States and adjacent Canada, the form considered here occupying the approximate eastern third of this territory. The common garter snake is ubiquitous locally, with records for all but four of the nineteen counties of the Chicago area.

References.—The Reptiles of Ohio. By Roger N. Conant. University Press, Notre Dame, Indiana, 1938. A good general account.

Mating of the Garter Snake *Thamnophis sirtalis sirtalis* (Linnaeus). By Frank N. and Frieda Cobb Blanchard. Papers of the Michigan Academy of Science, Arts, and Letters, vol. 27, pp. 215–234, 1942.

MASSASAUGA

Sistrurus catenatus catenatus

Plate 10

Recognition.—The rattle on the end of the tail makes this, the only poisonous snake of the Chicago area, recognizable at a glance. Conspicuous dark blotches and a heavy build serve to impress it on the memory. The scales, usually in twenty-five rows at the middle of the body, are heavily keeled.

The Sexes.—The average number of ventral plates in females (142) exceeds the average number in males by a few plates, but the overlap in range is so great that ventral counts do not help in determination of sex. The sub-caudal counts, on the other hand, are helpful in specimens from the same region; for example, Conant found that Ohio males have from 26 to 32 (average 28) subcaudal plates, whereas Ohio females have only 20 to 26 (average 23). The males have proportionately longer tails and attain a greater length, females being, on the average, only 92 per cent as long as males.

Reproduction.—Pertinent details of courtship have not been recorded, although a male was once seen paying court to a female by darting his tongue out, twitching his body, jerking his head, and wrapping his tail around hers. This behavior was observed in Iowa on May 7. Mating no doubt begins in April, since females carrying small embryos have been collected as early as May 13. It must be recalled, however, that some snakes become pregnant long after copulation, the sperm presumably remaining active for months in the female. Nothing is known about delayed fertilization in the massasauga.

Dissections of four gravid females and records of fourteen broods show that from five to fourteen, or an average of eight young are brought forth between August 16 and September 8. A female in the Chicago Natural History Museum had eleven young on August 30, 1940. Details of the last eight births were recorded, each one requiring from one and one-half to eight minutes for completion. The intervals between births increased with each successive one and varied from a few seconds to thirty-three minutes. The new-born remained in the foetal membranes up to nine minutes and soon after emergence were quick to vibrate the tail with its prebutton, though the motion was too slow to produce a sound. The skin, including the prebutton, which covers the true button (first permanent rattle), was shed within eight days of birth. A specimen caught by Wright had her eight young in an hour, a performance contrasting strongly with that of the female in the Chicago Natural History Museum.

Growth and Age.—In the Chicago area, the average length of new-born massasaugas is $8\frac{7}{8}$ inches. The smallest mature female on record measures $20\frac{1}{2}$ inches and the average lengths of adult males and females are, respectively, $26\frac{1}{8}$ and 24 inches. The male is known to reach a length of $36\frac{7}{8}$, the female 33 inches. The rattle is not ordinarily included in the total length because this appendage is so often incomplete.

Contrary to popular belief, the age of a rattlesnake cannot be told by counting the "rattles" or, more accurately, the segments of the rattle. Snakes that are still growing rapidly have tapering rattles, since the width of the segments increases with the diameter or girth of the snake. A segment is added every time the skin is shed and shedding occurs from three to five times a year, except late in life when the skin may be changed less frequently. An old snake never retains its first segments because a long rattle breaks readily; seldom is one of more than ten segments, additions of two or three seasons, found. A very long rattle is less efficient as a vibrator than one of moderate length.

On the basis of measurements of a series from the Chicago area, Wright has reasonably concluded that sexual maturity is reached during the third year. This snake would be expected to grow this rapidly, since Klauber has shown that the Pacific rattlesnake gives birth to young when three years old and not fully three times its birth-length. Nothing is known about the age attained by our local rattlesnake.

Habits.—Remarkably little has been written on the massasauga's habits. It is often seen abroad during the day, and in early spring numbers may be found basking on tufts of grass in their swampy habitat. I have noticed in the Chicago area that August is a period of activity— during this month these snakes are most often seen crossing Portwine Road, between Deerfield and Dundee Roads. The significance of this summer activity is not clear.

RIBBON SNAKE (*Thamnophis sauritus proximus*)

MASSASAUGA (*Sistrurus catenatus catenatus*)

The disposition of this moderately dangerous snake is good; many individuals make no effort either to defend themselves or to escape when closely approached. If thoroughly aroused, they strike viciously and sound the rattle, which, at a temperature of 65° F., vibrates at a speed of about 48 cycles per second and produces a hiss rather than a rattle. The rattle is beautifully and intricately made, its segments reinforced at points of possible weakness and asymmetrically shaped so that the last ones do not drag on the ground when the snake is crawling, or drop in a curve when the rattle is held at ten degrees from the vertical by an alarmed snake about to give its warning. Experiments have shown that one rattlesnake cannot hear another rattle.

Food and Feeding.—There is general agreement that the diet consists of frogs, mice, and, rarely, snakes; Conant concludes that it is chiefly mice that are consumed, whereas other investigators have named frogs as the preferred item. No one has examined more than a few stomachs, so the lack of agreement may be based on the discrepancies of casual sampling, or on differences that reflect a seasonal shift in habitat of the massasauga or its prey. Whenever these snakes are slaughtered in numbers, the bodies should be saved for stomach examinations. It may well be shown that, at least under some conditions, the rodents so regularly eaten more than compensate the occasional injury done to humans and livestock.

The deep cavity or pit in the side of the face of this and other pit-vipers has long puzzled anatomists, because its structure suggested a sensory function, but there was little evidence as to the actual purpose served. Experiments have now shown that this pit enables the snake to distinguish between very slight differences in temperature of near-by objects. The logical assumption is that warm-blooded prey can be located by means of the pit.

Enemies.—Man is of course the chief enemy of this poisonous snake. Students of animal behavior would like to know just how much caution is exhibited by such snake-eating mammals as raccoons and skunks when confronted by a massasauga. I made a crude experiment with a pet raccoon that had never before encountered a rattlesnake and concluded that the sound of the rattle put the raccoon on guard and kept it from approaching the massasauga as unhesitatingly as it approaches a garter snake.

Venom and Bite.—Although the venom of the massasauga is approximately as potent as that of the much larger Florida diamond-back, there is a vast difference between the abilities of these two rattlesnakes to injure a human being. Records show that nineteen out of seventy diamond-back bites resulted in fatalities, whereas there was not a single death among twenty-two massasauga victims. This difference is due to the inability of a small, short-fanged snake of a northern latitude (where limbs are well protected) to inject much venom. First, the capacity of the poison gland is not nearly as great; second, the fangs are only $\frac{7}{32}$ of an inch long or a third as long as those of a twice-as-long diamond-back; third, the greater strength and weight of the larger snake drives the needle-sharp fangs through clothing and deeper into flesh.

Habitat.—This reptile frequents bogs, swamps, and other poorly drained areas of the prairies. In the summer it appears to move into adjoining drier situations. It may have been generally distributed over the prairies until largely exterminated by man. The Indian name "massasauga" offers interesting evidence that swampy river mouths were a part of the original habitat. This word means "great river-mouth" in the Chippewa tongue, and the rivers of the Chippewa country have swampy mouths.

Occurrence.—The range of this small rattlesnake extends from central New York and western Pennsylvania westward to the northeastern corner of Kansas and the southeastern tip of Nebraska. To the north it is found in southern Canada, the lower peninsula of Michigan, and southern Wisconsin.

The counties of the Chicago area with records are: Berrien County, Michigan; La Porte and Porter counties, Indiana; Will, Du Page, Cook, and Lake counties, Illinois; Walworth County, Wisconsin. These records might lead one to believe that the massasauga is generally distributed locally, but such is not the case. In Indiana, it is restricted to the Indiana Dunes; in Illinois, to the flood plain of the upper Des Plaines River, from Des Plaines northward for about twenty miles; the vicinity of Wooddale in Du Page County; the country between Crete and Goodenow in Will County; and Palos Park, in Cook County. The Chicago Natural History Museum has material from all but the last of these four Illinois localities. Search for references to rattlesnakes in historical documents on the local region might give interesting results.

Reference.—Habit and Habitat Studies of the **Massasauga** Rattlesnake (*Sistrurus catenatus catenatus* Raf.) in Northeastern Illinois. By Bertrand A. Wright. The American Midland Naturalist, vol. 25, pp. 659–672, 1941. A good general account.

There is less aversion to turtles than to any other reptiles or amphibians. Most people look on a turtle as a harmless creature that deserves to be let alone; only the unpopularity of the snapping turtle proves this rule. Perhaps the importance of turtles to the national meat supply has counteracted any tendency to think of them as objectionable.

If turtles were known from fossils alone they would be exhibited as great curiosities because no other land animals with backbones have ever been as well protected. A visit to a collection of medieval armor will convince anyone that man has long been envious of the turtle's shell. This shell is the result of an experiment begun at least 175,000,000 years ago, about the time that the dinosaurs came on the scene to begin a development culminating in a world ruled by giant reptiles. The turtles kept calmly on their way and must have smiled their toothless smile as the great dinosaurs disappeared.

The reproduction of the turtle follows an ancient and uniform pattern. The eggs are buried on land, and neither nest nor young is attended by the parents. It is from the time of laying to the end of the hatchlings' first season that turtles pass through a bottleneck of existence: The eggs are relished by many mammals, the young devoured by a great variety of animals before the armor hardens.

Perhaps the most interesting turtle behavior is the laying and burying of the eggs. Each species has its own method of nest construction, and watching the details is a fascinating pastime. Most females, once they have begun, are not shy and may be closely approached. Inhabitants of tropical islands often sit by giant sea turtles and receive the eggs in the hand as they are laid. These robbers leave with full containers before the unwitting reptiles fill in the empty holes as carefully as though they contained eggs. A box turtle gently moved from her almost finished nest continued to tread the ground just as if she were still tamping her nest. Once the complex nesting mechanism has been released, it operates automatically, without benefit of reason.

Two kinds of turtles lay fertile eggs for three or four consecutive years after a single mating, an accomplishment that may be widespread in the group. The exact process involved in this remarkable ability has not been investigated.

Three names for these animals are in common use: turtle, tortoise, and terrapin. Among English-speaking peoples, there is little uniformity in the application of these terms, but in this country "turtle" is widely and generally applied, whereas "terrapin" is reserved for certain aquatic kinds sold in the markets, "tortoise" for the few large, wholly terrestrial species of the southern states, especially the arid southwest. I have reduced the nomenclature to its simplest terms by referring to all the local kinds as turtles.

The turtles comprise the Order Testudinata of the Class Reptilia.

My *Turtles of the United States and Canada* (1939) is the only general account of our turtles. This book is well illustrated and places special emphasis on habits.

Shape and pattern of head will identify turtles at a glance (Plates 11, 12). Since living turtles usually insist on hiding the head, and at times an empty shell must be classified, I have based the key largely on the shell. Very young individuals present difficulties because, in most species, the shell at hatching does not have its final rigidity, shape, and color. The hinge of the plastron or belly plate is never evident in baby box and Blanding's turtles. Fortunately, the head form and pattern can be relied on at all ages.

The flat part of the shell covering the belly is known as the plastron, the upper, dome-shaped part as the carapace.

Body enclosed in a hard, rigid shell; snout not a soft proboscis.

  Plastron small and cross-shaped, with four pairs of shields (Fig. 45).........................Snapping Turtle, p. 234

  Plastron larger, with five pairs of shields (Fig. 44).

                                       Musk Turtle, p. 230

  Plastron very large, with six pairs of shields.

    Plastron divided into two movable lobes by a hinge across it.

      Tip of upper jaw deeply notched....Blanding's Turtle, p. 241

      Tip of upper jaw beaked.

        Plastron with numerous, irregularly arranged yellow stripes.....................Ornate Box Turtle, p. 249

        Plastron without such stripes..Common Box Turtle, p. 244

  Plastron not hinged.

    Carapace black with small orange or yellow spots.

                            Spotted Turtle, p. 238

    Carapace without such spots.

      Red marks along margin of carapace..Painted Turtle, p. 255

      Margin of carapace without red marks.

        A yellow spot behind eye...........Map Turtle, p. 252

        A red area behind eye...........Troost's Turtle, p. 260

Body enclosed in a flexible, pancake-shaped shell; snout a soft proboscis.........................Soft-shelled Turtle, p. 263

Musk Turtle
Sternotherus odoratus
Plate 12 and Figure 44

Recognition.—No other local turtle has five pairs of shields in the plastron (not counting the side shields that connect carapace and plastron). The snapping turtle has but four (Fig. 45), whereas the other hard-shelled kinds have six. Only the musk and snapping turtles are without conspicuous shell markings. The vast difference in size will usually distinguish these two species. The adult snapper ordinarily weighs more than ten pounds, the musk turtle always less than half a pound.

The Sexes.—The tail of the male is longer and ends in a blunt spine; that of the female may have an acutely pointed one. The tail of the female, but not of the male, has a row of tubercles down the middle of its upper side and is the more tuberculate. The male has two patches of horny scales on the inner side of each hind limb and has a wider head. The plastron of this sex is smaller, and its shields are separated by wider areas of skin; consequently the plastral shields are noticeably larger in the female. The male's carapace is the narrower.

Reproduction.—Extensive researches by Risley on specimens from southern Michigan have shown that active sperm are present in males from September to May, hibernation merely interrupting the breeding activities. Copulation begins in the fall, to be continued with greater vigor the following spring when the sexes are together in the warmer water near shore. The males disperse after the middle of May, leaving the females in the shallows to await the laying season.

When ready to mate, the male follows the female around and finally mounts her from behind, grasping the edge of her carapace well toward the rear with all four feet. His head and neck are extended so that his throat and chin press against the slope of her shell in front. Presumably the patches of rough scales on the inner side of his hind limbs enhance his grip; no observations have been made to determine their use.

The eggs may be laid at any time during daylight hours. This reptile is remarkable for a general lack of

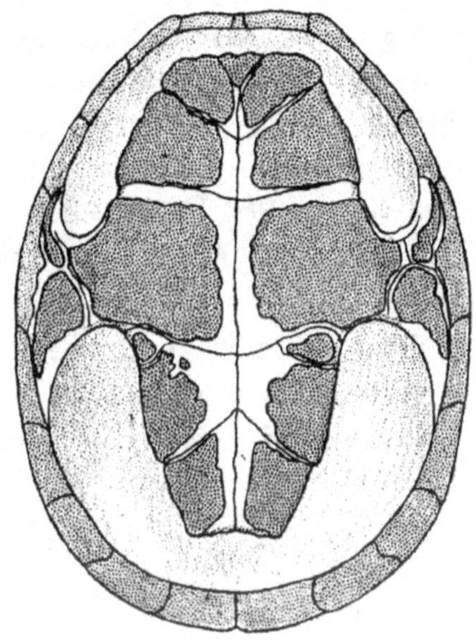

FIG. 44. Shell of musk turtle, seen from below.

uniformity in nesting habits, although some individuals dig a hole with alternate strokes of the hind limbs and bury their eggs in orthodox turtle style. In one case the whole process required forty-seven minutes. The following summary of scattered observations on nesting illustrates what a surprising lack of uniformity exists.

The site of deposition may be well above ground on top of a rotten stump, under a fallen log, in a pile of dead rushes, a cow-track, a mass of muck, or even on the bare ground. There is a strong gregarious tendency; dozens of nests may be mixed beneath a log or similar shelter. Muskrat houses are favorite sites for such aggregations.

The tendency to place the eggs under some large object is remarkable, since most turtles carefully select an open, sunny site. The mingling of clutches is also unusual.

From two to seven white, elliptical eggs measuring about $1\frac{1}{16}$ by $\frac{5}{8}$ inches are laid at a time. The thick, hard, brittle shell no doubt resists desiccation better than does the soft, thinner shell of most turtles. This assumption is supported by Cagle's discovery of surface-exposed eggs with normal embryos. In the latitude of Chicago, eggs are deposited during the last twenty days of June and the first week of July. Risley found that those kept at high temperatures (up to 98° F.) hatched in two to two and a half months, those kept some twenty degrees cooler, in about three.

Growth and Age.—At hatching, the highly arched carapace measures approximately $\frac{7}{8}$ by $\frac{3}{4}$ of an inch, and the lobes of the plastron are not yet movable. Males become sexually mature in their third or fourth year, females not until they are nine to eleven years old and have a carapace $3\frac{1}{8}$ inches long.

Measurements and weights of 171 specimens from Lake Maxinkuckee, northern Indiana, are as follows:

Longest carapace (inches; measured along curve) 5.37
Weight of its possessor in ounces 7.75
Number of additional carapaces 5 or more inches
  long. 10
Number 4 to 4.99 inches long. 104
Number 3 to 3.99 inches long. 52
Number less than 3 inches long. 4

The carapace of a typical adult female is $3\frac{3}{4}$ inches long by $2\frac{3}{4}$ wide. This shell was measured in the usual way, with a pair of calipers, disregarding its curve; the same carapace measured 4.31 inches along the curve.

One captive musk turtle lived twenty-three, another thirteen, and four more nine years. The age up to seven years can be determined by counting the growth rings on the shields of the carapace. A carapace more than $3\frac{3}{16}$ inches long indicates an age of ten or more years.

Habits.—This thoroughly aquatic, bottom-loving reptile is typically seen crawling on mud under quiet water. It is a poor swimmer and progresses clumsily on land to which it seldom goes except when about to lay. When frightened, it occasionally makes astonishingly quick dashes. The temperament is bad, most individuals being prone to bite at slight provocation.

Enormous aggregations of hibernating individuals are sometimes found. In central Ohio, for example, no fewer than 450 were taken from the bed of a canal when it was drained late in March. They were crowded into an area forty-five feet long by six feet wide.

Food.—A great many kinds of small, aquatic animals, such as crayfishes, mollusks, and insects, are devoured. Some carrion and vegetable matter are also consumed. The prey is normally caught and swallowed under water.

Enemies.—The not infrequent discovery of freshly emptied shells proves that, in spite of a protective odor, the adult has enemies. Probably muskrats are largely responsible for this destruction. The tiny hatchlings no doubt fall victim to a variety of mammals and birds; the former eat countless numbers of eggs.

Economic Importance.—Little praise and less blame can be laid at the door of this species. Anglers are often annoyed at its persistence in cleaning their hooks.

Habitat.—Almost any aquatic situation is frequented, but rivers, streams of all sizes, lakes, ponds, and ditches are preferred. A muddy bottom with abundant aquatic vegetation attracts large populations. In rivers and streams having strong currents the turtles frequent the deeper, quieter stretches.

Captivity.—The rather bad temperament, strong odor, secretiveness, and ungainly appearance detract from the musk turtle's popularity in the aquarium. It makes a hardy, easily fed pet that will take earthworms, chopped raw beef, or fish from the fingers, and will even mate in crowded quarters. There should be enough water to allow it to eat while submerged.

Occurrence.—This species has been found in the local area from Walworth and Racine counties, Wisconsin, to Lake County, Indiana, including five of the nine Illinois counties lying between. It is widely distributed over the eastern half of the United States and occurs in Canada from Georgian Bay southward.

References.—Turtles of the United States and Canada. By Clifford H. Pope. Alfred A. Knopf, New York, 1939. A general account.

Observations on the Natural History of the Common Musk Turtle, *Sternotherus odoratus* (Latreille). By Paul L. Risley. Papers of the Michigan Academy of Science, Arts and Letters, vol. 17, pp. 685–711, 1933. An excellent detailed account.

SNAPPING TURTLE

Chelydra serpentina serpentina

Plate 11 and Figure 45

Recognition.—The small, cross-shaped plastron leaves the fleshy under parts of this turtle largely exposed and the relatively flat carapace is serrated behind. The plastron has only four pairs of shields (not counting those on the side that connect carapace and plastron).

The Sexes.—The female apparently attains the greater size and its anus is farther from the tip of the tail. There is surprisingly little information on sexual differences.

Reproduction.—During copulation, the male rides the female, gripping her carapace with his four feet and pressing upon her retracted snout with his chin.

When ready to lay, the female leaves the water early in the morning. Selecting a site and depositing the eggs sometimes consume several hours and delay the return to water until late forenoon. A species that frequents such a variety of aquatic situations must be satisfied with nesting in almost any kind of soil that is not too hard to be dug into. An open, sunny, well-drained area is required, however. The considerable differences between accounts of nest construction mean either that the habits of this turtle are not uniform or that the females are often pre-

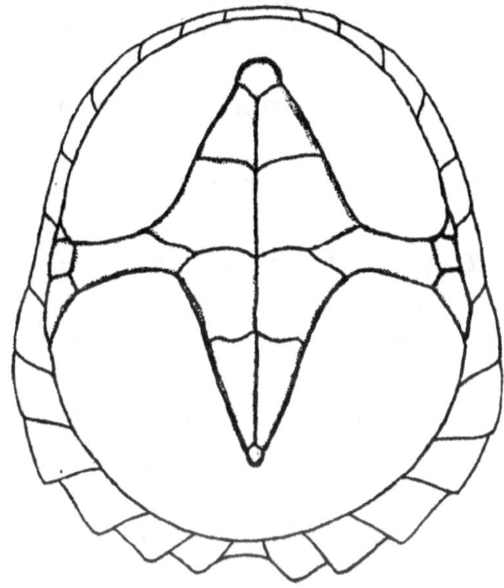

FIG. 45. Shell of snapping turtle, seen from below.

vented from making a perfect nest by hardness or dryness of the only available soil.

Most individuals lay from twenty to thirty eggs, although an occasional one produces about forty. There is such a tendency to exaggerate the number that many published records are best disregarded. Hamilton gives the number dissected from each of eleven New York females, the extremes being twelve and thirty, the average twenty-two; only one had fewer than seventeen eggs. His figures may be taken as representative for the northeastern states. It would be interesting to see whether there is a correlation between the size of the female and her clutch. If there is, persecution may be expected to affect reproductive capacity, since it is known to reduce the average dimensions of various large reptiles. The egg is spherical and usually a little more than an inch in diameter; its white shell is so tough that the egg bounces well on hard surfaces.

Hamilton saw a pair copulating on May 1 near Ithaca, New York. In the latitude of Chicago, eggs are laid in June, the middle of the month coinciding with the peak of the nesting season. Hatching and emergence occur in late September or early October except in the extreme north, where emergence at least may be postponed until spring.

Growth and Age.—At hatching, the carapace measures approximately 1¼ inches, at maturity 10 to 12. The tail, at first slightly longer than the carapace, is a little shorter than the carapace in the adult. Almost nothing is known about the rate of growth. Snappers, like fish, lose much of their weight when actually put on scales, but indisputable records prove that weights from three to four times greater than the 15-pound average are attained.

A few individuals have survived twenty years of captivity. Even Nip and Tuck, the two-headed freak raised by Grace Olive Wiley, has been her pet for ten years.

Habits.—When on land this reptile defends itself with jabs of head and neck too quick for the eye to follow; they often lift the whole body off the ground. This ferociousness disappears in water. Although thoroughly aquatic, the snapper is a poor swimmer and walks on the bottom a great deal. It basks by floating at the surface or entering shallows rather than by lying on log or bank. Apparent group migrations have been reported, but no studies of such have ever been made. Tagging and retaking large numbers would in time give interesting information on mass migrations, wandering of individuals, and rate of growth.

Food.—Long thought to be carnivorous, these reptiles are now known to eat much vegetable matter, a discovery that was not surprising because analysis of their digestive fluids had already proved them capable of digesting plants as well as animals. Lagler, who analyzed about a gallon of food from 186 Michigan stomachs, found that a third was made up of water plants, a third of game fishes, and a third of insects, crayfishes, snails, clams, dead fish and other carrion.

Enemies.—Man is the chief enemy of the snapper, destroying eggs as well as adults and young. Mature turtles seem to have no other important enemy, but the very young are eaten by crows, hawks, mink, raccoons, large fishes, and even bullfrogs. Countless eggs are dug up by skunks, raccoons, and other mammals.

Economic Importance.—Snapping turtles are widely used as an article of diet, even reaching the markets of big cities, especially those of Philadelphia, where certain restaurants specialize in snapper delicacies. It also renders service as a scavenger and a destroyer of noxious insects and undesirable fishes. Lagler's investigations do not bear out the contention that it devours large numbers of game fish and fowl. He believes that fish conservationists need not concern themselves about the little harm done by the snapper, since this is more than compensated by its usefulness. Commercial hunters may be depended upon to keep its population in check.

Habitat.—This ubiquitous reptile inhabits any permanent body of water large enough to support an association of aquatic plants, but shows a decided preference for sluggish water with a mucky bottom and profuse vegetation; clear lakes and deeps of swift streams are also frequented to some extent.

Captivity.—No turtle is more hardy or more easily fed in confinement, but its ungainly appearance and aggressiveness make it unwelcome in small collections. Enough water should be provided to allow food to be swallowed under the surface. A large specimen can even devour an adult barn rat whole, and little in the way of animal matter will be refused.

Occurrence.—Widely distributed over the eastern half of the United States and adjacent Canada, this subspecies also ranges southward into Mexico. It has been recorded from about half of the nineteen counties included in the Chicago area and no doubt occurs in all.

Reference.—Turtles of the United States and Canada. By Clifford H. Pope. Alfred A. Knopf, New York, 1939. A general account.

SPOTTED TURTLE

Clemmys guttata

Plate 12

Recognition.—This turtle is identified at a glance by the small, bright orange or yellow spots of its black carapace. Although, as a rule, many shields have more than a single spot, no general regularity in the arrangement of such additional spots can be detected. The plastron is yellow or orange with large black blotches usually on the outer parts of the shields; occasionally it is almost entirely black.

The Sexes.—The following remarkable differences in color of the head and throat may well prove to help the males recognize the females: The eye of the female is bright orange; the horny parts of the jaws are pale yellow (or pink); the lower jaw has a conspicuous yellow (or pink) stripe; the throat is spotted and streaked with yellow (Plate 12). In contrast, the eye of the male is dark brown; the horny parts of its jaws are dusky; the lower jaw almost or completely lacks a yellow (or pink) stripe; the black throat is finely speckled with orange or yellow.

The plastron of the male is concave, that of the female flat or even somewhat convex; when the tail is extended, the anus lies about a quarter of an inch beyond the edge of

SNAPPING TURTLE
(Chelydra serpentina serpentina)
COMMON BOX TURTLE
(Terrapene carolina carolina)
TROOST'S TURTLE
(Pseudemys scripta troostii)
BLANDING'S TURTLE
(Emys blandingii)

the carapace in the male, at or before the edge of the carapace in the female.

Reproduction.—The males are most evident in the spring during the mating season, which coincides with the last half of April in northern Indiana. Babbitt witnessed two wild males engaged in a spirited fight that probably had sexual significance. The excited warriors bit viciously at each other, and one succeeded in turning its opponent over only to be upset three times itself. At the end of half an hour, dusk obscured the fray and Babbitt left without being able to hail a victor. Males pursue the females before mounting them to copulate. Courtship and mating may take place either in or out of water. When ready to lay, the female selects in the late afternoon or evening a spot near water and digs a flask-shaped cavity with her hind legs. After depositing from one to four eggs, she fills the cavity and conceals it so carefully that little sign of her activity remains.

The white eggs are elliptical and measure about $1\frac{3}{16}$ by $1\frac{1}{16}$ inches. The laying period occurs during the last two-thirds of June in southern New England. The period of incubation under natural conditions has not been determined, but a clutch of eggs buried in sand by Babcock on June 16 did not hatch until September 6.

Growth and Age.—The carapace of the hatchling is a little longer than wide ($1\frac{1}{8}$ by 1 inch in an Ohio specimen taken on October 2) and each shield, except an occasional marginal one, has its orange or yellow spot. As growth proceeds, additional spots appear on the large shields. These spots are in reality tiny transparent areas that allow the yellow pigment of the underlying bone to show through. The entire center of the plastron is black at hatching, but the black migrates radially, leaving the yellow center of the adult plastron. Spotted turtles commonly attain a carapace length of $4\frac{1}{2}$ inches. One individual survived forty-one years of captivity.

Habits.—This is an aquatic species that often leaves the water to sojourn in wet woods or meadows. It cannot be induced to bite. Many years ago, Yerkes tested its ability to run mazes and found that it learned with surprising rapidity; in fact, its accomplishment was comparable to that of a rat.

Food.—Surface's report on the examination of twenty-seven stomachs indicates chiefly insectivorous feeding habits; the remains of beetles, flies, and dragonflies were most numerous. Other invertebrates had also been consumed, worms, snails, slugs, spiders, and crustaceans among them. There is evidence that small amphibians and some vegetable matter and carrion are at times devoured.

Habitat.—Bogs, swampy streams in woodland or meadow, ponds, and ditches are the preferred habitat of this species. It is but partly aquatic, sometimes wandering into wet woods and meadows that dry out at certain seasons.

Captivity.—Attractive colors and a gentle disposition make the spotted turtle a nice pet. It thrives in a vivarium if allowed enough water for complete submergence and will learn to eat mealworms, lettuce, and raw meat or fish.

Occurrence.—Locally, this reptile is known with certainty only from the dunes of the southern part of the Chicago area where it is not uncommon. There are records for Will County, Illinois, and Porter and La Porte counties, Indiana. Alleged evidence of its presence in Cook County, Illinois, and in Wisconsin calls for confirmation. The Chicago region marks the westernmost limits of the range, which extends eastward to the Atlantic Coast, reaching southwestern Maine in the north and the Carolinas or even Georgia in the south. In Ontario, it is found as far north as Georgian Bay.

Reference.—Turtles of the United States and Canada. By Clifford H. Pope. Alfred A. Knopf, New York, 1939. A general account.

BLANDING'S TURTLE

Emys blandingii

Plate 11 and Figure 46

Recognition.—The plastron is hinged, and the tip of the upper jaw notched. The box turtles likewise have a hinged plastron, but the upper jaw is beaked. Blanding's turtle also can be told by the uniform yellow of its throat

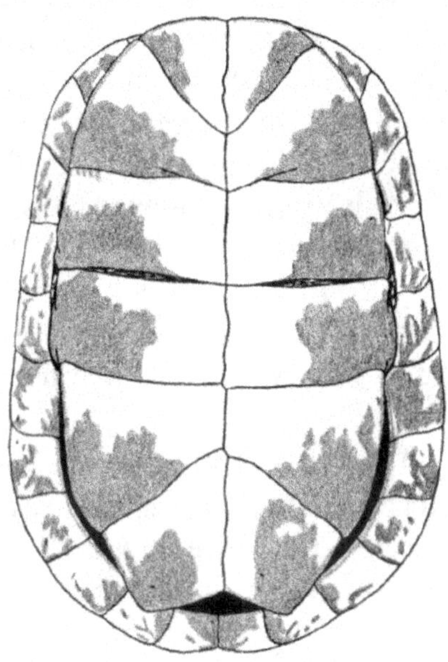

FIG. 46. Shell of Blanding's turtle, seen from below.

and lower jaw, the darker hues above contrasting with this light yellow and meeting it in a sharply defined line.

The Sexes.—No one has ever made a careful study of sexual dimorphism in this species, but a glance at the series in the Chicago Natural History Museum convinces me that at least two differences exist: When the tail is extended, the anus of the female lies under or in front of the edge of the carapace, that of the male beyond it; the male's plastron is slightly concave, in contrast to the flat or barely convex plastron of the female.

Reproduction.—Captive pairs have been seen to copulate under water, the male grasping the edge of his mate's carapace with all four feet and pressing his chin against her snout so that she has to keep her head withdrawn. May 22 and October 11 are recorded as mating dates in the Chicago region.

A few observations made in southern Ontario by Brown and others give us a good picture of nesting behavior. The season there extends at least from June 22 to July 17, and nests are constructed in the late afternoon. The flask-shaped cavity is dug and filled with alternate strokes of the hind legs, its depth being from five to seven inches. In one case, the digging required fifty minutes, the laying of eleven eggs twenty-eight minutes. The female was not disturbed by an audience of boys lying only a foot away, nor did she once glance at either eggs or nest. The white egg is elliptical, measuring in inches about 1½ by ⅞. There are from six to eleven in a clutch.

Growth and Age.—An Indiana specimen, obviously very young, is described as having a carapace 1⅜ inches long by 1 3/16 wide, and devoid of the numerous pale yellow spots so obvious on older individuals. The hingeless plastron is dark brown with a narrow yellow border, not boldly blotched as in the adult. The change from juvenile to adult plastron pattern is readily understood when we recall that each plastral shield has its own growing center around which the horny shell material is deposited. In the hatchling, the plastron is completely covered by these dark centers, but, as each shield grows, the spread of its dark pigment does not keep pace with growth, and the yellow appears wherever invasion of dark brown does not mask it. Thus the original growth centers come to lie in dark blotches that have failed to expand fast enough to cover the entire plastron.

The average adult carapace is from 7 to 8 inches long; a female with one measuring 9 7/16 by 6 7/16 is on record.

Habits.—When surprised on land, this shy turtle hisses and draws into its shell, which closes to give fair protection. If alarmed while basking over water, it quickly drops in and swims with agility to the bottom, where the somber colors of its carapace blend with bubble-filled growth or other aquatic vegetation. Hibernating individuals have been taken from under-water muskrat runways and the mud of spring-fed ditches.

Food.—On land, succulent vegetation, berries, earthworms, slugs, and insects are eaten; in water, chiefly crayfishes and insect larvae, but also leeches, snails, clams, carrion, and water plants.

Habitat.—Blanding's turtle frequents shallow, plant-grown water of ponds, swamps, sloughs, ditches, low fields, sluggish streams, and lake or river bays. It is sometimes described as terrestrial, but just how extensively it may live on land has not been determined; females in search of a nesting site have no doubt led some observers to consider it a land dweller.

Captivity.—Lettuce, earthworms, and chopped raw meat or fish may be fed to individuals kept in confinement. Their aquarium should have a large land section with a gentle slope leading to the water.

Occurrence.—The range of this reptile is not easily defined because it is not continuous. The body of the distribution extends from the lower peninsula of Michigan and the southern shore of Lake Erie southwestward to central Illinois and westward to Nebraska. More or less scant and isolated populations occur as far north as Lake Nipissing, Ontario, and as far east as New England. Locally, there are records for eleven of the nineteen counties of the Chicago area, from Walworth County, Wisconsin, to Kankakee County, Illinois, and Berrien County, Michigan.

Reference.—Turtles of the United States and Canada. By Clifford H. Pope. Alfred A. Knopf, New York, 1939. A general account.

Common Box Turtle
Terrapene carolina carolina
Plate 11 and Figure 47

Recognition.—The two sections of the plastron are hinged so that this turtle, when not too fat, can completely conceal its limbs and head by closing the shell. The plastron is yellow with more or less brown on it. An entirely yellow plastron occasionally occurs, but a striped pattern like that on the ornate box turtle's plastron is never evident.

The Sexes.—When the tail is extended, the anus of the male lies well beyond the edge of the carapace, that of the female under or scarcely beyond it. In the male, the hind section of the plastron has a noticeable concavity, whereas the plastron of the female is flat. In this sex, the carapace is more highly arched, making the female's height greater in proportion to its length. In all males the eye is red or pink. The more variable eye of the female is usually buff, straw yellow, gilt, dark purple, or purplish brown, but never the bright salmon-pink characteristic of males. There are additional but minor sexual differences.

Reproduction.—When ready to mate, the male follows the female about, pushing or lunging against her, viciously biting at her shell and soft parts, and trying to get his feet between her carapace and plastron. She may resist, and, if he has already mounted, render him temporarily helpless by closing her shell on his beak and feet. After sufficiently subduing her, the male, from his superior position, works his hind legs into the cavities between her shell and the front of her thighs. She in turn firmly grips his legs from the outside with hers. Their tails are thus brought together but, to effect union, the male must assume a vertical position with his tail turned to one side, hers to the other. The pair remain in copulation for many minutes, sometimes even more than an hour. Fertile eggs may be laid for three or four years after a single mating.

The common box turtle's nest is constructed in soft soil of an exposed area by three to five hours of laborious effort always begun in the late afternoon under a clear sky. The flask-shaped cavity is dug with alternate strokes of the hind legs while the front ones act as anchors for the body. Laying begins when the depth of the cavity equals the

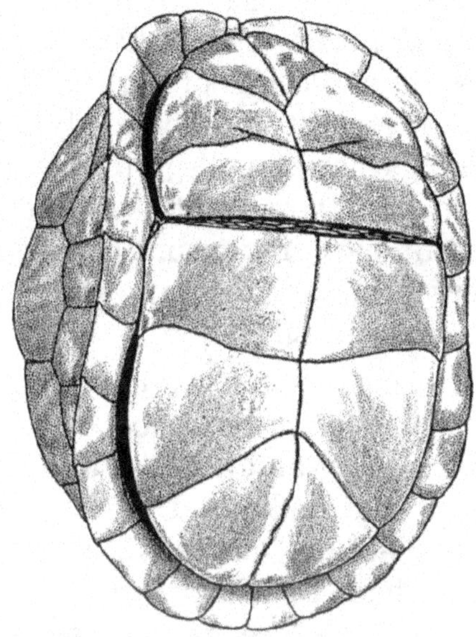

FIG. 47. Shell of common box turtle with both lobes of belly plate or plastron drawn up to protect enclosed soft parts.

length of the female's reach. After each egg has been dropped, a leg is lowered and swept around in the hole as if to feel whether all is well. The female usually rests between laying and filling. Alternate sweeps of the hind feet rake earth onto the eggs, and treading begins before the cavity has been completely filled. This laborious filling process, involving many nice variations in the use of the toes, feet, knees, and even plastron, leaves almost no visible traces of the nest.

The nesting behavior of the box turtle shows how automatic the actions of a reptile may be. Allard, who has written by far the best account of this species, tells of a female that worked the stump of a leg alternately with her complete limb to produce an asymmetrical nest. Another female, when gently moved some distance from her nearly finished nest, continued to tread the solid ground, entirely unconscious of what had happened.

The number of eggs in sixty clutches was found by Allard to range from two to seven per clutch and average 4.2, but most of the sixty had either four or five eggs; there are one or two records of eight. The white egg is elliptical and measures in inches about 1¼ by ¾. Although hatchlings have an "egg-tooth" on the tip of the snout, it is doubtful whether this temporary structure plays an important part in rupturing the shell. Hatchlings that emerge in the autumn apparently go into hibernation without eating.

Mating begins soon after emergence from hibernation and continues throughout the period of activity, with a major peak in the spring and a minor one in the autumn. I found a pair in the Indiana Dunes (Porter County) attempting to copulate on October 19, which was a sunny day with the noon shade temperature 67° F. In the region of Washington, D.C., where careful records have been kept, laying takes place during June and the first half of July; presumably it begins a little later as far north as Chicago. The hatching season is even more extensive than the laying one, because the rate of development after deposition depends so much on temperature. In nature, the young escape in approximately three months, but incubation periods as short as 69 and as long as 114 days are on record. Some nests retain their eggs or even hatchlings through the winter.

Growth and Age.—The carapace of the average hatchling measures 1⅜ by 1⅛ inches. The light yellow plastron has a dark brown center and its two sections are not yet hinged. Oddly enough, data on the rate of growth from hatching to maturity are scarce, but a few individuals have reached apparent maturity in four or five years.

adding annually a little less than an inch to the length of the plastron. Unfortunately, the exact conditions under which they lived are not known.

Nichols marked hundreds of common box turtles on Long Island, New York, from 1915 to 1937. Too few juveniles were included to establish the rate of growth to maturity, but his study proved that the majority of females and a large number of males have a plastron $5\frac{1}{4}$ inches long; that males attain the greater size; that most individuals with a plastron over $5\frac{1}{2}$ inches long are males, most grown ones with a plastron more than $\frac{1}{8}$ of an inch shorter than this are females; that the maximum plastral length is $6\frac{1}{8}$ to $6\frac{1}{4}$ inches, dimensions attained by only three specimens among the 843 marked.

The best method by which early development can be studied was recently introduced by Ewing, who made accurate plaster casts of the same individual for several successive years. If begun on hatchlings allowed to grow under natural conditions, this method would certainly lead to excellent results. It must be remembered that very small box turtles are exceedingly hard to find, because of their inconspicuousness and secretive habits.

There is a good deal of questionable information on longevity. Taking the studies of Nichols, already referred to, and of Flower, who tabulated data from zoo records, we may safely conclude that the common box turtle frequently amasses from forty to sixty years to its credit and may rarely pass the century mark.

Habits.—This interesting reptile is diurnal and solitary, its ordinary movements slow and deliberate. When approached, it usually closes up tightly but may remain on the alert or may attempt to escape through flight. Rarely, one is found that snaps, but its bite can scarcely injure even a small child. The young are much more secretive than the adults.

It is a general belief that each individual has a home territory to which it will return when transported to a distant point. Nichols has shown that normally there is for the adults a home territory with a diameter of 250 yards or less and that most adults exhibit definite homing tendencies. All of the eleven that he moved—from one-half to three-fourths of a mile—went 1,000 to 1,400 yards back toward home.

Hot, dry weather sends box turtles in search of boggy places where they bury themselves in wet earth or forest débris, great numbers sometimes congregating in a small, muddy area bordering a woodland pool or pond. In the winter, they sometimes hibernate under water but usually burrow into soft earth or decaying vegetation.

Food.—The great variety of food eaten is about equally divided between plant and animal matter. A few preferred items are mushrooms (apparently including poisonous varieties), insects, earthworms, slugs, snails, myriapods, carrion, and strawberries. The young seem to have stronger carnivorous tendencies than the adults.

Enemies.—Automobiles and forest fires destroy great numbers of common box turtles. Various mammals eat the eggs and juveniles, or even older individuals that have grown too fat to be well protected by the shell.

Economic Importance.—This species has some value as a destroyer of noxious insects and is one of the most inoffensive and quaint elements of our local fauna.

Habitat.—Although most at home in the woods, this turtle is not averse to wandering into meadows and fields adjacent to woodlands. In rolling or hilly country, it prefers hillsides and other upland situations.

Captivity.—No reptile more readily adapts itself to close captivity or to confinement in a limited area such as a yard. Ideal living quarters can be made by providing vegetation for shade; shallow water for drinking and soaking; piles of leaves or other decaying vegetation for nocturnal retreat, aestivation and hibernation; and, for nesting, loose, sandy soil exposed to direct sunlight.

Occurrence.—The box turtle, *Terrapene carolina,* is widely distributed over the approximate eastern half of this country, except some parts of the extreme north and probably all of the territory west of Lake Michigan. The species is divided into a few subspecies, the most familiar one, the common box turtle, ranging eastward and southeastward from Porter County, Indiana, to the Atlantic Coast. It is common in the dunes of La Porte and Porter counties, Indiana.

References.—Turtles of the United States and Canada. By Clifford H. Pope. Alfred A. Knopf, New York, 1939. A general account.

The Natural History of the Box Turtle. By H. A. Allard. The Scientific Monthly, vol. 41, pp. 325–338, 1935. An excellent account.

ORNATE BOX TURTLE
Terrapene ornata
Figure 48

Recognition.—The two sections of the plastron are hinged so that this turtle, when not too fat, can completely conceal its limbs and head by closing the shell. The plastron is boldly marked with numerous yellow stripes of different lengths extending in various directions on a dark brown ground color.

The Sexes.—When the tail is extended, the anus of the female lies under the edge of the carapace, that of the male beyond it; the distance from anus to tip of tail is greater in the male. The first claw on the hind foot of this sex is turned abruptly forward.

Reproduction.—Judging by the behavior of captive individuals, males court the females by biting them. Copulation takes place in May and, to a limited extent, from then through the summer. According to Anderson, the eggs are laid in the evening during the latter half of June. His report, the first field account of breeding ever published, is based on observations made in western Missouri midway between the north and south boundaries.

Growth and Age.—An apparent hatchling in the Chicago Natural History Museum, from Cleveland County, Oklahoma, has a carapace only 1¼ inches long by 1⅛ wide. In spite of the puzzling May 18 collection date, this individual lacks signs of growth, and bears the remnants of an umbilical scar. The light yellow plastron has a dark

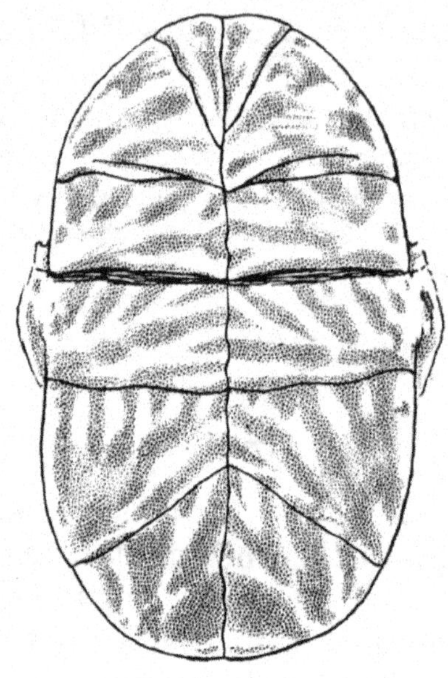

FIG. 48. Plastron of ornate box turtle.

brown center. A Chicago Natural History Museum juvenile from central Illinois has a carapace barely 1¹¹⁄₁₆ inches long, and yellow areas have already invaded the noticeably expanded dark center of the plastron. As might be expected, both carapace and plastron show distinct signs of growth. The hinge has not yet appeared.

The carapace rarely attains a length of 5¾ inches and a width just one inch less. These are, in fact, the dimensions of a Chicago Natural History Museum specimen from Brewster County, Texas. Such a size is not reached east of the Mississippi River, where a carapace measuring 4¼ inches is of average size.

Habits.—The ornate box turtle wanders about on the surface or rests in natural cavities, beneath objects, or in the shallow burrows that it occasionally digs. It is often found abroad during daylight hours. Like other box turtles, it is incapable of inflicting more than very slight injuries on man; some individuals, when annoyed, hiss and open the mouth instead of retreating into the shell.

Food.—Vegetable matter, beetles, and ants have been found in the few stomachs examined; field studies indicate that earthworms, caterpillars, robber flies, grasshoppers, and cantaloupe also form part of the diet. This turtle is especially fond of grasshoppers and shows astonishing agility in getting them. One lively adult even caught a large lubber grasshopper on the wing by stretching the neck and actually jumping.

Enemies.—The speeding automobile takes an enormous toll of box turtles as they laboriously cross wide highways; for example, in western Missouri, Anderson observed along one new concrete stretch a decrease from year to year in number of dead specimens. Apparently the local population was being slowly wiped out; it is improbable that they were learning to shun the road.

Economic Importance.—Where really abundant, this species destroys large numbers of noxious insects. It does damage to cantaloupe patches by biting into the ends of the melons.

Habitat.—The ornate box turtle, typically an inhabitant of prairies, is partial to sandy, dry, or even semiarid regions. It is also found in open hilly country and in light woodland but shuns forests and other kinds of heavy cover. No aquatic tendencies have been detected. It is often astonishingly abundant and in southern Kansas was once branded "a nuisance as a cumberer of the ground."

Captivity.—Strecker kept three in his backyard where they hid under the coal shed but always appeared at feeding time. He gave them strips of raw beef. An adult from western Texas, cared for by one of my sons for more than three years, has remained in perfect condition on a varied diet that includes lettuce, earthworms, raw meat and fish. It wanders at will about the house, usually keeping near a certain radiator that it has little trouble in locating even if removed some distance. Anderson kept one in captivity for twelve years.

Occurrence.—Widely distributed in the central part of this country between the Mississippi River and the Rocky Mountains, this turtle reaches northern Mexico in the southwest. East of the Mississippi, isolated populations occur in sandy areas as far as Lake Maxinkuckee, Indiana. The species is absent from the Indiana Dunes of our area but has been found farther south in Jasper and Starke counties, Indiana, and Kankakee County, Illinois.

Reference.—Turtles of the United States and Canada. By Clifford H. Pope. Alfred A. Knopf, New York, 1939. A general account.

MAP TURTLE

Graptemys geographica

Plate 12 and Figure 49

Recognition.—An oval or triangular yellow spot lies behind the eye, and numerous stripes of the same color extend along the head and neck. A network of greenish-yellow lines adorns the dull-olive or brown carapace, but the plastron of the adult is without markings or with faint remnants of the juvenile pattern. In young individuals, conspicuous dark areas cross the plastron, reaching its margin along the sutures of the shields.

The Sexes.—The female attains a much greater size and has a relatively larger head than the male. The male's tail is longer and its carapace less rounded behind.

Reproduction.—Females with fully developed eggs come out of the water early in the morning and often travel hundreds of yards before deciding where to lay.

The flask-shaped nest cavity is dug with alternate strokes of the hind legs, and filled with ten to sixteen white, elliptical eggs measuring about 1⅜ by ⅞ inches and having a soft, thin shell. The nest site is carefully concealed.

In the latitude of Chicago, mating takes place in April and probably again in the fall. The eggs are laid from

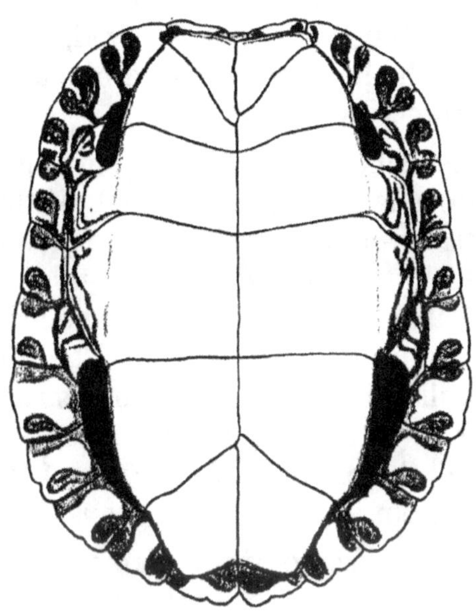

FIG. 49. Shell of **map turtle**, seen from below.

late May through June, with a peak in the second and third weeks of June. Those laid in this month hatch during the latter half of August or in early September.

Growth and Age.—The smallest specimen in the Chicago Natural History Museum is from Lake Maxinkuckee, northern Indiana, and has a carapace 1¾₆ inches long by 1⅛ wide. In spite of having been collected on June 16, it appears to be a hatchling. The discovery of other very small individuals in late spring and early summer was formerly explained by the assumption that some nests are made later than June and retain their contents through the winter. This assumption seems to be well founded.

The smallest breeding female on record had a carapace only 7½ inches long, but there is no indication of its age. Females attain a maximum carapace length of 10¾ inches, but males do not exceed 5¼ inches in this dimension.

Habits.—This thoroughly aquatic turtle seldom leaves the water except to bask or to deposit its eggs. It is an agile swimmer but a slow mover on land. Extreme shyness makes it inoffensive; when annoyed, instead of snapping, it retracts the head with a loud hiss and depends on the shell for protection.

Newman describes in detail the gregarious sunning habits of the once large population of Lake Maxinkuckee. Scores of turtles would crowd onto a narrow ledge until they were piled in two or even three layers. There, when no danger threatened, they stretched the legs out behind and relaxed to enjoy the warm sun. The slightest alarm sent them tumbling into the water only to reappear one at a time when the "all clear" feeling returned. Constant sunning certainly helps to rid the turtles of leeches and no doubt benefits them in many other ways.

In this same lake some of the map turtles hibernate in the soft mud of the lagoons; others apparently remain active through the winter months and may be seen crawling slowly about on the lake bottom beneath ice.

Food.—The broad crushing surface of the jaws gives a clue to the mollusk-eating habits of this species, which subsists chiefly on snails and clams. Crayfishes are also devoured, as well as a few small fishes, insects, carrion, and even some aquatic vegetation. The young eat chiefly the thin-shelled mollusks but the adults are able to cope with the shells of the tougher kinds.

Enemies.—Various mammals dig up and eat vast numbers of the eggs of this and all other local turtles.

Economic Importance.—Although a distinctly second-rate food for man, map turtles sometimes find their way to market.

Plate 12

SOFT-SHELLED TURTLE
(*Amyda spinifera spinifera*)

PAINTED TURTLE
(*Chrysemys picta marginata*)

SPOTTED TURTLE
(*Clemmys guttata*)

MAP TURTLE
(*Graptemys geographica*)

MUSK TURTLE
(*Sternotherus odoratus*)

Habitat.—An inhabitant of substantial bodies of water, this reptile frequents rivers, large streams, and lakes. It abounds in marshes and shallow bays of big rivers and lakes, in river backwaters and overflow ponds. Muddy, plant-grown bottoms are preferred, clear, swiftly flowing streams avoided.

Captivity.—This turtle has the reputation of being excessively shy and hard to feed in captivity but some individuals will take snails, clams, and even meat if provided with deep water into which to retreat.

Occurrence.—The map turtle occurs in the southern part of our local area but it is not common. There are records for Berrien County, Michigan; Porter and Lake counties, Indiana; Kankakee and Grundy counties, Illinois. An old record for Lake County, Illinois, calls for confirmation. The total distribution covers approximately that part of the United States lying between the Appalachian Mountains on the east and the Chicago area and central Texas on the west. In adjacent Canada, it reaches Georgian Bay and the Ottawa region.

Reference.—Turtles of the United States and Canada. By Clifford H. Pope. Alfred A. Knopf, New York, 1939. A general account.

PAINTED TURTLE

Chrysemys picta marginata

Plate 12

Recognition.—There are red markings along the edge of the black carapace, and an elongate, dark blotch occupies the center of the yellow (or red-stained) plastron.

The Sexes.—The longest claws of the male's front feet are two or three times as long as the claws of its hind feet or the claws of the female's front feet. When the tail is extended, the anus lies well beyond the edge of the carapace in the male, below it in the female. Males are noticeably smaller than females.

Reproduction.—It is not surprising that this species and Troost's turtle have the same type of courtship, since the males of both possess the long claws used in this performance as described on page 260. Substantiating field observations are much needed for these two species because in neither has courtship under natural conditions been studied.

Painted turtles have been known to select such a variety of nesting sites that it is hard to decide just what basic conditions they require. It is probable that any open, elevated place satisfies their desire. The "expectant" female invariably starts her search for a site late in the afternoon. Stromsten described in great detail nest construction by an Iowa female of the western painted turtle, which is so closely related to our Illinois population that the use here of his account is fully justified. He brought out the following points of special interest:

The hole was started by the hind feet, first one and then the other scratching the surface dirt away. When a depression had been made, the hind feet continued to work alternately, each lifting out on its palm and pushing far back the earth it had dislodged. Frequent ejections of water from the cloaca interrupted this digging and soon gave the surface soil the consistency of thick cream. The mouth of the completed flask-shaped cavity was just large enough to allow ready passage of the eggs. The hole was dug in an hour and a half.

Actual laying proved to be as careful a performance as excavation; each egg, as it came out and slid gently into the hole, was followed by a foot, which apparently arranged it. Six eggs were laid in five minutes, mostly at intervals of thirty seconds, actual extrusion of an egg taking only half a second. Filling and packing were also accomplished by alternate efforts of the hind limbs. After being raked in, the dirt, if dry, was pressed down; if wet, it was kneaded by the knuckles; at the very end, even the plastron was used. As a finishing touch, more dry dirt was scraped in. Her task completed, the female seemed to awake as if from a trance and become suddenly aware of Stromsten's light. Covering the eggs had taken thirty-two minutes.

The egg is white and elliptical, measuring in inches from $1\frac{1}{8}$ to $1\frac{1}{4}$ in the greater diameter, from $^{11}\!/_{16}$ to $^{13}\!/_{16}$ in the lesser. The vast majority of nests contain from five to eight eggs.

Mating takes place in the spring and, to a limited extent, in late summer and early autumn; there is some doubt about the fruitfulness of summer and fall copulation. The eggs are laid during June and the first three weeks of July, the height of the nesting season covering the last two-thirds of June and the first third of July. The incubation period has not been determined and is undoubtedly variable in extent, some nests even retaining their contents until spring. It is safe to guess that hatchlings begin to appear early in September.

Growth and Age.—The hatchling's carapace is about 1 inch long. During the first year, this length is a little more than doubled, and subsequently about half an inch is added annually. Since the males breed when just over 3 inches long, it is safe to conclude that breeding begins at an age of $3\frac{1}{2}$ to 4 years. The larger females do not breed until they are more than 5 inches long, but little is known about their growth rate. This picture of development has been put together from data secured by Cunningham and Pearse, who worked on turtles from southern Wisconsin where the western and central painted turtles intergrade. Substantiation of the male's growth rate and determination of the female's rate are much to be desired and can be secured by marking hatchlings and recapturing them for measurement at regular intervals.

The average carapace length in males is about $4\frac{1}{2}$, in females about $5\frac{1}{2}$ inches. The former sex attains a maximum length of $6\frac{7}{8}$, the latter of $7\frac{3}{8}$ inches.

Habits.—This turtle is diurnal, shy, and wary. When picked up, most individuals wave the feet frantically, others withdraw into the shell, and a few even bite. Though aquatic, it sometimes wanders hundreds of yards from water. The winter is spent in bottom mud and débris. Basking is one of the most characteristic habits, numbers often crawling up on the same log to sprawl out and enjoy the sun's warmth.

Few kinds of turtles are so universally abundant. There is a record of a catch of 280 specimens by one haul of a 35-foot seine in northern Indiana. In view of this abundance, it is not surprising that certain aspects of behavior have been studied in field and laboratory. Results of the most interesting investigations are summarized below:

A study of migration by marking free individuals convinced Pearse that painted turtles are sedentary and will stay in one place for years if the environment remains favorable. The specimens tagged and immediately released wandered less than those held for a short time. This work was done at Lake Mendota, southern Wisconsin. Cagle is now tagging large numbers of turtles in southern Illinois.

Laboratory experiments carried on by Casteel proved that well-tamed individuals can learn to choose between black and white, and between black and white lines of different width and direction. Efforts to teach simple design discrimination gave only negative results. The reward provided in these experiments was food; the punishment was electric shock.

Food.—Water plants make up one-half to two-thirds of the food, aquatic insects most of the remainder. Some carrion, leeches, earthworms, crayfishes, mollusks, and small fishes are also eaten. This information is based on extensive studies of stomach contents, the feeding habits of no other American turtle having been so thoroughly investigated.

Enemies.—In June, a crushed painted turtle is one of the commonest sights on highways along rivers, streams, and lakes, the automobile thus taking an enormous toll of nesting females. The eggs are dug up and eaten by such mammals as skunks, squirrels, and raccoons. Adults are frequently infested with leeches.

Economic Importance.—The habit of feeding on insects makes this a beneficial species. It is a ubiquitous and picturesque element of the pond and stream life so dear to the heart of every nature-lover. As an article of diet, it scarcely warrants consideration, since it has never had a market value.

Habitat.—Ponds, lakes, streams, canals, river bays and backwaters, swamps, and marshy meadows are frequented, the chief requirement being quiet, shallow water supporting an abundance of aquatic vegetation. A marked degree of natural stagnation is no deterrent, and, at the other extreme, sluggish, plant-grown sections of cold, swift streams are inhabited.

Captivity.—The chief requirements for captives are a temperature of at least 72° F. and enough water to allow the food to be swallowed below the surface. The natural food items can be supplemented with lettuce and chopped fish or meat. Vitamin B given in yeast promotes growth. One individual survived twelve, another nine years of captivity.

Occurrence.—This subspecies intergrades in Illinois with the western painted turtle; in New York, Pennsylvania, and Virginia with the eastern painted turtle; at unknown points with the southern painted turtle of the lower Mississippi Valley.

The central painted turtle is of general occurrence in the Chicago area, the local population, except perhaps in the Indiana Dunes, showing some characteristics of the western form, *Chrysemys picta bellii*.

Reference.—Turtles of the United States and Canada. By Clifford H. Pope. Alfred A. Knopf, New York, 1939. A general account.

TROOST'S TURTLE

Pseudemys scripta troostii

Plate 11 and Figure 50

Recognition.—An ovate, blood-red area lying behind the eye identifies this turtle. There are conspicuous, solid or light-centered spots on the yellow plastron (usually one spot to a shield) except in some old males, the patterns of which are obscured by profuse dark pigment.

The Sexes.—The longest claws on the male's front feet are twice as long as those on its hind feet or on the front feet of females. When the tail is extended, the anus of the male lies beyond the edge of the carapace, that of the female under or in front of it. The males are noticeably smaller than the females, and, as already stated, sometimes have such dark shells that little or no pattern is discernible.

Reproduction.—The courtship, which strongly resembles that of the painted turtle, has never been observed under natural conditions, but three herpetologists have watched captives go through the astonishing performance that explains why the male has long claws. After placing himself in front of his mate so that his extended fore limbs, their palms turned outward, can just reach her face, the male proceeds to brush his nails against her chin and lores like a hypnotist. These movements last only a second or two but are frequently repeated. The male maintains his relative position by swimming to and fro before his apparently indifferent mate. Several males may simultaneously pay court to the same female.

When ready to lay, the female seeks, usually in the early morning or late afternoon, an elevated, well-drained spot, preferably a sandy one somewhat protected by low vegetation but exposed to direct sun. The hind legs are used in digging the flask-shaped nest cavity, and the front ones act as anchors for the body. If the site proves to be hard, the surface is softened by water from the cloaca and bladder. After the eggs have been dropped, the hole is filled and sealed by the moist soil that came from it. The copious supply of water poured on the nest may do more than facilitate digging. Nests are dug in Illinois from about the middle of June through the first part of July, but, as far south as Tennessee, the laying season is more extensive.

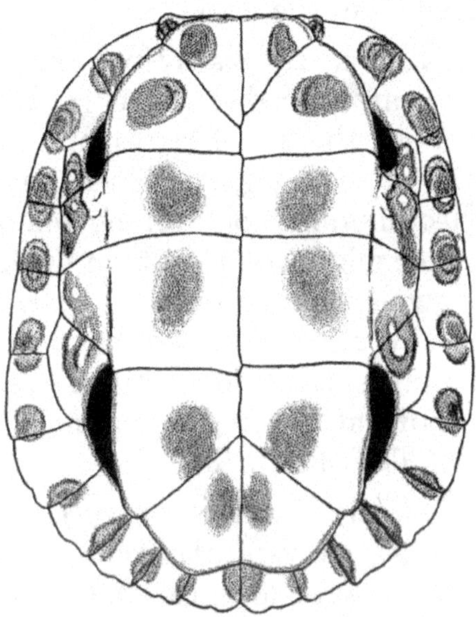

FIG. 50. Shell of Troost's turtle, seen from below.

In western Tennessee, Cagle found from five to twenty-two eggs in each of forty-seven nests, the average number per nest being 10.5. The white, elliptical eggs vary considerably in size and shape, the lesser diameter measuring from $\frac{3}{4}$ to $\frac{7}{8}$, the greater from $1\frac{1}{2}$ to $1\frac{3}{4}$ inches.

Growth and Age.—The carapace of the hatchling is about $1\frac{3}{16}$ inches long and wide. Sexual maturity is probably attained when the female is seven or eight years old and has a carapace 7 to $7\frac{1}{2}$ inches long. This information is based on so few data that it requires confirmation. Nothing is known about sexual development of the male. In Illinois, a large female has a carapace $9\frac{1}{2}$ inches long, whereas a large male has one about an inch shorter. The subspecies attains a length of almost, if not fully 11 inches.

Habits.—This shy, thoroughly aquatic reptile is a fast swimmer. Most individuals when annoyed draw into the shell for protection rather than defend themselves by biting. Large numbers often sun together on logs or other objects projecting from the water.

Biologists have recently discovered that the breeding cycles of many warm-blooded vertebrates change with the seasons because these cycles respond to lengthened or diminished hours of daylight. Birds kept under artificially controlled illumination can be made to migrate out of season, since migration is in turn dependent on the initiation of a new cycle; raccoons mate earlier than usual under certain carefully regulated conditions of light. Burger has now presented evidence that even reptiles are no exception, artificial lighting apparently affecting the breeding cycle of Troost's turtle.

Food.—This largely carnivorous species eats insects, mollusks (especially snails), crayfishes, tadpoles, small fish, various water plants, and, to some extent, carrion.

Enemies.—Man must be rated as the greatest enemy of Troost's turtle. The adults are eaten, the young are collected for the pet trade, and, at least in Tennessee, countless thousands of eggs are dug up each year to be used as fish bait. Smaller mammals such as raccoons and skunks also dig up the eggs but do not give them to fish.

Economic Importance.—The flesh is often eaten by country folk and not infrequently reaches the dinner table via markets of large cities.

Habitat.—Ponds, lakes, rivers, streams, and large springs are the preferred habitat of this reptile, which likes quiet, plant-grown water. Swampy bays of lake and river support large populations. The adults inhabit water of various depths, but the young shun deep places.

Captivity.—This, *the* common pet-shop reptile, is even handled by department and ten-cent stores. Thousands of hatchlings are shipped annually from Louisiana alone. Individuals with gaudily painted backs are not likely to survive unless the paint, which interferes with growth, is removed. Needless to say, it is a hardy captive if kept warm (about 75° F.) and allowed to bask in direct sunlight from which it is free to retreat. Fresh, tender vegetables, chopped meat or fish, and earthworms will do for food but not the prepared "ant eggs" sold by pet shops. Like most aquatic turtles, it prefers to swallow under water.

Occurrence.—Troost's turtle ranges from southeastern Iowa, the Chicago area, and southern Ohio southwestward to the Louisiana and Texas Gulf Coast. Somewhere east of Louisiana, it intergrades with *Pseudemys scripta scripta,* a common form of the southeastern coastal plain. Locally, Troost's turtle is known only from the Kankakee drainage of Kankakee County, Illinois, and of Porter County, Indiana. It is especially interesting as an addition to the list of reptiles that range to but not beyond the Chicago area.

Reference.—Turtles of the United States and Canada. By Clifford H. Pope. Alfred A. Knopf, New York, 1939. A general account.

SOFT-SHELLED TURTLE
Amyda spinifera spinifera

Plate 12

Recognition.—The flattened form and round, flexible shell identify this species at a glance. The snout ends in a soft proboscis and the lips are fleshy.

The Sexes.—Females attain much the greater size, sometimes being two or three times as bulky as males. The tail of the male is thicker and, when extended, projects well beyond the edge of the carapace; the female's tail scarcely projects beyond this edge.

Reproduction.—No details of courtship and copulation are known. The few accounts of nesting enable me to describe it briefly as follows:

When ready to lay, the female leaves the water late in the morning and, with an air of extreme caution, selects a sunny spot on a sloping bank or in an open field. After planting the front feet firmly on the ground, where they act as an anchor, she scratches some soil loose and flicks it far away with a violent kick of one foot. This scratching and flicking are repeated alternately by the hind limbs until a flask-shaped cavity about three inches wide at the bottom and fully six deep has been completed. The eggs are then dropped, a process hard to observe in detail. Newman states that, as soon as a few have been laid, the female first arranges them with the feet and then, using the knuckles, carefully packs about them some earth; before being scraped in, the earth is moistened with water from the accessory bladder and cloaca. When the hole has finally been filled, the soil at the surface is so carefully tramped down that the site dries out and becomes all but invisible. In one case, the entire process required seventy-five minutes, in another, only about half an hour. A clutch may contain from nine to twenty-five (rarely as many as thirty-two) eggs, the average number being eighteen. The nearly spherical, white shell varies from 1 to $1\frac{1}{4}$ inches in diameter and is thick, hard, and brittle.

In Illinois and Indiana, nests are made from the second week of June through the third week of July. Hatching occurs in September or late August; only rarely is emergence postponed until spring.

Growth and Age.—Hatchlings are about $1\frac{1}{2}$ inches long but not quite this wide. Among seventy-one specimens from Ohio examined by Conant, the largest female had a carapace $14\frac{1}{2}$ inches long, whereas that of the largest male measured but $6\frac{1}{2}$. A large Indiana female weighing seven pounds had a carapace 13 by $10\frac{1}{2}$ inches. Lagler records a 16-inch Michigan carapace. Cahn believes that females mature, at a length of 9½ inches. A specimen once lived 10½ years in Paris.

Habits.—This thoroughly aquatic reptile is a powerful and agile swimmer. On land its movements are astonishingly quick; steep banks are ascended with ease. It is fond of lying in water just deep enough to allow the snout to reach the surface. Before settling down, it rocks from side to side so that it stirs up mud or sand that settles on and completely conceals the leathery shell.

These turtles can submerge for hours on end because the lining of the pharynx is able to remove oxygen from the water and expel carbon dioxide into it. Streams of water are pumped in and out of the mouth and throat by movements of the hyoid apparatus. In view of this ability, it is not surprising that the winter is spent in bottom mud or sand.

During the warmest weeks of the summer, specimens may be seen basking on sandy or grassy banks, rarely on objects projecting from the water. Numbers are sometimes encountered in a small area, but they keep such a constant watch that the slightest disturbance sends all of them scuttling into the water, which is never more than a few feet away. The habit of always facing about before settling down greatly facilitates this quick escape. The posture assumed while sunning is often a relaxed one, with neck and legs extended and the webbed toes spread apart.

The disposition is not good. Most individuals when captured put up a vigorous struggle, projecting the head violently forward to bite a distant object, or frantically clawing and biting if picked up. The jaws of a large soft-shell can inflict a painful though not a dangerous wound.

Food.—The food consists chiefly of crayfishes and aquatic forms of insects. Other animals such as tadpoles, earthworms, and mollusks, or even small fish, are occasionally taken. There is a little evidence that this turtle may at times feed on vegetable matter.

Economic Importance.—Wherever it occurs in abundance, this species is considered a table delicacy and brings a good price in local markets. Conant found this to be true in Ohio, and the State of Illinois has even put a minimum size limit of seven inches on soft-shelled turtles. These reptiles are not sent to distant markets of large cities apparently because they do not ship as well as does their competitor, the snapping turtle, and because there is great local demand for them.

Habitat.—Rivers and large streams are the favorite haunts, but lakes and small streams are also frequented, the latter chiefly by the young. Relatively shallow water with a sandy or soft-mud bottom is preferred; thick, aquatic vegetation is not a special attraction.

Captivity.—Small soft-shelled turtles make interesting pets because they are so alert and quick in their movements. High temperature (at least 75° F.) is desirable. The aquarium should have a thick layer of sand on the bottom and a smooth slope by which the turtles can leave the water without scratching their tender plastrons. Chopped raw meat and fish will do for food when the animals named above as natural food are not available.

Occurrence.—This species is widely distributed in the United States from the Appalachian to the Rocky Mountains, and from the Gulf to the region of the Great Lakes. The exact limits of its range are now being determined by Conant and Goin, who believe that good subspecies exist. The name *Amyda spinifera spinifera* will certainly apply to the population of the Chicago area throughout which this turtle probably occurs. Actually, there are records for only Cook and Kankakee counties, Illinois; Lake County, Indiana; and Berrien County, Michigan. The difficulty of capture is probably responsible for the dearth of records.

Reference.—Turtles of the United States and Canada. By Clifford H. Pope. Alfred A. Knopf, New York, 1939. A general account.

Acris, 90
  gryllus, 86–90, text fig. 19
Algae in egg envelopes of spotted
    salamander, 37
  in egg mass of wood frog, 107
  as food of tadpoles, 78, 94, 99,
    104, 118, 126, 131, 139
Allard, H. A., 245
Allen, A. A., 91
Ambystoma, 50
  jeffersonianum, 29–34, text fig.
    6, pl. 4
  maculatum, 34–41, text figs.
    7–9
  opacum, 41–46, text figs. 5, 10,
    11
  tigrinum, 50, 51
  tigrinum tigrinum, 46–52, text
    figs. 2, 12, 13
American toad, 68, *69–81*, 82,
    139, text figs. 15–17
*americanus, Bufo americanus, 69–
    82*, text figs. 15–17
Amphibians, 13, 15, 17
  as food of green frogs, 126; of
    common water snakes, 167;
    of spotted turtles, 240
Amphipods as food of siren, 64
*Amyda spinifera spinifera, 263–
    266*, pl. 12
Ants as food of American toads,
    78; of ornate box turtles,
    251; of salamanders, 38, 54;
    of six-lined race-runners,
    152; of swamp tree frogs, 94
Anura, 65
Aronson, Lester R., 82, 113, 122,
    135, 138
Axolotl, 50

Babbitt, Lewis H., 129, 131, 239
Barden, Albert, 152
Beetles as food of. American
    toads, 78; of lizards, 152,
    158; of salamanders, 38, 45,
    54, 60; of turtles, 240, 251;
    (staphylinid), of four-toed
    salamanders, 57
Bellrose, F. C., 181
Berries as food of Blanding's
    turtle, 243
Beyer, George E., 188
Birds as enemy of bullfrogs, 119
  as food of bullfrogs, 118; of
    snakes, 167, 173, 176, 178,
    186, 218
Birds' eggs as food of snakes, 173,
    176, 178, 186
Bishop, Sherman C., 44, 47, 49,
    56
*bislineata, Eurycea bislineata, 57–
    60*, text figs. 3, 5
Bitterns as enemy of American
    toads, 80; of plains garter
    snakes, 210
Black snake, pilot, 164, *174–177*,
    pl. 8
Blacksnake, 171, 172
  as enemy of six-lined race-
    runners, 152
Blair, Albert P., 82, 86, 93
Blanchard, Frank N., 94, 169,
    195, 196, 202, 215, 216, 219
Blanchard, Frieda Cobb, 215, 219
*blanchardi, Opheodrys vernalis,
    169–171*, pl. 6
blandingii, Emys, 241–243, text
    fig. 46, pl. 11

Blanding's turtle, 228, 229, *241–243*, text fig. 46, pl. 11
Blue racer, 164, *171–174*, pl. 7
  as enemy of glass-snakes, 148
Blue-tailed skink, *153–159*, text fig. 36
Box turtle, 227, 228
Boyer, Dorothy A., 88
Bradley, Helen Teale, 150, 154
Brady, Maurice K., 41
Bragg, Arthur N., 102
Breder, Charles M., 82, 125
Breder, Ruth B., 82, 125
Brown, J. Roland, 242
Bufo americanus, 75, 76, 82, 85
  americanus americanus, 69–81, text figs. 15–17
  americanus copei, 80
  fowleri, 80
  woodhousii fowleri, 81–86, text figs. 17, 18
  woodhousii woodhousii, 86
Bugs as food of six-lined race-runners, 152; (homopterous), of four-toed salamanders, 57; (potato), of leopard frogs, 140
Bullfrog, 68, *111–120*, 121, 126, 127, text figs. 25–28
  as enemy of pickerel frogs, 131; of snapping turtles, 237
Bullheads as food of bullfrogs, 118
Bull snake, 164, *179–184*, text figs. 38–40, pl. 8
Burt, Charles E., 151, 152
butleri, Thamnophis, 204–207, text fig. 42
Butler's garter snake, *204–207*, text fig. 42
Butterflies as food of six-lined race-runners, 152

Cagle, Fred R., 22, 24, 61, 154, 166, 175, 232, 261
Cahn, Alvin R., 264
Cantaloupe as food of ornate box turtles, 251
carolina, Terrapene carolina, 244–249, text fig. 47, pl. 11
Carr, Archie F., 63, 64
Carrion as food of snakes, 176, 210, 218; of turtles, 233, 237, 240, 243, 248, 254, 258, 262
catenatus, Sistrurus catenatus, 220–225, pl. 10

Caterpillars, 139
  as food of ornate box turtles, 251
catesbeiana, Rana, 111–120, text figs. 25–28
Catfish as food of common water snakes, 197, 198
Caudata, 18
Centipeds as food of spotted salamanders, 38
Chelydra serpentina serpentina, 234–238, text fig. 45, pl. 11
Chicago area, 11, fig. 1
Chickens as food of pilot black snakes, 176
Chrysemys picta bellii, 259
  picta marginata, 255–259, pl. 12
cinereus, Plethodon, 52–55, text figs. 2, 11, pl. 4
clamitans, Rana, 121–127, text figs. 29, 30
Clams as food of turtles, 237, 243, 254
Clausen, Harry J., 196, 206, 218
Clemmys guttata, 238–240, pl. 12
Cnemidophorus sexlineatus, 149–153, text fig. 35
Coluber constrictor, 171
  constrictor flaviventris, 171–174, pl. 7
Common box turtle, 229, *244–249*, text fig. 47, pl. 11
Common garter snake, 205, 208, *213–220*
Common water snake, 164, *194–199*, 212, text fig. 41, pl. 9
Conant, Roger N., 153, 157, 165, 171, 173, 177, 191, 192, 193, 196, 202, 203, 205, 215, 218, 221, 264, 266
constrictor flaviventris, Coluber, 171–174, pl. 7
contortrix, Heterodon contortrix, 165–168, pl. 6
Cope, Edward Drinker, 63
Copperheads as food of snakes, 173, 186
Courtship of salamanders, 17, fig. 5
Craneflies as food of siren, 64
Crayfishes as food of frogs, 89, 118; of mudpuppies, 23; of snakes, 189, 193; of turtles, 233, 237, 243, 254, 258, 262, 265

Cricket frog, 65, 68, *86–90*, text fig. 19
  as food of ribbon snakes, 212
Crickets as food of spotted salamanders, 38
Crows as enemy of snapping turtles, 237
crucifer, Hyla crucifer, 95–100, text figs. 22, 23
Crustacean eggs as food of American toads, 78
Crustaceans as food of frogs, 126, 131, 139; of Graham's water snakes, 189; of salamanders, 45, 63; of spotted turtles, 240
Cunningham, Bert, 257

Davis, D. Dwight, 207
dekayi wrightorum, Storeria, 200–201, pl. 9
DeKay's snake, 164, 196, *200–201*, 218, pl. 9
Dempster, Wilfrid Taylor, 40
Diamond-back rattlesnake, 224
Diatoms as food of frogs and toads, 78, 99, 104, 118, 126, 131, 139
Dickerson, Mary C., 74, 75, 82, 125, 136, 138, 139
Dinosaurs, 226
Ditmars, Raymond L., 146
Dogs, 131
Domestic fowl as enemy of American toads, 80
Dragonflies as food of spotted turtles, 240
Drake, C. J., 139
Dunn, Emmett R., 51

Earthworms as food of frogs, 78, 126; of salamanders, 33, 45; of snakes, 178, 191, 200, 206, 210, 218; of turtles, 243, 248, 251, 258, 265
Eastern green snake, 170
Edelmann, Abraham, 108
Elaphe obsoleta obsoleta, 174–177, pl. 8
  vulpina gloydi, 178
  vulpina vulpina, 177–179, pl. 1
Emys blandingii, 241–243, text fig. 46, pl. 11
Eumeces, 158
  fasciatus, 153–159, text fig. 36
Eurycea bislineata bislineata, 57–60, text figs. 3, 5

Eurycea bislineata major, 60
Ewing, H. E., 247

Farris, Edmond J., 106
fasciatus, Eumeces, 153–159, text fig. 36
Finster, Ethel B., 216
Fish, 18
  as enemy of American toads, 80; of frogs, 119, 139; of snapping turtles, 237
  as food of bullfrogs, 118; of salamanders, 23, 38; of snakes, 189, 193, 197, 198, 210, 212, 218; of turtles, 237, 243, 254, 258, 262, 265
Flagellates as food of American toads, 78
flaviventris, Coluber constrictor, 171–174, pl. 7
Flies as food of American toads, 78; of salamanders, 45, 60; of six-lined race-runners, 152; of spotted turtles, 240; (drosophilid), of four-toed salamanders, 57; (robber), of ornate box turtles, 251
Flower, Stanley S., 247
Four-toed salamander, 20, 21, 53, *55–57*, text fig. 6, pl. 4
fowleri, Bufo woodhousii, 81–86, text figs. 17, 18
Fowler's toad, 68, 69, 80, *81–86*, text figs. 17, 18
Fox snake, 164, *177–179*, 184, 185, pl. 1
Frog, 13, 17, 65
  cricket, 65, 68, *86–90*, text fig. 19
  as food of bullfrogs, 118; of snakes, 167, 173, 189, 197, 210, 212, 218, 223
  green, 68, 109, *121–127*, text figs. 29, 30
  larvae, recognition of, 19
  leopard, 68, *133–142*, text figs. 32, 33
  pickerel, 68, 115, *127–133*, text fig. 31
  swamp tree, 68, *90–95*, text figs. 20, 21
  tree, 68, *100–105*, pl. 5
  use of term discussed, 65
  wood, 68, *105–111*, text fig. 24
Frost, S. W., 76, 99, 109, 125, 126, 139

Garter snake, 164, 196, 220
  Butler's, *204–207*, text fig. 42
  common, 205, 208, *213–220*
  as enemy of toads and frogs,
    80, 94, 131, 139
  plains, 169, 203, *208–211*, text
    figs. 42, 43, pl. 9
geographica, Graptemys, 252–255,
  text fig. 49, pl. 12
Glass-snake, 145, *146–148*, text
  fig. 34
Gloyd, Howard K., 176, 182, 183,
  212
Goin, Coleman J., 266
Gophers as food of bull snakes,
  181
grahamii, Natrix, 188–189
Graham's water snake, 164, *188–
  189*
Grant, Chapman, 194
Graptemys geographica, 252–255,
  text fig. 49, pl. 12
Grasshoppers as food of leopard
    frogs, 140; of lizards, 148,
    152, 158; (lubber), of ornate
    box turtles, 251
Greenberg, B., 87
Green frog, 68, 109, *121–127*, text
    figs. 29, 30
  as enemy of pickerel frogs, 131
Green snake, 164, *169–171*, 203,
  210, pl. 6
Grobman, Arnold B., 170
Ground squirrels as food of bull
  snakes, 181
gryllus, Acris, 86–90, text fig. 19
guttata, Clemmys, 238–240, pl. 12

Hall, F. G., 141
Hamilton, William J., 60, 74, 76,
  235, 236
Harper, Francis, 84, 90
Harrison, Ross G., 40
Hausman, Sibyl A., 26
Hawks as enemy of snakes, 182,
    210; of snapping turtles, 237;
    (broad-winged), of toads,
    79; (red-tailed), of snakes,
    203, 219
Heinze, Albert A., 88
Hemidactylium scutatum, 55–57,
  text fig. 6, pl. 4
Herons as enemy of American
  toads, 80
*Heterodon contortrix contortrix,
  165–168*, pl. 6

Higginbotham, A. C., 75
Hinckley, Mary H., 98, 99, 108,
  110
Hisaw, Frederick L., 182, 183
Hog-nosed snake, 164, *165–168*,
  pl. 6
  as enemy of toads, 80
Holbrook, John Edwards, 146
Hudson, George E., 208
Hurter, Julius, 63
Hyla crucifer, 100
  crucifer bartramiana, 100
  crucifer crucifer, 95–100, text
    figs. 22, 23
  versicolor, 105
  versicolor chrysoscelis, 105
  versicolor versicolor, 100–105,
    pl. 5

Identification, 13
  of frogs, 67; of salamanders,
    19; of snakes, 162; of turtles,
    228
Ifft, J. D., 25
Ingram, William Marcus, 116,
  118
Insects as enemy of American
    toads, 80; of leopard frogs,
    139
  as food of blue-tailed skinks,
    158; of frogs, 78, 89, 94, 99,
    104, 118, 119, 126, 131, 139,
    140; of salamanders, 23, 33,
    38, 45, 54; of snakes, 167,
    173, 197, 210, 218; of turtles,
    233, 237, 248, 254, 258, 262,
    265
intermedia nettingi, Siren, 61–64,
  text fig. 14
Isopods as food of blue-tailed
  skinks, 158

*jeffersonianum, Ambystoma, 29–
  34*, text fig. 6, pl. 4
Jefferson's salamander, 20, *29–
  34*, 35, 37, 48, text fig. 6, pl. 4

Key to frogs and toads, 68; to
    reptiles and amphibians, 13;
    to salamanders, 20; to
    snakes, 164; to turtles, 229
kirtlandii, Natrix, 189–191, pl. 8
Kirtland's water snake, 164, *189–
  191*, pl. 8
Klauber, L. M., 222
Kumpf, K. F., 47

Lacertilia, 145
Lagler, K. F., 237, 264
Lampropeltis triangulum triangulum, 184–188, pl. 1
Leeches as enemy of painted turtles, 259
  as food of Butler's garter snakes, 206; of turtles, 243, 258
Leopard frog, 68, *133–142*, text figs. 32, 33
Lizards, 13, 17, 145
  as food of blue racers, 173; of glass-snakes, 148
Logier, E. B. S., 206
London Zoological Gardens, 22
louisianensis, Triturus viridescens, 24–29, text fig. 5
Lueth, Francis X., 210
Lynn, W. Gardner, 108

McAtee, W. L., 118
maculatum, Ambystoma, 34–41, text figs. 7–9
maculosus, Necturus maculosus, 21–23, text fig. 4, pls. 2, 3
Mammals as enemy of frogs, 119, 139; of snakes, 219, 226; of turtles, 237, 248, 254, 259, 262
  as food of snakes, 167, 173, 176, 178, 181, 182, 186, 197, 218
Man as enemy of leopard frogs, 139; of snakes, 168, 198, 223, 224; of snapping turtles, 237
Map turtle, 229, *252–255*, text fig. 49, pl. 12
Marbled salamander, 20, 36, *41–46*, 51, text figs. 5, 10, 11
marginata, Chrysemys picta, 255–259, pl. 12
Marshall, Byron C., 61
Mason, E. R., 146
Massasauga, 164, *220–225*, pl. 10
Mayflies as food of six-lined race-runners, 152; of two-lined salamanders, 60
Maynard, Elliott A., 70
Metamorphosis, 65
Mice as food of bullfrogs, 118; of snakes, 176, 181, 186, 223
Milk snake, 164, 177, *184–188*, 203, pl. 1
Miller, Dorothy C., 136, 138
Miller, Newton, 70, 71, 72, 74, 76, 78

Millipeds as food of salamanders, 33, 38; of wood frogs, 109
Mink as enemy of snapping turtles, 237
Minnows as food of siren, 64
Mites as food of American toads, 78
Moles as food of bullfrogs, 118
Mollusks as food of leopard frogs, 139; of siren, 63; of turtles, 233, 258, 262, 265
Moore, John A., 98, 107, 115, 129, 130
Mosquitoes as food of six-lined race-runners, 152
Moths as food of four-toed salamanders, 57; of six-lined race-runners, 152
Mudpuppy, 20, *21–23*, 46, 55, text fig. 4, pls. 2, 3
Munz, Philip A., 78
Mushrooms as food of common box turtles, 248
Muskrats as enemy of musk turtles, 233
Musk turtle, 229, *230–234*, text fig. 44, pl. 12
Myriapods as food of common box turtles, 248

Naso-labial groove, 19, text fig. 2
Natrix grahamii, 188–189
  kirtlandii, 189–191, pl. 8
  septemvittata, 192–194, pl. 8
  sipedon, 198
  sipedon sipedon, 194–199, text fig. 41, pl. 9
Necturus maculosus maculosus, 21–23, text fig. 4, pls. 2, 3
  maculosus stictus, 23
nettingi, Siren intermedia, 61–64, text fig. 14
Newman, H. H., 254
Newt, 20, *24–29*, text fig. 5
  as enemy of leopard frogs, 139
Nichols, John T., 247
nigrita triseriata, Pseudacris, 90–95, text figs. 20, 21
Noble, G. Kingsley, 41, 61, 97, 106, 135, 138, 146, 150, 154, 157, 196, 206, 214, 218

obsoleta, Elaphe obsoleta, 174–177, pl. 8
occipitomaculata, Storeria occipitomaculata, 201–204

odoratus, Sternotherus, 230–234,
    text fig. 44, pl. 12
opacum, Ambystoma, 41–46, text
    figs. 5, 10, 11
Opheodrys vernalis blanchardi,
    169–171, pl. 6
    vernalis vernalis, 169, 170
Ophisaurus ventralis, 146–148,
    text fig. 34
ornata, Terrapene, 249–252, text
    fig. 48
Ornate box turtle, 229, *249–252,*
    text fig. 48
Ortenburger, A. I., 173
Owls as enemy of American
    toads, 80

Painted turtle, 229, *255–259,* pl.
    12
palustris, Rana, 127–133, text fig.
    31
Parker, G. H., 104
Patterson, Thomas L., 118
Pearse, A. S., 257
Perch as food of ribbon snakes,
    212
Piatt, Jean, 70, 72
Pickerel frog, 68, 115, *127–133,*
    text fig. 31
picta marginata, Chrysemys, 255–
    259, pl. 12
Pilot black snake, 164, *174–177,*
    pl. 8
pipiens, Rana pipiens, 133–142,
    text figs. 32, 33
Pituophis sayi, 184
    sayi sayi, 179–184, text figs.
    38–40, pl. 8
Plains garter snake, 169, 203,
    208–211, text figs. 42, 43,
    pl. 9
Plankton as food of siren, 64
Plethodon cinereus, 52–55, text
    figs. 2, 11, pl. 4
Pocket gophers as food of bull
    snakes, 182
Pollister, Arthur Wagg, 107
proximus, Thamnophis sauritus,
    211–213, pl. 10
Pseudacris nigrita, 94
    nigrita triseriata, 90–95, text
    figs. 20, 21
Pseudemys scripta scripta, 263
    scripta troostii, 260–263, text
    fig. 50, pl. 11
punctatum, Ambystoma, 40

Quail as food of pilot black
    snakes, 176
Queen snake, 164, 188, *192–194,*
    pl. 8

Rabbits as food of snakes, 176,
    181
Raccoons, 131, 168
    as enemy of bullfrogs, 117; of
    snakes, 210, 219, 224; of
    turtles, 237, 259, 262
radix, Thamnophis, 208–211, text
    figs. 42, 43
Rahn, Herman, 215, 216
Rana, 76, 107, 115, 130, 141
    catesbeiana, 111–120, text figs.
    25–28
    clamitans, 121–127, text figs.
    29, 30
    grylio, 119
    palustris, 127–133, text fig. 31
    pipiens, 140
    pipiens pipiens, 133–142, text
    figs. 32, 33
    sphenocephala, 136
    sylvatica, 105–111, text fig. 24
    sylvatica cantabrigensis, 111
Raney, Edward C., 116, 118
Rats as food of bull snakes, 181,
    182
Red-backed salamander, 20, *52–*
    55, 57, 58, text figs. 2, 11,
    pl. 4
Red-bellied snake, 164, 169, *201–*
    204, 210
    as food of milk snakes, 186
Redmond, Albert C., 82, 125
Reptiles, 13, 143
    as food of blue racers, 173; of
    green frogs, 126
Reptilia, 145, 227
Reynolds, A. E., 154
Ribbon snake, 164, *211–213,* pl.
    10
    as enemy of frogs, 89, 94, 110,
    131
Robins as food of pilot black
    snakes, 176
Root, R. W., 141
Rugh, Roberts, 40, 51, 99, 133,
    134, 136
Ruthven, Alexander G., 208

Salamanders, 13, 17, 65, 186, 202
    as enemy of American toads,
    80

Salamanders as food of bullfrogs, 118; of snakes, 167, 170, 178, 189, 197, 218
    four-toed, 20, 21, 53, *55–57*, text fig. 6, pl. 4
    Jefferson's, 20, *29–34*, 35, 37, 48, text fig. 6, pl. 4
    larval, recognition of, 19
    marbled, 20, 36, *41–46*, 51, text figs. 5, 10, 11
    red-backed, 20, *52–55*, 57, 58, text figs. 2, 11, pl. 4
    spotted, 20, *34–41*, 46, 48, text figs. 7–9
    tiger, 20, 34, *46–52*, text figs. 2, 12, 13
    two-lined, 20, 52, *57–60*, text figs. 3, 5
Salientia, 65
Sauria, 145
sauritus proximus, Thamnophis, 211–213, pl. 10
sayi, Pituophis sayi, 179–184, text figs. 38–40, pl. 8
Schmidt, Karl P., 12, 90, 109, 173, 212
scripta troostii, Pseudemys, 260–263, text fig. 50, pl. 11
scutatum, Hemidactylium, 55–57, text fig. 6, pl. 4
Senning, W. C., 22
septemvittata, Natrix, 192–194, pl. 8
serpentina, Chelydra serpentina, 234–238, text fig. 45, pl. 11
sexlineatus, Cnemidophorus, 149–153, text fig. 35
Shrews as food of milk snakes, 186
Shumway, Waldo, 138
sipedon, Natrix sipedon, 194–199, text fig. 41, pl. 9
Siren, 18, 20, 46, *61–64*, text fig. 14
Siren, 62, 63
Siren intermedia intermedia, 64
    intermedia nettingi, 61–64, text fig. 14
    lacertina, 63, 64
sirtalis, Thamnophis sirtalis, 213–220
Sistrurus catenatus catenatus, 220–225, pl. 10
Six-lined race-runner, 145, *149–153*, text fig. 35

Skink, blue-tailed, *153–159*, text fig. 36
Skunks, 131, 168
    as enemy of bullfrogs, 117; of snakes, 219, 224; of turtles, 237, 259, 262
Slugs as food of American toads, 78; of salamanders, 38, 45; of snakes, 191, 203; of turtles, 240, 243, 248
Smith, B. G., 47
Smith, Hobart M., 87, 92
Smith, Philip E., 61
Smith, Robert Emrie, 25
Snails as food of frogs, 109, 126, 131; of lizards, 148, 152, 158; of salamanders, 38, 45, 54; of turtles, 237, 240, 243, 248, 254, 262
Snakes, 13, 132, 160, 186, 202
    bull, 164, *179–184*, text figs. 38–40, pl. 8
    Butler's garter, *204–207*, text fig. 42
    common garter, 205, 208, *213–220*
    common water, 164, *194–199*, 212, text fig. 41, pl. 9
    DeKay's, 164, 196, *200–201*, 218, pl. 9
    eggs of as food of milk snakes, 186
    as enemy of bullfrogs, 119
    as food of bullfrogs, 118; of glass-snakes, 148; of snakes, 173, 186, 218, 223
    fox, 164, *177–179*, 184, 185, pl. 1
    Graham's water, 164, *188–189*
    green, 164, *169–171*, 203, 210, pl. 6
    hog-nosed, 164, *165–168*, pl. 6
    Kirtland's water, 164, *189–191*, pl. 8
    milk, 164, 177, *184–188*, 203, pl. 1
    pilot black, 164, *174–177*, pl. 8
    plains garter, 169, 203, *208–211*, text figs. 42, 43, pl. 9
    queen, 164, 188, *192–194*, pl. 8
    red-bellied, 164, 169, *201–204*, 210
    ribbon, 164, *211–213*, pl. 10
Snapping turtle, 226, 229, 230, *234–238*, text fig. 45, pl. 11

Snedigar, Robert, 220
Soft-shelled turtle, 229, *263-266*,
    pl. 12
Sowbugs as food of two-lined
    salamanders, 60
Sparrows as food of pilot black
    snakes, 176
Spermatophores, 18
Spiders as enemy of spring
    peepers, 99
    as food of lizards, 148, 152,
    158; of salamanders, 33, 38,
    54, 57, 60; of spotted turtles,
    240; of toads and frogs, 78,
    89, 94, 99, 126, 131, 139.
*spinifera, Amyda spinifera, 263-
    266*, pl. 12
Spotted salamander, 20, *34-41*,
    46, 48, text figs. 7-9
Spotted turtle, 229, *238-240*, pl.
    12
Spring peeper, 68, 93, *95-100*,
    text figs. 22, 23
Springtails as food of four-toed
    salamanders, 57
Squirrels as enemy of painted
    turtles, 259
Star gazers as food of common
    water snakes, 198
Sternotherus odoratus, 230-234,
    text fig. 44, pl. 12
Storeria dekayi dekayi, 200
    dekayi wrightorum, 200-201,
    pl. 9
    occipitomaculata obscura, 203
    *occipitomaculata occipitomacu-
    lata, 201-204*
Strawberries as food of common
    box turtles, 248
Strecker, John K., 182, 189, 251
Stromsten, Frank A., 256
Stull, Olive Griffith, 180
Suckers, white, as food of com-
    mon water snakes, 198
Swamp tree frog, 68, *90-95*, text
    figs. 20, 21
sylvatica, Rana, 105-111, text
    fig. 24

Tadpoles as food of plains garter
    snakes, 210; of turtles, 262,
    265
    identification of, 19
Taylor, Edward H., 153
Terrapene carolina, 249

*Terrapene carolina carolina, 244-
    249*, text fig. 47, pl. 11
    ornata, 249-252, text fig. 48
Terrapin, 227
Testudinata, 227
Thamnophis butleri, 204-207, text
    fig. 42
    radix, 208-211, text figs. 42, 43
    sauritus, 212
    sauritus proximus, 211-213,
    pl. 10
        as enemy of swamp tree
        frogs, 94
    sirtalis, 220
    sirtalis sirtalis, 213-220
        as enemy of swamp tree
        frogs, 94
Thrips as food of American
    toads, 78
Tiger salamander, 20, 34, *46-52*,
    text figs. 2, 12, 13
*tigrinum, Ambystoma tigrinum,
    46-52*, text figs. 2, 12, 13
Toad, American, 68, *69-81*, 82,
    139, text figs. 15-17
    Fowler's, 68, 69, 80, *81-86*,
    text figs. 17, 18
    as food of snakes, 167, 173, 193,
    197, 200, 212, 218
    use of term discussed, 65
Tortoise, 227
Trapido, Harold, 201
Tree frog, 68, *100-105*, pl. 5
*triangulum, Lampropeltis triangu-
    lum, 184-188*, pl. 1
*triseriata, Pseudacris nigrita, 90-
    95*, text figs. 20, 21
Triturus viridescens, 28
    viridescens dorsalis, 28
    viridescens louisianensis, 24-29,
    text fig. 5
    viridescens viridescens, 24, 26
*troostii, Pseudemys scripta, 260-
    263*, text fig. 50, pl. 11
Troost's turtle, 229, *260-263*,
    text fig. 50, pl. 11
Turtle, 13, 226, 227
    Blanding's, 228, 229, *241-243*,
    text fig. 46, pl. 11
    common box, 229, *244-249*,
    text fig. 47, pl. 11
    as enemy of bullfrogs, 119
    as food of bullfrogs, 118
    map, 229, *252-255*, text fig.
    49, pl. 12

Turtle, musk, 229, *230–234*, text
fig. 44, pl. 12
ornate box, 229, *249–252*, text
fig. 48
painted, 229, *255–259*, pl. 12
snapping, 226, 230, *234–238*,
text fig. 45, pl. 11
soft-shelled, 229, *263–266*, pl.
12
spotted, 229, *238–240*, pl. 12
Troost's, 229, *260–263*, text
fig. 50, pl. 11
western painted, 256
Two-lined salamander, 20, 52,
57–60, text figs. 3, 5

ventralis, Ophisaurus, 146–148,
text fig. 34
*vernalis blanchardi, Opheodrys,
169–171*, pl. 6
*versicolor, Hyla versicolor, 100–
105*, pl. 5
*viridescens louisianensis, Tritu-
rus, 24–29*, text fig. 5
vulpina, Elaphe vulpina, 177–179,
pl. 1

Walker, Charles F., 93
Water-boatmen as food of spotted salamanders, 38

Waterbugs as food of spotted
salamanders, 38
Water snakes, 198
common, 164, *194–199*, 212,
text fig. 41, pl. 9
as enemy of toads and frogs,
80, 131, 139
Graham's, 164, *188–189*
Kirtland's, 164, *189–191*, pl. 8
Western painted turtle, 256
Wilde, Walter S., 218
Wiley, Grace Olive, 236
Wood frog, 68, *105–111*, text fig.
24
woodhousii fowleri, Bufo, 81–86,
text figs. 17, 18
Woodpeckers, downy, as food of
pilot black snakes, 176
Worms as food of salamanders,
54; of spotted turtles, 240;
(annelid), of salamanders,
23, 60; (lumbriculid), of
siren, 64
Wright, Albert Hazen, 72, 82, 91,
92, 96, 97, 98, 101, 103, 108,
113, 114, 117, 124, 136, 138,
141
Wright, Bertrand A., 222
*wrightorum, Storeria dekayi, 200–
201*, pl. 9

Yerkes, R. M., 240